FIND YOUR F*CK YEAH

FIND YOUR FUCK YEAH

STOP CENSORING WHO YOU ARE AND
DISCOVER WHAT YOU REALLY WANT

ALEXIS ROCKLEY

P

CHRONICLE PRISM

This book contains advice and information relating to health and inter-personal well-being. It is not intended to replace medical or psychother-apeutic advice and should be used to supplement rather than replace any needed care by your doctor or mental health professional. While all efforts have been made to ensure accuracy of the information contained in this book as of date of publication, the publisher and the author are not responsible for any adverse effects or consequences that may occur as a result of applying the methods suggested in this book.

Library of Congress Cataloging-in-Publication Data available.

ISBN: 978-1-4521-8332-9

Manufactured in Canada.

Design by Sara Schneider.
Typesetting by Cody Gates, Happenstance Type-O-Rama.

10 9 8 7 6 5 4 3 2 1

Chronicle books and gifts are available at special quantity discounts to corporations, professional associations, literacy programs, and other organizations. For details and discount information, please contact our premiums department at corporatesales@chroniclebooks.com or at 1-800-759-0190.

CHRONICLE PRISM

Chronicle Prism is an imprint of Chronicle Books LLC, 680 Second Street, San Francisco, California 94107

chronicleprism.com

TO THE EXHAUSTED MISFITS,
THE BORED CREATIVES, THE PEOPLE WHO WERE TOLD THEY
WERE "TOO _____," AND ANYONE TIRED OF CENSORING,
STIFLING, AND EDITING WHO THEY ARE—
I WROTE THIS FOR YOU.

CONTENTS

PART III: FUCKYEAH

WTF IS FUCKYEAH?

It's the kind of happiness you've only heard about in rumors. And yeah, *it's real.*

Fuckyeah is having a clear sense of purpose without having all the answers. It's the clarity of mind and resolute focus that gives you the motivation to work your ass off, stick with it when shit hits the fan, and recognize which problems are the worth-it problems.

It is a life filled with real, electric joy—the kind that can't be stifled, shoved down, or censored—a joy that persists without pretending that a bubble-wrapped, pain-free life is possible. It is everything that lights you up inside; it's the version of being alive in which you can't help but think *"Fuck yeah!"* all the time.

I know, I know. It sounds fake, like a wild-eyed happiness that demands detachment from reality or a creepy half-smile plastered on your face at all times. But that's because you and I have forgotten what "fuckyeah" actually *feels* like.

We've been searching for fuckyeah since our first taste of ice cream, first drawing pinned proudly on the fridge, first time we cried laughing—since our first taste of joy. But with every day that we get older, finding it seems less likely. We would have given up the search a long time ago if it weren't for the rumors that some people have actually found their fuckyeahs in their adult lives; if they can, we can, right? But fuckyeah is so much blurrier and further away, somehow, than when we were kids.

Raise a hand if this sounds like you:

You regularly bounce back and forth between total boredom and overwhelming stress, only to level out at a vegetative, exhausted state. It's not that you're never happy; you are—while out with friends, chilling at home, after great sex, eating a mouthwatering meal, or waking up from a really good night's sleep. But that version of "happy" peaks around 70 percent—never fully hitting true contentment or raw joy, a fleeting state of satisfaction at best. The rest of the time? You're going through the motions, feeling kind of . . . numb.

You find yourself annoyed that your time isn't your own because you're busy "making a living"—but when you finally have free time, you have no clue what to do with it (other than binge-watch TV shows in bed). You like having time to yourself, but *hate* being alone without an Internet connection; you can only tolerate a few minutes of being completely alone with your thoughts because when you are, the persistent question sneaks in: *Hey—is something missing here?*

Sometimes you feel confident in the life choices you've made (i.e., education, career, relationships), but you can't help but feel like where you're "at" in life is somehow *not enough*. If you had just done A, B, or C, you could be much further along in your career; maybe even happier, or healthier. You know, deep down, that you can change your life, but *how*?! You've shape-shifted, filtered, muted, and edited who you are at work, online, in relationships, in friendships, and with family for so long that you're no longer certain what your real, uncensored self actually looks, sounds, or feels like.

Is your arm tired from all the aggressive hand-raising? I thought so. We spend most of our modern lives bored or stressed, thinking, *"I guess this is just what adulthood is? I guess this is me now?"* I know I definitely did.

At just twenty-eight years old I had a drool-worthy, creative, and steady job. I managed the styling and visuals for a colossal hipster retail business, directly supervising double-digit millions of dollars in annual volume and leading a huge network of people. I was in a happy long-term relationship. I was surrounded by good friends. I lived in a beautiful apartment in a beautiful place that people spend their precious vacation days visiting. I was living the millennial dream—but that didn't stop me from swinging wildly between numbness and anxiety, living in dread of Monday mornings, or experiencing some version of a quarter-life crisis.

>> *"Really? Because it sounds like you're just bragging and ungrateful."*

Nope. Just giving you some background, so you know that I've done the whole "be impressive while you're young" thing . . . and well, it's not always all it's cracked up to be.

There was a time when I LOVED my job, but things had changed. As infatuation with my career began to fade into the distance, it was quickly replaced by exhaustion and frustration. I discovered that twelve years of pulling yourself up by your bootstraps while simultaneously climbing the corporate ladder is complicated *and* tiring.

Being great at my job meant I earned plenty of external validation and promotions—but it also buried me under mountains of new responsibilities outside my job description and unrealistic expectations from my peers. I was burnt out and full of questions. *What do you do when you discover your dream job is making you miserable? How do people figure out WTF they want to do with their lives? Why are so many of us depressed? Why are we bored out of our minds but too scared of failure to try anything new?* I was floating outside my body, watching myself slip silently into a lame adult life—and I needed to do something about it, ASAP.

So, I got to work.

On myself.

I tried every self-help strategy known to humankind. I braved a cloud of toxic morning breath to practice "simhasana" breathing and "access my inner power." I bought tickets to career-focused women's conferences. I journaled. Made a vision board. Meditated. Took my "inner artist" on a date. I wrote a letter to myself, from myself, giving myself permission to be myself. I did a lot more than I care to list, and I was *still* burnt out and unhappy. More than anything, I was annoyed.

First of all, most of the health and wellness experts telling me to "practice self-care" were clearly also trying *to sell me something*. Excuse me, but how will a fair-trade, cruelty-free, organic rosehip and lavender bubble bath help me cope with overwhelming feelings of existential dread or anxiety? Anybody notice that at its worst, self-care is just the self-help industry rebranded and repackaged for millennials? UGH.

Second, where was the hard science in all this WooWoo? The more I read, the more I noticed a pattern: the most popular advice acknowledges our pain (or desire to grow) in a way that makes us feel seen, while also baiting us with the promise of "proven" solutions to our problems. But instead of grounding these strategies in science, we are often left with generic, vaguely spiritual platitudes. When these "strategies" do nothing to help us, we aren't angry at the source of our advice—*we're disappointed in ourselves.* Why? Because we were made to believe this journey to happiness is complex and elusive. If we failed to "create work-life balance," or "follow our bliss," or "practice self-care," it must be our own damn fault that we're still unhappy, right? *UGHHHHH.*

Pissed off at the huge gap between scientific research and the warm-fuzzy brand of #selfcare dominating pop culture, I decided to roll up my sleeves and do the research for myself. You know those scholarly medical journals with groundbreaking scientific studies that no one has time to read? I read them. (So many, actually, that when I type a medical question into my browser, Google assumes I want a scholarly article and not WebMD.) You know the shelves of informative but painfully boring books on cognitive therapy and positive psychology? I read them too. Maybe all of them? And when books, conferences, and rituals weren't enough, I decided to study the science of happiness, joining a certificate program led by the founder of positive psychology (Martin Seligman) and digging deep into the scholarly world in a search for real, concrete answers. Turns out I am an obsessive researcher.

Guess what I discovered after all that reading, research, and trial and error?

My fuckyeah.

And you know what? It wasn't because I found some exact recipe for happiness by blending hard science and WooWoo spirituality. The research helped. The mindfulness helped. But it wasn't what led me to my fuckyeah. It's because I *unlearned* the bullshit that had tangled my brain into knots and found my way back to that little-kid, first-ever-ice-cream-cone, raw *joy*. A year into my self-help quest, the universe handed me an opportunity: stick it out at my fully formed boss-lady career or quit my job and reinvent my life.

Spoiler Alert: *I reinvented my life*. Five stars, thumbs-up, would recommend. And now? Now I'm going to save you years of reading, research, trial and error.

I KNOW INTRODUCTIONS HAVE A RICH HISTORY OF BEING BORING, BUT PLEASE DON'T SKIP THIS.

The thing is . . . the "experts" are lying to you. They mean well, but they're lying.

They don't have the formula for your happiness. They don't know which six superfoods will unlock the secret to your youthfulness. They have no idea how to help you land your dream job. They don't know what morning routine will transform your life, or what twelve signs of compatibility you should look for in your partner, or how to get you where you want to go.

But these formulas, superfoods, morning routines, and listicles are *compelling*. Convincing. Promising. These accidental lies are yummy and well-researched and look suspiciously like the road map to your dream life.

As soon as we consider the possibility that fuckyeah *might* be real, "experts" appear in our lives, maybe on a podcast or in our Instagram feed, telling us that they have, in fact, found their fuckyeahs. They gush about how drop-dead amazing it is; how deeply, like as-deep-as-the-ocean deeply, fulfilling it is to finally be living their best lives. They also insist on telling us exactly *how* they found their fuckyeah, especially since it can be summarized, Buzzfeed-style, in twelve bullet points or less. And that's when all the lying begins.

Their autobiography isn't a lie—but the twelve steps required to repeat their results definitely are.

The happiness road map drafted by experts, gurus, and titans of industry will never be your road map. Your fuckyeah is different than mine, and theirs, and everyone else's. It is specific, individual, and not a copy > paste kind of situation.

And that's the problem with "self-care" advice today—it's a protocol for happiness that has become a one-size-fits-all, confusing, vaguely spiritual, science-phobic, brain-tangling, well-meaning, and yummy *lie*. And sure, the power stances, charcoal detoxes, and me-time bubble baths may offer some relief in the moment, but they *keep us chasing* a joy that we can't seem to find, or hold on to, in our adult lives. This is because the "experts" can't tell you how to find that drop-dead amazing, deep, like as-deep-as-the-ocean, magically fulfilling, and lasting happiness.

AND NEITHER CAN I.

None of us, myself included, have the secrets to your happiness. I don't have a clear-cut road map for you—of course, I don't—because I don't know where you are now, or where you're going, and I don't know how you'd like to get there. *But I can tell you how to create YOUR OWN map that will get you there. I can show you what self-limiting beliefs and habits—biological and societal—are censoring who you are and what you really want out of your life.*

Why? Because I know you; because I *am* you. I have equal parts lofty goals and time invested in my Netflix account. I lose track of time reading double-blind clinical studies, and I also lose hours scrolling my Instagram feed. I've been both an overachieving honors student and a college dropout. I've spoken at retreats, I've built my own business from the ground up—and I've also been fired, broke, and too overwhelmed to get out of bed some mornings. I think the wisdom that comes with age is a warm and fuzzy acceptance that we know and control nothing, and I *know* I'll never know as much as I'd like about this wild and crazy universe. But what I *do* know is how I feel, and how *many* of us feel.

I know we're tired of being pressured to be better, do more, and work faster, to self-optimize and fall in line in order to be happy. I know we're fed up with condescending self-help books telling us to just "be ourselves," and of hyper-filtered social media posts telling us to chase our "best lives." We're ready to stop bouncing back and forth between boredom and stress; ready to take our lives off "autopilot." We want to be happier, more confident, and more alive. We're ready to rediscover the raw joy of fuckyeah *as* we are right now, *where* we are right now. Not later, not when we get that next promotion, or when we're "finally in shape," or when we evolve into this so-called "best" version of ourselves. Not then—but *right . . . now.*

You *can* start building a well of inner resources that won't fade. You *can* find out what it is you want to "say," with or without words—that something which is uniquely yours to give—and share it with the rest of the world. *All you need is a willingness to change your mind.*

Really. That's it.

Over the course of this book, we're going to clear away the mental haze that's preventing you from realizing *what you want to do* (what I'm calling your fuckyeah), and *how to find it for yourself.*

Traditionally, the "experts" start by asking you a series of questions about what you want out of your life, starting with "What are you passionate about?" and then advise you to pursue that thing. That's great—*except for when you have no idea what you're passionate about.* How are you supposed to "follow your bliss" if you have no clue what "your bliss" is?!

If you were *starving*—quite literally dying of hunger—and someone told you, "I have the solution to your problem! All you need to do is eat!" wouldn't you be furious? When someone is starving, they don't need someone else to state the obvious; they need someone to (a) give them food, or (b) show them where to find it. *I'm going to do both.*

PART I: DETANGLE YOUR BRAIN

We like to call life a "journey" (**eye roll**) because we begin somewhere and end up somewhere else. Or maybe it's more accurate to say we begin as *someone* and end up *someone else*; we're changed by the journey. This lifelong transformation can be magical and deeply satisfying . . . unless the experience is a colossal waste of time spent wandering in aimless circles.

We can't get clear on where we want to go in life unless we're also clear on where we're starting from. What motivates your decisions, and what do you actually give a fuck about? What do you believe about yourself? Do you know why you believe that? Is it even true? To find fuckyeah we need to start by untangling the cultural, economic, and biological bullshit throwing off your innate sense of direction. Wouldn't it be nice to stop hating yourself for where you're "at" in your life and career? To live without regret over your past choices or fear of your future decisions? To be crystal clear on what you want and to have the confidence to go after it? Part I will prove that's not as crazy as it sounds.

PART II: UNCENSOR YOURSELF

"Be yourself." "Follow your bliss." "Live your best life." "Do what you love; love what you do."

>> *Okay, but HOW?!*

In an attempt to present an appealing, hireable, friendable, dateable, and acceptable version of ourselves to the world, we've spent our lives smothering, stifling, censoring, and editing who we really are—and in the process, shoving what we truly want deep into our subconscious and just beyond our reach.

To discover what we actually want out of life, we have to *unlearn* automatic self-censorship and *relearn* how to play, experiment, and take risks, befriending our intuition in the process. Part I will clear away the haze that makes what you want in life seem blurry and impossible. Part II will give you the courage, clarity, and scientifically proven strategies (*yes, for real*) to make it happen.

We'll step out in search of your fuckyeah—avoiding pitfalls, exhaustion, self-help clichés, and preachy books about eating paleo—*together*.

PART III: FUCKYEAH

You know what's missing from self-help, self-improvement, and self-care? The truth about "happily ever after."

Seems the high priests of self-improvement have plenty to say about finding joy, seeking happiness, and pursuing purpose, but nothing to say about what inevitably comes afterward: *change*. How do you *sustain* happiness? How do you *recover* fuckyeah after you've lost it? What do you do when you accomplish your goals and achieve your dreams—and it turns out you want a different dream altogether? How do you weather the storm when positive change *creates* chaos?

When shit hits the fan—because life guarantees that it will—you'll need the inner resources and practical tools to get through it unscathed (hopefully with a smile on your face), and that's what part III is all about.

When you understand the difference between the market's version of gimmicky #selfcare and the real deal, discover how to choose a team of people who will champion you and your fuckyeah, and no longer fear the chaos life hurls your way because you're fully equipped to keep finding your fuckyeah and never stop fighting for it—*you're finally free.*

Part I will give you clarity, part II will give you courage, and part III will give you resources you need to finally live your life on purpose.

No more bullshit. No more apathy. No more beating yourself up, tearing yourself down, stalling, stressing, or shrinking. It's time to uncensor yourself. It's time to find your fuckyeah.

Ready? I brought snacks.

I:
NGLE
YOUR
BRAIN

THE BRAIN TANGLE

Fuckyeah is your particular mash-up of sparkly universe dust, a form of self-expression that's *dying* to get out. It is your Art.

Fuckyeah comes from unpretentious, *literal* creativity—from your very human impulse to create something from nothing. This kind of Art is born out of that little-kid urge to dig something up from the intersection of your brain and soul, to mold it into something, and then share it with the world. It happens any moment you decide to make a connection with someone else; any moment you give instead of take. Sure, it might be conveyed through some traditional form of self-expression. But, then again, maybe not. It's possible your fuckyeah has nothing to do with what we think of as regular "creativity." Clay, glitter, or open-mic audience not required.

What if your Art is connecting with people? Or maybe your Art manifests in creating space: maybe digital space, through coding new software; or mental space, through practicing cognitive therapy; or physical space, through practicing architecture. Maybe your Art lies in merchandising, or gardening, or something else? It isn't necessarily a job. This kind of Art might make you money, or it might not. Your fuckyeah might not be for sale. It might not be an object. It might be an idea. A gesture.

You have something to say, with or without words—something uniquely yours to give—and this is your fuckyeah.

Fuckyeah isn't a thing or a job description; *it's the magic you bring into your world.*

Does that sentence make you want to roll your eyes? That's okay. It makes me feel that way too. But the truth is, fuckyeah lives somewhere between *raw joy* and *uncensored self-expression.* You may have noticed that the two go hand in hand: when we're free to exist without filters, we experience real happiness.

So, the question is, do you know what makes you feel that way? Maybe not. Maybe you *know* that you've felt fuckyeah before, but whatever made you feel that way seems blurry and far off now. *That's okay. You don't have to have all the answers.* But to figure out what it is you really want out of life, you do need to know *where to go looking* for your Art. Let's start by doing something irrational together; let's see what happens when you try to uncensor your dream life.

UNCENSOR YOUR AMBITIONS

Using the following blank space, complete the exercise below. (If you're someone who prefers their books un-messed-with, any blank piece of paper will work: a napkin, the note-taking app on your phone—anything, really.) After reading the prompt, write what comes to mind onto the page *as quickly as you can.* Make an orderly list or scribble all over the place—whatever comes naturally to you.

RULE NO. 1:	*Be honest, even if it's embarrassing. Nobody sees this but you.*
RULE NO. 2:	*Do not edit, censor, or tweak your answers. Do not rationalize with yourself; do not disqualify anything.*
RULE NO. 3:	*Set a timer for five minutes, read the prompt, then start the clock.*

Imagine that you have an endless supply of money. We're talking about B-I-G money here: you won the lottery—all the lotteries, everywhere, actually—and for some reason, the government decided *not* to tax you on any of it. You will never need money *ever* again. No catch. You can do whatever you want with this money, and because of that, literally anything you want with your time. Let's also assume you buy everything you need for yourself and your loved ones. Knowing that you and everyone you care about are financially set for life, answer this question:

If you could have, create, do, build, or try anything, and be anyone, what would you have, do, or be?

GO.

_____
_____
_____
_____
_____
_____
_____
_____
_____
_____

Note: If you doodled on a piece of paper and not in your book, hang on to it. Fold it up and wedge it between the book's pages or snap a quick photo of it. You'll need it later!

THE BRAIN TANGLE

So, how did drafting up your dream life go?

I'm guessing you thought of plenty of things you'd like to have, a few things you'd like to do or try, and petered out around what you'd like to do with your life. Maybe you tried to fill that five minutes with your dreamiest dreams, but lost steam after just two or three minutes, because thinking about "the how" was too overwhelming. Don't feel bad, because there's a damn good reason we struggle to clearly visualize our dream lives: we're caught up in reality. And the reality is, *we can't afford to dream BIG.*

We have *no idea* what we'd do with all the cash and time in the world, because we haven't had many chances to consider it seriously. And more importantly, because suddenly winning the lottery, or all the lotteries in the world, will NEVER happen. And that's the catch, isn't it? If we had all the money in the world, it *wouldn't matter* that we don't know what we want to do with our time, because we'd finally have time to find out. Time to be ourselves, to relax, and to screw around with hobbies. Time to see the world and learn new languages. Time to become game-changing entrepreneurs, or to start philanthropic foundations that wipe out world hunger.

But we don't have the luxury of that kind of time.

Think about it: If your "time" was somehow magically transformed into a pie, what would the biggest slice be? *Work.* Are you in school? Then school is your work. Are you in school and holding a job? Go ahead and take an even bigger slice. The majority of our time "pie" is work-flavored (eww), and we're starting to question *if we can stomach it.* If we are in a job where we struggle to find meaning, why would we spend up to 54 percent of our waking hours doing it?

Oh, right. Bills.

Whatever dreams we have for our lives—whatever things we want to learn, or try, or change—we view through the filter of "cost." Not because we're all greedy, soulless assholes, but because what we can't buy *costs us our time.* For example, you could walk to work each morning, but you'll have to decide if walking forty-seven miles is *worth* your time. A car payment costs hundreds of dollars per month, while walking to work would cost you fifteen hours per day. Walking just isn't practical in this scenario. But which do you currently have more of, money or time? Maybe a car payment is out of the question, but a bus ticket isn't. Everything *costs* something.

In other words, *we're only as free as our last paycheck.* Kind of explains why we grit our teeth and roll our eyes at these "exercises" asking us to "dream big," as if we had all the money in the world, doesn't it? But there's another, deeper, well-hidden reason it's so difficult to picture the life you want:

You're not allowed to want it.

Have you ever spent fifteen minutes playing with a five-year-old? They have no problem fully embodying a princess who is also a firefighter who *also* has a crack team (comprised of Spider-Man, a plush turtle, and a headless Bratz doll) protecting the kingdom from the evil monster (the family golden retriever). Why is it so easy for kids to see a world of possibilities in this fluid way? It's not because they have underdeveloped brains, though that would be easy to claim. *It's because they haven't learned how to censor themselves yet.*

You've been lied to, remember? By people who meant well, of course. Well-meaning, yes, white lies, yes, but lies nonetheless—subtle little knots that become catastrophic brain tangles, limiting the person you want to be, holding you back from the life you want to live. A lifetime of systemic pressure, social expectations, and cultural feedback has taken its toll on you, tying tight little knots in the part of your brain that knows how to dream and execute on those dreams. It's not your fault; to be a functioning human in the modern world requires *a lot* of censorship.

But let me put it this way: You know your dangling-but-twisted earbud headphones? (For those of you who have embraced our cordless future, you remember these, right?) The ones you just yanked up from the bottom of your bag, all knotted up in a jumbly clusterfuck of a cord tangle? After years of "refining" and editing your look, language, beliefs, and self, *those are your brains.*

As we grow up, we're taught that princesses can't also be firefighters, that turtles don't talk, and that our Art probably won't pay the bills. We learn that forty-plus hours of work a week is tiring, and that we're *all* far too tired to deal with the potential resistance, or possibility of failure, that comes with chasing our dreams. So, in an effort to protect our finite energy and ensure our safety, we automatically smother our irrational ideas, edit our dreams, and filter our presentation of ourselves to the world, surprised that we eventually find ourselves *numb.*

That exercise you did at the beginning of this chapter? It wasn't a punchline for some cruel joke about how your dreams can't coexist with modern life. You don't know *how* yet, but the life you want to live—you can live it. It all starts by detangling those knots in your mind.

THE PROBLEM WITH AUTOPILOT

Autopilot: a complex system that allows a plane we're sitting inside of to fly itself through the air. A plane. That we're sitting inside of. Can fly itself. *Through the air!*

Human pilots input settings like speed, altitude, and direction; in turn, the autopilot maintains those settings for as long as the plane has fuel. Unlike people, the autopilot won't get tired; it will maintain any preprogrammed course with mathematical precision. By juggling multiple complicated tasks for long stretches of time, autopilot systems give human pilots the freedom to fly the plane without compromising their concentration, thus ruling out countless forms of human error. Autopilot is the *perfect* pilot.

Except, of course, when a flock of birds is up ahead, or a massive storm, or zero fuel. Sure, the autopilot has plenty of warning bells, whistles, and blinking lights to inform a human pilot about the oncoming danger, *but it's not going to do anything about it on its own.* This is why we aren't flying around in self-flying airplanes without a crew: only the *pilot* is capable of taking adaptive action. Autopilot's lack of self-awareness and inability to change can put the people on board and the surrounding world in *real* danger.

Guess what?

Your life is on autopilot.

Unfortunately, your brain's goal is to automate huge facets of your life. It's been evolving for millennia, fine-tuning your ability to absorb, assess, and respond to the world, all in less than an instant. Your brain and body have manufactured a near-perfect system to keep you from dying—a thing you're always *almost* doing—and you don't even have to pay attention for it to work.

Just think of everything your brain has to manage while you're driving a car: keeping you alive without distracting you (breathing, circulation, digestion), sensory perception (touch, vision, hearing), memory access (rules of the road and a mental map of your neighborhood), *and* motor reflexes, *and* a stream-of-consciousness internal monologue, *and* language (especially since some asshole just cut you off). That's a lot of things to juggle at once, and yet, you do it beautifully, regularly.

Autopilot is an incredible evolutionary miracle. In fact, it's probably the reason our ancestors survived the horrors of early human life, while the other relatives of *Homo sapiens* did not.

It's also the reason you're unhappy.

This automatic system—designed to lengthen your life, lighten your workload, and streamline your decision-making—is deeply flawed. *Autopilot can't turn itself off.* Not ever. Not even when your health, sanity, or happiness depends on it. Autopilot is the foundation of all habits, the source of all self-sabotage, the brain tangle to end all brain tangles, and the oldest, most powerful, fully autonomous function of your mind.

RUSSIAN NESTING DOLLS

Have you ever seen these things? They're these little egg-shaped, hand-painted, wooden dolls that split in half to reveal a smaller doll inside, and another inside that, all the way down to an adorable, itty-bitty little doll nugget. Yeah, so ... that's your brain.

When I say "brain," you are likely visualizing a football-shaped, squiggly pinkish-gray blob with two halves—but that's just *one part* of your brain. You're picturing the largest, outermost nesting doll, called your *cerebrum*—the new kid on the evolutionary block, and the part responsible for the "higher thought" activities unique to humans. To keep things simple, we will call this your *Pilot Brain*. Pilot Brain handles logical thinking, language, inventing, calculating, planning, and integrating sensory input with action and movement. Pilot Brain is "book" smart: the brain processing the words you're reading on this page; the brain that sets goals; the brain that schedules things on calendars; your conscious mind. Your Pilot Brain likes to believe it's in charge of your life—but that's because it doesn't know about the other nesting dolls yet.

Deep within the Pilot Brain are two more "brains," each smaller, less civilized, and more powerful than the last—together they make up your *Autopilot Brain*. The middle nesting doll includes your *cerebellum* and *brain stem*; these structures handle the automatic bits of being a human—breathing, heart rate, sleeping, digesting, sneezing, puking, and so on. Although these involuntary bodily functions are 100 percent on autopilot, they're not why autopilot is making you unhappy. To uncover the source of our stress, exhaustion, confusion, and apathy, we need to travel deeper into the center of the Autopilot Brain—to the final, smallest, and most powerful of the nesting dolls: *the limbic system.*

This little troublemaker handles your animal instincts (like "fight or flight"), the drives behind hunger, sex, parenting, aggression, and dominance, and the creation of all your complex emotions. Neuroscientist Paul MacLean, the guy who discovered the limbic system in the 1950s, called the tiny structures within it our "reptilian" brain, because they were similar in appearance and function to the brains of reptiles (and a few birds). This "reptilian" brain was the earliest part of the human mind to evolve, making it more powerful and dominant than any other part of your brain. Imagine giving a skittish little lizard the authority to direct your decisions and override logical thought in favor of instinctive, fear-based feelings? Yeah—that's your Autopilot Brain.

Autopilot Brain is the reason you are afraid to take risks, make changes, and take a chance on your dreams. When we leave our comfort zones, Autopilot kicks into survival mode.

Have you ever stood in front of an audience and struggled to get the words out? You can't stop sweating, blushing, and stuttering through your speech. You're not in real danger and you *know* that—but your Autopilot Brain doesn't and is reacting in the same way it would if you saw a raging grizzly bear. If your inner lizard has any reason to believe you are taking a risk, it will happily override logical thought, sabotage your decision-making, and paralyze you with fear. Survival mode worked for millions of years for our evolutionary ancestors; why would biology quit now?

Autopilot Brain is street-smart, nonverbal, and intuitive: the brain that blocks out distractions so you can focus on reading this book; the brain that imagines, daydreams, and worries; your *subconscious* mind. And because it was the first section of your brain to form in your mama's womb, Autopilot is faster, more efficient, and better at multitasking than Pilot Brain, which means Autopilot is in charge of your life by default.

And that's the key—the way out of this mess—the magic words: "by default." Autopilot isn't your only mode; it's your default mode. Autopilot isn't your only brain *for a reason.*

See, your life experience is real, but it isn't "happening" to you. You're not observing a preexisting reality; Autopilot is constructing it. *Autopilot Brain is ghostwriting your life.*

THE GHOSTWRITER

Vast amounts of information bombard your brain every second of every day.

Ever tried holding a conversation with friends in a roaring, dimly lit, full-capacity bar on a Saturday night? You could argue it takes all your focus just to piece together what your friend is saying, let alone make sense of all the other stuff going on.

Scientists estimate our senses are sending 11 million bits of information to our brains *per second,* while the amount of information we can consciously handle is between only 60 and 120 bits per second. Listening to just one person talk requires processing up to 60 bits of info per second, which means listening to two people at once in that noisy bar puts us at our *maximum concentration capacity.* But something doesn't quite add up here . . . that leaves roughly 10,999,880 bits of data flooding our brains *every second.* Where the fuck is all this other sensory data going?!

It is going into autopilot territory—*your subconscious mind.* When we hear terms like *subconscious* or *unconscious,* we think of a mysterious subbasement of our brains, full of repressed emotions and weird, NSFW desires. This wet and wild image of a secret self was brought to you by Sigmund Freud, the twentieth-century founder of psychoanalysis who popularized a theory of the self being built on a dark and twisty psyche. Contrary to many of Freud's theories, modern science now knows that your subconscious mind is healthy and a pretty damn awe-inspiring master sorter, analyst, and processor, but it took a minute (okay, more like several hundred years) to get here.

Your subconscious isn't one location or a specific structure inside your brain; it's a network of lightning-fast communication between Autopilot and Pilot Brain, constantly operating behind the scenes of your life. Things that are subconscious (like breathing) can be brought up into consciousness as long as you are thinking about it, but a huge percentage of Autopilot activity *stays* subconscious.

Neurologists have some surprising news: we're clueless when it comes to nearly 95 percent of what's happening in our minds at any given time, leaving only 5 percent of our lives within our conscious awareness.

So your brain isn't throwing out those 10 million–plus bits of data per second—it's sorting them obsessively, searching for patterns that might mean something to your survival. Your brain is a hoarder, saving that random song lyric, elementary school poem, and newspaper headline from a week ago—just in case you might need it—all ready to be brought up into your conscious thoughts instantaneously. And really, it's doing you a favor; if you had to process everything your senses picked up all at once, you'd crash faster than my first-generation iPod. This is the beauty of the subconscious mind—it narrows down what we need to focus on, making it easier to be a human—just like autopilot streamlines what a pilot needs to focus on. But autopilot doesn't just filter out excess data; it can also refuse to acknowledge new data and stick to old formulas—and, without a pilot's intervention, overcorrect in flight and put the plane and crew in unnecessary danger.

Keeping most of reality out of focus makes your life easier, but this means your subconscious perceptions, emotions, memories, and beliefs get to ghostwrite your life story, and you have to deal with the resulting plot.

Lawyers advocate for their clients, right? They're great at collecting evidence relevant to their case and downplaying what would hinder their argument. They blend tangible proof with compelling storytelling, connecting the dots for the listening judge or jury. They reconstruct reality for the audience and on behalf of their client. They are the perfect blend of scientist and storyteller.

And so is your brain.

Except for late-night conversations while high off our asses, we believe our physical senses reflect an *objective* reality. And while our senses of sight, smell, hearing, taste, and touch are incredibly sophisticated, it turns out they're not accurate. What we see is not, in fact, what we get.

Your subconscious mind, responsible for sorting nearly all the sensory data coming at you, is filling in the gaps and inventing your reality.

Don't believe me? *You have a blind spot in your vision.* You are incapable of seeing anything in this area, because it's where the bundle of optic nerves from your brain connects to your eye's retina, and there are zero-zilch-nada photoreceptors at that pinpoint.

So, why isn't a black hole blocking out someone's face while you talk with them? Because your subconscious fills in the gap, making its best guess about what *might* be in the void based on what surrounds it.

Here, I'll show you: Hold this book at arm's length, and cover your right eye with your free hand. Focus on the big **X** below with your left eye, and keep your focus on it as you slowly pull the book toward you. While you're looking at the **X**, you'll still be able to see the **O** in your peripheral vision, up until a certain point when it disappears. It usually vanishes about ten inches away from your face and then reappears again as you bring the book closer. Find the spot where it disappears; that's your blind spot. Go ahead, try it with the other eye too.

O   **X**

Crazy, right? Now draw a straight line directly through the **O** and **X**, all the way across the page, horizontally. (If you like your books pristine, draw these two markings on a notecard about four and a half inches apart; then draw the horizontal line through them.) Once again, bring the book toward you, and when you find your blind spot, notice that the line you drew *appears* unbroken. I say "appears" because, remember, *you cannot see anything at that blind spot*; you have no photoreceptors there. It is a black hole, but your brain is filling in the void with the *illusion* of a line, using information collected from your central focus (in this case, a line).

Our subconscious minds are reconstructing reality based on our central focus. (Remember that; it's going to be important later.)

Oh, also: *your vision is shaking violently, all the time.* But our brains are so good at lying, I mean *processing images*, you'd never know it. Your eye muscles are making lightning-fast movements—over one hundred thousand a day—to take in the scenery around you. If *Cloverfield* and *The Blair Witch Project* had a movie baby and then you watched that movie while off-roading in the mountains, it *still* wouldn't be as shaky as your eyeballs naturally are. But your auto-pilot smooths it all out by *suppressing reality*; it does you a favor by tricking you. And that's just your sense of sight!

Your sense of hearing is a game of Mad Libs, played by your brain. Case in point: the "phantom words" experiment created by Diana Deutsch, a professor of psychology at the University of California, San Diego. By looping two-syllable sounds slightly out of sync on a recorded track, Deutch created a world of sound bouncing from ear to ear, unnerving the listener. Subjects reported hearing specific strings of words in their native language. Even weirder? What people hear is usually related to something they're thinking about subconsciously; researchers were surprised to find out that people who heard words related to food were on a diet and people who heard things like "No time" or "I'm tired" were under serious stress at work. Whatever Autopilot Brain is subconsciously focused on (food cravings, exhaustion, sex, you name it) will become the conscious reality of what we hear.

AUTOPILOT IS GHOSTWRITING YOUR LIFE

Now, let's test *your* memory (and maybe catch the lawyer in action). Pay very careful attention to the following list of words; study them for at least thirty seconds. Ready?

Sour, candy, sugar, bitter, tooth, good, taste, nice, soda, honey, chocolate, cake, heart, eat, and pie. Did you really study this list? Okay, now don't look at the list while you read the next paragraph.

All you need to do is identify which of the upcoming words appeared on the previous list. Your answer doesn't have to be just one word—maybe all of them were on the list; maybe only one or two were. Don't decide on a word until you can visualize where the word was on the list. Choose from the following three words: taste, point, sweet. Take a moment to think about this. Okay, revisit the list. How'd you do?

That was a different kind of phantom word experiment, one that theoretical physicist and author Leonard Mlodinow has given to countless groups of his students over the years. According to Mlodinow, the majority of people remember with absolute certainty that "point" was not on the list, but are pretty sure that "taste" was. Most also recall, confidently, that "sweet" was on that list. Were you one of those people? Yeah, so was I. "Sweet" was not on the list, but most of the words on it were related to sweetness as an *idea*. We remembered a phantom word because our memory was built around *the gist* of the words we saw, not the actual words.

Your Autopilot Brain isn't as concerned with accuracy as it is with speed. Being fast and efficient ensures survival, and that's how your memory has evolved: to fill in the blanks as quickly as possible.

We tend to think of our memories like video files saved on a computer—when we need them we look for the correct folder and file, replaying it back in our conscious thoughts. In actuality, our memories are more like an editable PDF. You, as the initial author, lay down the first round of content, but a new version overwrites the original every time the document is opened. Whenever we access a memory, our autopilot can't help but make dramatic edits, especially if the experience is at odds with our beliefs or expectations, or if we know something now that we didn't know then.

This memory distortion happens all the time. Just think back on the game of "telephone" that we all played as kids, in which a message is whispered from one person to the next, inevitably transforming into something totally different. Frederic Bartlett, an early twentieth-century psychologist, famously used this game in an experiment to prove we don't only lose memories, but we also have "additive" memories. As our original memory fades, we *fabricate* new memory data that immediately streamline and *erase* anything our brains consider "nonsense." This is how the phrase "vroom dinosaur" becomes "dining room floor" by the end of the game. In other words, your "memory" is much more an act of creation than recollection.

You remember your Pilot Brain has a right and a left hemisphere, yes? Good. The left brain is famous for logic, speech, and analytical thinking, while the right brain is famous for nonverbal, creative, and emotional thinking (these qualities are stereotypes, but generally true). These two halves pass essential sensory info to each other across the *corpus callosum* (let's call it your *brain bridge*) so that your whole brain can process it. Split-brain patients, however, cannot share information between their two hemispheres, because their brain bridge is either damaged or destroyed.

In several famous studies, researchers first asked split-brain patients to complete a task via their right brain, and then asked them to use their left brain to explain why they did what they did. When they asked a patient (via his right hemisphere) to laugh, he did. His left hemisphere heard and felt the laughter, *but did not know any instruction to laugh had been given*, so when asked why he laughed, he said it was because he thought the researchers were being funny. His left brain completely invented a reason for his behavior! When the researchers asked a patient via his right hemisphere to wave, and then asked his left hemisphere why he waved, the patient told them he had seen someone he knew. Even though these patients' left brains had no clue where these actions had come from, they were still compelled to explain, even defend, their actions. Ultimately, the researchers of these experiments—and of similar experiments involving patients with "connected," healthy brains—discovered that *our Pilot Brain doesn't merely acknowledge our Autopilot emotions and actions, but also tries to explain them, even if those explanations aren't true.*

The skewed and inaccurate stories we tell ourselves are the biological origin of our self-sabotaging beliefs.

When we allow negative, seemingly true, stories to become our reality, we are censoring our dreams with false perceptions of ourselves, granting Autopilot permission to tear down our confidence and strip us of our power to succeed.

Like a lawyer, your mind connects disparate pieces of evidence to tell a story *it has already determined is true,* because it thinks that story is in your best interest.

Sensory illusions are the result of our brain trying to match new "data" to a preexisting mental template; when it can't find a match, it fills in the blanks with something else. Our subconscious Autopilot is just doing its job, looking for patterns or connections that mean something to our survival—even if they're not there. Your ghostwriting Autopilot Brain isn't censoring your dreams or changing your life's plot points to be an asshole; it thinks it's protecting you.

Our reality is constructed, not reflected. If we want to find the raw joy of fuckyeah, we have to rewrite the stories that are being automated.

CANCEL YOUR SUBSCRIPTION TO BULLSHIT

Let's say you fall down an HGTV rabbit hole and decide to build your own house, from scratch. (Impressive.) Once the home is finished, you move in. You'd say then that you live in this house, right? *Right.* Would you also say that this house happened to you? *Nope.* You live in this house, but it didn't "happen" to you. In fact, you built it.

Your life experience is real, but it isn't "happening" to you. You're not observing a preexisting reality; you are building it.

And the framework of this reality house? Your beliefs.

In fact, your beliefs determine your actions, *whether you are aware of them or not.* If I believe that earning money is an uphill battle, then *I will make* earning money an uphill battle. If you believe your life is exhausting, then *you will make* your life exhausting. If I believe I have an audience, then *I will make* my life a performance. If you believe you are your job, then *you will make* your life an endless pursuit of the "dream job." We don't realize we're constructing these realities—but Autopilot is busy hammering away, just out of sight, in our subconscious minds. Beliefs determine everything we do (or don't do), because they're tied to something far more powerful than just sensory data: *our emotions.*

"Beliefs" are a set of instructions for your brain and body to follow, based on a set of emotionally color-coded memories. Let's say you touch a hot stove and experience searing pain. Youch. Thanks to the sensory data you picked up (touch: *hot!*) and your emotions color-coding the memory (*pain! fear! danger! RED FLAG!*), you now believe touching a hot stove should be avoided. (Good call.) Since you don't need to be thinking about hot stoves all the time, your brain files this away in your subconscious; the next time you see a hot stove, you're looking at it through this *filter* of belief.

Belief = Sensory Information + Emotional "Proof"

Your brain ultimately decides how to store information based on how emotionally relevant it is to your survival—a concept called "somatic marker theory." Since there is an absurd amount of data to sort and store (11 million bits per second, you'll recall)—and since your hoarder-brain wants to keep it all—your belief "instructions" and the memories they're based on will all need to be *compressed*.

The ideal way to compress a file—or shrink a memory—is by creating shortcuts; by erasing anything that can be communicated accurately with less data. Memory shortcuts are the reason you can drive home from work without thinking (you've done it so many times) and why the smell of baked cookies always reminds you of your Nana (baking cookies with Nana is an emotionally colored memory). To make room in your memory for everything important, bits of information are removed, shortcutting one thing to another, making your brain both faster and roomier at the same time. It's the efficient kind of shit your Autopilot Brain lives for.

Shortcutting redundancies can only be done so many times though. Once information is as simplified as possible, the next, less ideal option in file compression is to remove *valuable* data. Files that are overcompressed look pixelated and blurry, sound garbled, or read like jumbled nonsense. What do you think happens to your over-compressed memories? How many times over would you guess your childhood experiences have been compressed in this way?

I've always hated the Steven Spielberg classic *E.T.* with a fiery conviction. When asked why, I'd explain, "It's overhyped, you know? E.T. is a creepy alien, and the whole plot is depressing." My answer always confused people, since *E.T.* is a universally loved, heartwarming eighties family sci-fi movie. When my hatred for *E.T.* came up in a conversation with my mom, she interrupted my airtight defense, "Punkin, that's not why you hate this movie. Don't you remember?

When we took you to get allergy tested, this movie was always on loop in the patient room. You watched *E.T.* lying on your stomach, with fifty-plus needle pricks running down your spine, itching in pain as your little body reacted to the allergens. That's why you hate *E.T.*" Um . . . color me surprised. My brain had saved a vague memory of watching *E.T.* and the emotional "color" of watching it but *wrote out the rest of the info.* Whenever called upon to explain, my Pilot Brain did its best, even though it had to fill in the blanks with made-up reasons. I didn't really hate *E.T.*, I hated the experience of allergy testing—but missing data in my compressed memory left me with just the vague feeling: *E.T.* = pain.

We don't act on data; we act on what we believe about the data—even if we can't remember why we believe it.

While we have no problem labeling someone else's belief as fact, personal preference, or flat-out bullshit, we can't filter our beliefs in the same way. Your brain doesn't file your experiences logically, from "subjective opinion" to "objective fact." *It organizes them by emotional color codes*—by whatever experience made the most noise, was most awe-inspiring, or horrifying, or earth-shattering. The more intense the emotion of an event, the more factual it seems, and when things have to be compressed, as they always do, your brain counts the emotional experiences as more important than any of the actual details.

So, there are two ways for information or an experience to become a "fact" (aka a belief) in your mind:

1. *It is something so emotionally neutral and so universally agreed upon at that time that it would be embarrassing to refute it (like, for example, the belief that the earth revolves around the sun).*

2. *It is something so loaded with emotion that it earns permission to overwrite the contents of a memory (like, for example, the belief that you are unworthy of love because you have been dumped four times in the last year).*

Once your mind has decided "this is true" it files all your beliefs in a folder labeled "facts" within your subconscious and then treats them all with equal validity, as if to say: *I can and will act on this.*

This means an idea that you're a loser-piece-of-shit can carry the same factuality in your brain *as the laws of physics.*

The beliefs we know to be the truest about ourselves and our life's possibilities are not necessarily the most true or even the least bit accurate—they just happen to be the noisiest.

GRILLED ONIONS AND LIMITING BELIEFS

Something grabs your attention after you roll down the car window: the mouthwatering scent of grilled onions and barbecue floating through the air.

Your subconscious Autopilot Brain instantly scans the "facts" folder and concludes, *"Hungry! Grilled onions and barbecue are food. Yum. Get food."* For a split second, your conscious Pilot Brain starts planning: *"Get a Double-Double Cheeseburger with grilled onions from In-N-Out for lunch!"* But before you can determine how this will reorganize your day, your Autopilot Brain scans the "facts" folder again, at lightning speed, and makes the final call:

>> *"I can't have that."*

Wait, *WTF*? On the second pass, your Autopilot Brain found a compressed, red-flagged memory that had been grandfathered in to the "facts" folder because of its emotional intensity: a belief that eating burgers makes people fat, and that being fat is bad.

This secret belief is buried so deep in your subconscious *you don't even realize you believe it.* It was buried there when you were a little kid—your mom made a big deal about weight, often fat-shaming people whose bodies she disapproved of, including yours. Even though your conscious mind completely disagrees with Mom's closed-mindedness about which bodies are beautiful, you absorbed this belief into your subconscious background as a kid. Even though you would never fat-shame anyone, your subconscious accepted limitations about what is okay or not okay *for you to eat.*

So what happens? You keep drooling, but you still don't allow yourself to get the Double-Double. When the burger idea is redirected to your conscious mind, memories of your mom's opinions and fat-shaming were nowhere to be found, long since compressed into a pixelated blur. All you know is: *"I can't have a burger right now."* Your desire (*Hungry!*) still needs to be met, so you decide to eat a granola bar that you hate just to satisfy the need, oblivious to why.

And that, right there? That's a limiting belief.

Here's why limiting beliefs fuck us over: *they make sense on the surface—which makes us buy into them.* When you made that split-second decision, it wasn't conscious. It was an Autopilot *feeling* that you shouldn't eat burgers, followed by a Pilot Brain *explanation*. In this case, the explanation is totally logical: there *are* serious health consequences to eating fast food; it *would* be healthier to eat something else. It's wise to avoid artery-clogging fast food. But, in this particular instant, you didn't choose that granola bar to promote your health;

you chose it because your belief is *you are not allowed to have, do, or be anything associated with "fat."* This limiting belief forced you to make a decision from a place of shame, rather than finding satisfaction with choosing something healthy for your body.

Remember the split-brain patients, accidentally bullshitting about why they waved or laughed? When looking for a reason to direct your behavior, your brain reached into the "facts" folder, pulled out "Fast food is unhealthy," and conveniently left "If I am fat, I am unloved" hidden in your subconscious. This action (skipping the burger) *validated* that toxic belief. This is how self-sabotaging beliefs spread into different areas of our lives. The more you buy into this damaging belief around beauty and body image, the more you find yourself denying yourself the clothing you'd like to wear and fixating on becoming the "perfect" physical version of yourself by someone else's standards—the more the world misses out on getting to appreciate the real, authentic you.

The good news: If you're capable of constructing your reality, you're capable of reconstructing it too.

Recent research in neuroscience has proven that the human brain is "plastic," meaning thoughts *alone* are capable of changing the function and physical structure of the brain. Thoughts have the power to trigger depression and sabotage our lives—but they also have the power to heal stroke survivors, conquer learning disabilities, overcome mental disorders, and cure diseases. NO JOKE. Science has proven that changing our thoughts actually changes our body chemistry, our behavior, and, ultimately, our lives. (Yay science!) I can also confirm, from personal experience, that it's possible to unravel the tangle of limiting-belief garbage in your messy brain and start living the life you really want.

Once you discover what self-limiting rules your Autopilot has been diligently following—which limiting beliefs have edited your dreams and censored who you really are—you can rebuild your reality, rewrite your stories, and redirect your life toward fuckyeah.

Ready to dispel some bullshit?

2.

I'M ONLY AS FREE AS MY LAST PAYCHECK

We live our lives in installments.

We eat, and then we need to eat all over again. We sleep and then need to sleep again. Pay rent and then pay rent again. Today, spending our days hunting and gathering, as our ancestors did, is not the most efficient way for us to continuously pay rent or eat. So, instead, we spend our time working for a paycheck. In this reality, what we "do for a living" becomes *really important.*

But you knew that.

You remember answering the question, "What do you want to be when you grow up?" at least a hundred times for friendly grown-ups and grade-school homework assignments. More often than not, you were rewarded for having an answer, and that positive reinforcement was deeply ingrained into your spongy little-kid brain. And today?

After the name swapping, nice-to-meet-yous, and handshakes, the question is always, "What do you do?" It's clear you're not being asked how you spent the last few hours either (*ahem* Netflix). You're being asked to explain what you're doing *with your life*. Even if the answer you give feels like icky bullshit the moment it comes out of your mouth, it somehow feels less icky than having no answer at all.

Since we spend most of our time at work, and our time off the clock is spent depleting the resources we earned at work, and since working is a necessity for most of us, it makes sense we're all a smidge obsessed with (1) earning as much cash as possible, and (2) finding a job that doesn't make us want to rip our hair out.

We want to love what we do for a living, but life in the "real world" doesn't always present us with this possibility—and we have Wi-Fi to pay for. We dream of the "dream job," where our passion pays the bills and our free time is full of things we love to do; we exhaust ourselves hustling to get there. It's a tug-of-war. This back and forth is so familiar that we've even invented a popular expression for it: *work-life balance.*

Imagine an old-timey, scales-of-justice kind of scale. On one side of the scale, in a category we'll call JOB, we've got boring concepts: pays the bills, the nine-to-five, the hustle, and working for the man. On the other side, in a category we'll call ART, we've got fun, dreamy concepts like passion, calling, creative autonomy, purpose, and your fuckyeah. JOB is not exclusively negative and ART is not exclusively positive; but each time the scale tips further in the direction of JOB, we experience more *work* and less *life*, often leading to resentment and burnout, dragging us further away from modern life's best-case scenario: living our fuckyeahs.

Modern Life: Worst-Case to Best-Case Scenarios

1. *No job and no Art. Financially screwed and creatively miserable.*

2. *Job pays the bills but drains the life out of you. No energy to live Art off the clock.*

3. *Job pays the bills. If Art happens, it happens off the clock.*

4. *Art pays the bills, at least some of the time. Pretty dreamy.*

5. *Your job and your free time are Art! Your finances are solid, and you've found creative fulfillment.*

We don't want to just pay the bills; we want to like *how* we pay the bills. We want to be creatively stimulated and satisfied. Maybe change the world, even if it's just an itty-bitty corner of it. We want to find our fuckyeah and share our Art. Unfortunately, we spend our lives tipping this scale back and forth, searching for work-life balance on the JOB versus ART seesaw, daydreaming about the dream life (no. 5) and struggling to make the most of things as they often are (somewhere between no. 2 and no. 3). This work-life balance seesaw—in addition to making us tired, confused, and a little nauseous—has had an unexpected side effect:

We've come to believe we *are* our jobs.

We wear our jobs like a second skin, the first layer of our personalities—whether proudly or begrudgingly. It's even coded into our language. The more we like the work we do, the more comfortably we identify ourselves with it: "*I am* a graphic designer." The less we like the work we do, the further we distance ourselves from it: "Right now? I, uh . . . I just . . . bus tables. Just for now, you know . . ." If we like the work, we're proud of ourselves; if we hate the work, we're disappointed in ourselves. You can see how that might be problematic, right?

I couldn't.

In the four years leading up to that stress-meltdown and quarter-life crisis turned self-help-quest that I mentioned in the introduction, I was *slaying* at work. I liked my job, which meant I enjoyed working really hard. I showed up early. I stayed late. I went above and beyond. My bosses took notice, and since the company was steadily growing, I was promoted year after year. I liked the validation, creative freedom, positive feedback, and increased responsibility. I *liked* wrapping my identity up in my job, because I liked the work, because other people thought I was good at my job, and because it came easily to me.

When my biggest promotion pushed me far outside my comfort zone, stretched my skill set, and tested my relationships, I took it in stride. "It's just part of a new challenge," I thought. I continued to approach my new gig the way I had before: I showed up early. I stayed late. I went above and beyond. I treated mundane tasks with the same enthusiasm; I thought of my coworkers as family. I was the same, the company was the same, but something had changed: *the circumstances.*

The company's growth had slowed along with the economy, spreading its resources thin. It had to adapt, as all good companies should, which meant my bosses had to adapt, as did my job responsibilities. I struggled to keep up my standard breakneck pace. The external validation dried up, the creative freedom disappeared, and the increased responsibility weighed on me. I became more and more insecure by the day. *"Am I just not cut out for this? Was I fooling myself?"* I became anxious and defensive, often lashing out in my personal life. I was exhausted, and it showed. I was putting myself under intense pressure to maintain the excellence that came so easily in my previous roles, and as a result, I began to go totally *numb.*

Do you know why I slowly started to implode? Why I was so full of self-doubt and self-loathing? Because I believed I was my job, *and I was no longer good at my job*. It's not that I was incapable or overpromoted—but I was inexperienced, limited by a redistribution of company resources, *and* trying to be a perfectionist. Perfectionism bred shame, which sucked all the fun out of the work. I had accidentally tied my self-worth to external validation in my job, and when it disappeared, so did my value.

When our identities are tangled up in our jobs, we're forced to censor who we are to fit a job description—and when our work defines our worth, our self-esteem is at the mercy of the market.

By believing we are our jobs, we're living like commodities, not humans. How the hell did we get here?!

HOW THE HELL WE GOT HERE

Before the Industrial Revolution, it was standard procedure to grow your own food, spin your own yarn, make your own clothes, and trade or sell whatever you created directly from your home. Your quality of life was limited by your skill set (not to mention the race and class you were born into). You worked for yourself, your family, or a more affluent family (and very possibly without your consent). In other words, the nine-to-five didn't exist. Regular paychecks didn't exist. Resumes didn't exist. Machines changed all of that, immediately and forever.

Production by machine was cheap as hell and dramatically improved the standard of living. Cities boomed. Capitalism boomed. Lots of booming, all around. Instead of becoming a pro at whatever your family's trade was, you could now do entry-level work in a factory and bring home cold hard cash. *This was game-changing.*

If you're a capitalist in the nineteenth century, you want your machines to work efficiently and precisely. That's the whole point; machines are expensive at first but reduce costs in the long run because they are much faster and cheaper than people. But if a machine is comprised of unique parts—and that machine breaks down from wear and tear—you lose money. You can't have that; you like money! What if you could make *uniform* machine parts, so that if one thing breaks you can easily replace it? Great. Now, what if you could standardize the things your machines are producing too? What if each of your *products* was uniform and had interchangeable parts? By the time you've answered that question, you're richer than Scrooge McDuck diving into his Olympic-size swimming pool full of gold coins. (Don't look at me like that; I'm a nineties kid.)

The massive profitability of replaceable parts meant that bosses also began to *prefer replaceable employees.* Why pay two people the big bucks for their expert skills, when you could pay hundreds of people almost nothing for their entry-level skills and produce more? If the assembly line was perfect, the employees didn't need to be. *They just needed to know how to follow directions.*

Art was not necessary for the factory to succeed. Employees didn't need to be passionate about their iron rivets, just efficient. Assembly-line workers didn't need to increase their knowledge, just their speed. What happens when people are paid for uniformity, efficiency, and speed, but not for passion, or knowledge, or Art?

They leave their Art at home.

Fast-forward a couple hundred years and here we all are, posting passive-aggressive GIFs about our bosses, hashtagging #TGIF so often that Instagram had to temporarily *ban it,* and leaving our Art at home.

OKAY . . . BUT WHAT DO FACTORIES HAVE TO DO WITH ME?

That's easy: you're working for one. You don't have to be wearing a hairnet or standing at an assembly line to work for the Modern Factory. (We'll call it the MF.) In fact, most of today's businesses and government agencies are versions of the Factory: the post office, your health insurance company's call center, big box superstores, restaurant franchises, retail . . .

HERE'S HOW YOU KNOW YOU WORK FOR THE MODERN FACTORY:

THERE'S A NONNEGOTIABLE HIERARCHY

Workers report to a boss, who reports to another boss; that boss probably reports to a board, and the board reports to the shareholders (and, let's be real, to profit margins). Instructions are passed down the chain of command and must be followed.

WORK IS CENTRALIZED

Employees come to a building where they punch in and out; if you don't show up to work in this building, you're fired. Even remote work is centralized through vast email chains, software chat groups, or online video meetings.

TRAINING IS UNIFORM

Handbooks and manuals are compiled and updated continually. Managers have little say in the restrictions they place on their employees.

Look familiar? Factories are just workplaces that maximize profits by prioritizing a *system* over the potentially messy creative output of *people*. Does someone in charge tell you exactly what to do and exactly how to do it? Then you work for the MF. Welcome to the club.

We know, deep down, that working for the MF is not our "calling" or "life's work." It's hard to cold-call, mass-email, burger-flip, and paper-push *wholeheartedly*. It's a means to an end, a way to finance the cost of being a human in the modern world. When it comes down to it, we all just want to be happy and comfortable in our own skin. Unfortunately, we don't know what will make us happy or what we can offer to the world, or how to be 100 percent ourselves *yet*. As best we can tell, our life's work is *to find out*. So fuck it, we'll pay bills however we need to along the way, even if that means working for the MF.

On the days at the MF that you love your coworkers, and your boss isn't a micromanaging asshole, you kind of forget to dream about the Dream Job.

>>   *"This isn't so bad, is it?"*

But on the days you're stuck cleaning up someone else's mess—the days your boss publicly humiliates you in the meeting that you finally had the courage to speak up in, the days you want to smash your computer with a baseball bat, à la *Office Space,* because you can't believe how mind-numbing these tasks are—on *those* days, you're desperate for the Dream Job.

>> *"That's it. I can do better than this. What are my options?"*

It's on our worst days at the MF that we recognize how powerless and alienated from our work we really feel. *Especially* when the work is dictated, top-down, from a bureaucracy that treats us like pieces of machinery. Since the hierarchy pits us against each other, real community rarely forms among our coworkers (except in shared commiserating). Our work can feel meaningless when it's broken down into micro-tasks—only a handful of which require any expertise— leaving our contribution to the "final product" tiny and impersonal. And when we sense the resulting product or service is just for profit and not for fulfilling any real human need, our work feels even more pointless. So why do we keep showing up?

Two reasons, mostly: (1) YA NEED CASH, and (2) it's easier than the alternative.

EASIER THAN THE ALTERNATIVE

At this point in history, the MF has automated as much as is financially viable; we've assembly-lined, mechanized, and outsourced everything we can to machines. (Think: automated call centers; customer service chat bots, HR software, literal assembly lines.) The Factory jobs that remain require a human but aren't necessarily appealing or lucrative. In order to fill those positions, the MF lures people in with its best bargaining chip: *Come enjoy being told what to do.*

See, the benefit of being disconnected from your work is *disconnecting from your work.*

You don't think this is appealing? Everyone wants to be off the hook. If a project falls apart, we can claim we were "just following directions." If we can't keep up, we can blame our lack of training; our bosses didn't prepare us adequately. If a product fails, we can blame the person whose idea it was. Wait, it was your idea? Then it failed because you didn't get the resources you needed to make it work.

Being told what to do is a lot easier than the alternative: having to think, taking real risks, and being held accountable—maybe even accepting blame.

It's not that Factory work, whether literal blue-collar or metaphorical white-collar, is inherently shitty or beneath us—it's not. If it weren't for this system, we wouldn't have the ridiculous material prosperity we take for granted today. *There's nothing wrong with exchanging a paycheck for following clear-cut directions.*

But do you want to? Because you do have a choice.

I DON'T HAVE A CHOICE

Or, "I'm only as free as my last paycheck."

We show up for work at the MF because we know what happens when our paycheck runs out. We know how seeing our bank account in the red makes us feel (stressed the F out), and the kind of food it relegates us to eat (cheap junk), and we'd like to avoid both, thank you very much. But we don't show up at the MF *just* because we need the cash; we also show up because *we made a deal.*

In *Linchpin*, possibly the most perfect book ever written on the MF and our choices in the new economy (seriously, go read it), author Seth Godin describes the "Take-Care-of-You Bargain" that our grandparents signed up for: In exchange for paying attention, following the rules, working hard, and showing up on time, the Factory would take care of them. They wouldn't need to be "brilliant or creative or take big risks." They would be paid well, given health insurance, and offered job security. They could go to school, get a job, work for one company for thirty-plus years, and retire with a full pension. Work was stable, more or less, because companies typically stuck around for more than thirty years.

Thanks to the Factory, our grandparents could be big fish in a small pond. And since the Bargain had been upheld, more or less, for close to a century, it seemed like a safe bet—so our grandparents signed our parents up for it too. But then globalization happened, and the Internet happened—and the pond scaled to the size of the entire planet. Suddenly, everyone was connected to everyone, technology turned entire markets upside-down on a daily basis, and our parents were very small fish in a huge pond, which brings us to today.

You and I believe that in exchange for paying attention, following the rules, showing up on time, and working hard, we should get a fat paycheck, health insurance, and job security too.

Except the MF can no longer hold up its end of the "Take-Care-of-You Bargain." The goal of any Factory is to generate profit, and in what Godin calls a "race to the bottom" of labor costs, the MF *doesn't have* fat paychecks, comprehensive health insurance, matched 401ks, or job security to offer us. They definitely can't make taking care of us their focus; *they're just trying to stay in business.*

But I have some (sort of) good news.

The MF? The one you work in, the one that doesn't want your fuck-yeah? *It's dying.*

THE MF IS DYING

If you're a capitalist today, efficiency and profit are no longer enough to compete. Globalization and technology mean that someone, somewhere, can do what you're doing waaayyy cheaper than you are, and produce it faster than you can too. Let's say, for example, you run a delivery business; you *profit* from people paying for shipping. How do you compete with the company that just made free, borderline instantaneous shipping *the status quo?* How do you beat same-day, or outright free? If a new Factory can turn a whole industry upside down, like Amazon has, how do you compete? *You don't.* Yeah, it might be a slow death, but the old Factories that can't produce cheap enough and fast enough are as good as dead.

The only alternative to cheap and fast?

Fuckyeah.

To offer something that speaks to people's insides. Something unique. Something people will *gladly* pay big money for. Something that connects people. Something authentic. The good news? The businesses and entrepreneurs that are flipping entire markets upside down *are taking fuckyeah seriously.* They're hiring and collaborating with rule-breakers, people who try things, people who take risks, people who give a shit. *People who bring their Art to work.* Why? Because it's suddenly lucrative. We, the public, are suspicious of ads, fed up with product homogeny, and disgusted by cold, inhuman interactions with corporations. We're putting our money where the authenticity is. The MF only chases profit, and, shockingly, Art has become the single best way to become profitable. Go figure.

So, except for the "too big to fail" giants, the MF is dying, businesses are beginning to prioritize Art, and this leaves us with a new choice: stay with the slow sinking MF ships or start bringing our Art to work.

I know you need a paycheck. I do too. This is the world we live in. But what would happen if you brought your humanity, creativity, and sparkly universe dust to work on Monday? Would you get fired? Criticized? Laughed at? Would you get promoted? Have you already tried? Did it backfire? Are you unsure what your Art even is? If I'm defining fuckyeah with words like *passion, purpose, calling, creative autonomy*, and *Art*—and I'm telling you to bring it to work—I imagine you're having one of two reactions:

1. *"Look, if it were possible to bring my 'Art' to work, don't you think I'd be doing it? And how am I supposed to squeeze 'creative autonomy' into my job description?!"*

   OR

2. *"I've been looking for my passion/purpose/fuckyeah since I could form sentences. I have no idea what it is. I'm burnt out looking for it, and at this point, I'm pretty sure it's a setup to be disappointed. I don't have 'Art,' whatever that is, AND AREN'T YOU SUPPOSED TO TELL ME HOW TO FIND IT?!"*

I know *exactly* how you feel. Firsthand. I also know *why* you feel this way. The reason we struggle to find a place to share our Art and still earn a paycheck? The reason fuckyeah feels like self-help semantics, a gimmick, or a myth? The reason we have no clue what our Art even is?

Because you and I went to Factory School.

3.

SOMEONE WILL TELL ME WHAT I NEED TO DO

I was #fashun at a young age. A faux off-the-shoulder white dress, complete with massive lace collar and pink ribbon rose on the neckline. A cobalt blue jersey romper with pink and white beading, puffy paint, and horse decal. A floral ribbon hot-glued to the front zipper pocket of my baby blue JanSport backpack. So when uniforms came into my life at my new middle school, I knew I'd need to get creative with the whole self-expression thing. I had tasted the sweet, sweet freedom of picking out my outfit each morning with care, and now? Now I was trapped by a steady diet of white polo shirts, navy pleated skirts, and itchy polyester sweaters. You can imagine my tween delight, then, when I discovered slap bracelets, butterfly hair clips, and socks with "flair"—you know, socks with "100% Angel" in sassy lettering. Apparently, the kind of flair that gets you detention. *This is a uniform-clad institution, young lady. Think on your sins.*

What did I learn in school? That standing out leads to trouble. That rules should be followed blindly, without concern for their context. That there's not a lot of room for your Art. No, I didn't learn all that from one afternoon of detention. These lessons came from years of studenthood, and I picked up a few other things along the way too.

Raise your hand if anything on this list sounds familiar:

Things (Factory) School Taught Me

- The Pledge of Allegiance.

- "F" is for failure. Don't fail.

- This will be on the test.

- This is going on your permanent record.

- You have a permanent record.

- You know nothing, and the adults in authority know everything (ergo when you are finally an adult you will have things figured out).

- Ask for permission—to speak, to go to the bathroom, and so on.

- Showing up every day is more important than being involved every day.

- Tests are mostly memorization, so cramming is fine. No need to learn the material.

- Do NOT write in pen, for fuck's sake.

- Follow the instructions. All of them.

- The only problems worth solving are problems that already have answers (and your teachers have those answers).

- Avoid standing out.

- Fear boredom and wasted time above all else (i.e., detention).

- Look good on paper, on report cards, in the yearbook, on college applications, on a resume, and so on.

> - *Raise your hand once every few weeks; otherwise, avoid saying or doing anything that might embarrass you.*
>
> - *Speaking of embarrassing yourself—don't challenge your teachers; they will wipe the floor with you.*
>
> - *The only way to get 100 percent is by not making any mistakes. Not one.*

You too? Yeah, I thought our lists might be similar.

HOW FAR BACK CAN YOU REMEMBER?

Left alone with crayons, I guarantee Art poured out of Little You; maybe on a piece of paper, maybe on the walls. Creativity had no strings attached when you were a kid. It bubbled up and up and out of you, to the joy (and sometimes frustration) of the grown-ups who raised you. You effortlessly invented nonsensical stories, weird songs, and games with perpetually changing rules.

And then your crayons were replaced with standardized tests.

Suddenly, bubbling, doodling, and daydreaming were discouraged. You found out you'd be punished less (and rewarded more) if you would just sit down, shut up, and fit in. Demand for your fuckyeah shrank; demand for your obedience grew. By your teens, you'd picked up some unspoken advice from the rest of us:

"It's not that we don't want you to express yourself—by all means, please do—but if you could find a way to express yourself within the shut-up-and-follow-directions framework, then you'll be a happy, well-liked, pillar-of-society kind of adult someday. Make 'Art' if someone asks for it; otherwise, be useful."

It made sense at the time, but this strategy has yet to pay off. You're not sure what happiness is, the jury is out on whether you're a well-liked "pillar of society," and all signs point to you being a grown-up. Like I said, I know *exactly* how you feel.

HERE'S HOW YOU KNOW YOU WENT TO FACTORY SCHOOL

THERE'S A NONNEGOTIABLE HIERARCHY

Students report to teachers, who report to their principal or administrator; the administrators report to the school board (and let's be real, to politically motivated donors). Instructions are passed down the chain of command and must be followed.

EDUCATION IS CENTRALIZED

Students come to a building where they answer roll call Monday through Friday. If you don't show up to class in this building, you're kicked out of the system.

THE CURRICULUM IS UNIFORM

Expensive textbooks and standardized tests are mandatory and updated continually (except in low-income schools, where curriculum is uniform, but materials are often out-of-date). Teachers have little say in the material they present to their students.

A CLASS SYSTEM IS IN FULL EFFECT

Each student is assigned a grade year and set of benchmarks (measuring their intelligence) that they are expected to attain. Though it's frowned upon, saying "I'm not good at [insert subject here]" is perfectly understandable.

If a student fails, they will be replaced. If a teacher fails to teach curriculum on the test, they will be replaced.

Factory School pays lip service to creativity but beats it out of us in practice. It rewards us for zero errors, for perfect regurgitation, for giving it back exactly as it was given. Not a lot of room in there for your sparkly universe dust. *Not a lot of room for fuckyeah.*

We spent our youth treated like empty vessels, waiting for an all-knowing authority to pour knowledge into us, caught in a feedback loop: *receive, memorize, regurgitate, repeat.* This loop teaches us that we are *spectators* in the world instead of *creators*; we "receive" education, and life "happens to us."

Creators recognize their own autonomy (freedom, control); they can tweak, redefine, or change what they create, because they created it. Spectators, however, have no autonomy, except to decide *how to react* to what is *happening to them.*

Think back to your early days in a classroom. Were you and your classmates seated like an audience, facing your teacher (the performer)? And when you were told to participate, was it to create something wholly your own, or to *react* with the correct answer? Even in a "creative" space, like drama club or art class, how often were you being totally inventive, and how often were you instructed to make a version of something that had already been made, like performing Shakespeare or painting sunflowers like van Gogh? Were there times when it was not socially, emotionally, or even physically safe for you to speak up, create, invent, or stand out?

Now think about your experience as an adult. How much of your time is spent *reacting* to what is *happening to you?* How often does it feel like you can't catch up—scrambling to respond to a flood of emails, putting out fires at work, or reeling from some drama between coworkers, friends, or family? Now consider what a relief it is to be a passive *audience member* after an exhausting day—scrolling through your social feed, binge-watching TV, revisiting photos of your last vacation (#flashbackfriday).

When we believe living life as a spectator is our only option, we "participate" by being reactive and "relax" by being passive audience members.

But fuckyeah isn't passive; if we want to actually enjoy our lives, we need to actively seek and create the life we want.

Of course, we *can't* control the workings of the universe, every event in our lives, or the way people choose to treat us. And, of course, fearing what we can't control is part of being a human. But when we internalize spectatorship, we fling open that door to fear and *jam* it open. If we believe we're powerless to affect an outcome, then why take any risks? Why get hurt? Wouldn't it be easier to be told what to do, or what the "right" answer is, to save us pain, time, and energy? This is a logical approach, coming from our skittish little lizard brain—but it's narrow-minded and damaging to us in the long run to be driven by a survival mentality rather than seeking to thrive, grow, and explore.

What if spectatorship wasn't our only option? (Hint: It isn't!) What if we could instigate, create, invent, problem solve, and bring our Art to work? (We can!) Better yet, make our Art our life's work? (We will!) But in order to learn how to tap into our powerful, innate, active creativity, we have to *unlearn* some deeply internalized, dark and twisty, self-censoring MF bullshit.

I SHOULD PROBABLY EXPLAIN WHAT I MEAN BY "FACTORY SCHOOL"

Fun fact! The public school system in the United States was designed to serve the needs of postindustrial capitalism. *No joke.* The curriculum. The schedule. The hierarchy. The testing methods.

School was designed to produce excellent factory workers.

Let's see if I can smash two hundred-ish years of history into something only *slightly* longer than your mom's standard Facebook post:

By the time the Civil War was over in the 1860s, the factory system had become the economic status quo. Beta testing of "public school" was also well underway: school was mandatory, free, tax-funded, bureaucratic, class-based, and very racist. School was less about the "spirit of learning" or "individual development" and more about straight-up *discipline.*

While public school was getting its systematic shit together, the MF was dealing with two new problems: (1) overproduction and (2) understaffing. Mechanized production was wildly efficient; factories were cranking out stuff of all shapes and sizes faster than it could possibly be assembled, packaged, or sold. Factories needed more employees to keep up the grueling pace, and America would need to learn the art of "consumption" so products wouldn't go unbought. Then came advertising, and the desire to buy, buy, buy skyrocketed. Problem no. 1 was quickly solved.

Problem no. 2 was trickier. If bosses wanted to keep the cash flowing, they'd need to keep up the whirlwind production pace. To do that, they'd need a reserve army of skilled laborers, hungry for work. Sure, plenty of people had already switched to factory labor (since their mom-and-pop businesses couldn't compete with the new industrial giants), but they were pissed off about the forced subordination in their new jobs and intent on doing something about it. Turnover was high. Protests were constant. Unions formed. Social reformers called "progressives" demanded labor laws that protected workers. For turn-of-the-century capitalists, this was *annoying AF*. How do you convince people that the fate of the majority (i.e., workers) should be subjected to the control of a wealthy minority (i.e., bosses and owners)? It's no easy feat, considering that's the exact opposite of America's collective headspace: that the minority (elected leaders) should subject itself to the decisions of the majority (citizens). You know, *democracy*?

Bosses would do their best to squash worker revolt, but one thing was clear: if they wanted a future workforce, they'd need to introduce future generations to social hierarchy and class division at work. *And they'd need to be subtle about it.* Their best option? *Public school.*

It's not like a bunch of monocle-wearing old white dudes piled into a room, twisted their mustaches, and shared a round of evil laughter before plotting the takeover of the education system; the champions of Factory School were no Illuminati. In fact, institutionalized subordination was a concept that everyday Americans were aware of, and sort of *liked*. As President Woodrow Wilson put it in an address to New York City high school teachers in 1909:

> *"We want one class of persons to have a liberal education, and we want another class of persons, a very much larger class, of necessity, in every society, to forego the privileges of a liberal education and fit themselves to perform specific difficult manual tasks."*

Yikes. Has the quality of public education and our understanding of child psychology improved since this era? Yep, and by a huge margin. Do more people have equal access to education, both formal and informal, than ever before? Double yep. Am I waaaaay oversimpli-fying a few hundred years of socioeconomic change? Definitely. But that doesn't mean I'm exaggerating.

You.

Me.

Factory School.

Grossed out again? Expecting me to tell you to burn your diplomas and toilet paper your nearest educational facility? *Nah.* Modern edu-cation is twisted up, but—and this may surprise you—I'm not inter-ested in making it a scapegoat.

First of all, good teachers are out there, working their asses off to create change. They make school bearable; they draw leadership out of us and challenge us to solve problems that don't necessarily have answers. They change kids' lives for the better, often despite the sys-tem they have to work within. To every good teacher and administ-rator out there, working to change the world: *Thank you, thank you, thank you.*

Second, the truth is that school will always be a reflection of a *cul-ture's* expectations and norms, especially the socioeconomic ones. Until more businesses demand that fuckyeah replace the MF, school will keep being great at "producing Factory workers."

I don't pretend to have a solution for this Artless, joyless pickle we've gotten ourselves into as a society. And actually? I don't even want you to worry about solving it right now.

I just want you to know you're not crazy.

PLEASE TELL ME WHAT TO DO

You've been getting mixed messages for years, and it's crazy-making. Paralyzing, even. Messages like:

Take risks.
Don't make mistakes.

Always ask for permission; it's a sign of respect.
Be bold. Better to ask for forgiveness than for permission.

Be authentically yourself.
Don't take up too much space. Actually, shut up.

Seek out and follow the instructions.
Solve problems; carve your own path.

Stand for something.
Don't make a scene.

There's a good reason we're conflicted or bored or stressed, or sometimes all three: We were *trained* to be passive, to admire the status quo. We were taught to do everything in our power to not rock the boat. And yet, today, at work, we're also expected to be creative and flexible, to take risks, have an opinion, and stand out among our peers.

We were taught to fit in, but we keep noticing all the "successful" people found a way to stand out. We were taught to follow the rules, but it seems like the "successful" people broke them. Or wrote new ones. Or invented a whole new game. *We're justifiably confused.*

This next part is important, *SO LISTEN UP.*

You are not your education. You're not your grade point average. You're not your extracurriculars. Your value as a human being is not equal to your ability to follow directions, sit still, or pass tests. You don't have to let your Factory School education determine how you are supposed to learn and grow. You don't need answers before you try something new. *No one* has the answers before trying something new. None of us can tell you what you should do. That doesn't mean you're fucked; *that means it's time to get curious and start experimenting.*

If you're currently better at being passive than creative, it is not your fault, nor is it irreversible. If you signed up for the "Take-Care-of-You Bargain" and got a job at the MF, it doesn't mean you're a gullible lost cause of a human, destined to live a boring life.

It likely means your grown-up soul is very, very tired—because you think it's too late. Too late to discover what you want to "do with your life." Too late to slow your breakneck pace at work and still maintain the respect of your peers. Too late to find the love(s) of your life. Too late to gracefully pivot careers, successfully launch a business, or bring your Art to work. Too late to make a lasting impact on the world. Too late to find your fuckyeah.

If you're reading this, it's *not* too late. (Drake was wrong.)

You were *born* creative, remember? The crayons, the wall doodles, the stories? Art is your natural state. So you've got a PhD in Passivity . . . so what?! I've got a degree in Fashion Design, and I'm not currently using that. You know what else you and I have? *Our Art.*

Something to say, with or without words; something uniquely ours to give. Our personal and particular mash-up of sparkly universe dust; the combustible spark of our fuckyeah. And we need you to share yours.

We want to throw all our money at your fuckyeah, to wait in line for it, to be a part of the community it creates. We've been waiting for your Art for what feels like *ages*. We think your Art is amazeballs. *We don't care what the MF wants.* We. Want. Your. Art.

If working mindlessly for the MF was the only way to make a living, then yeah, your Art could stay on lockdown forever. But machines have nearly replaced us on the assembly lines, and they're coming for us at the paper-pushing gigs, the cold-calling jobs, and the rest of the so-called white-collar work. Machines cost less than you do, and systematically reducing costs to increase profit is what the MF system lives for. So unless you want to spend your life being paid to do mindless stuff (stuff that machines are better at anyway), you gotta figure out how to unleash your Art *on the clock.*

Now let's see if I can get everyone reading this to roll their eyes, all at once:

You are a magical, unique snowflake. You actually are special.

No one in the history of EVER has shared the same exact genetic makeup, molecular connections, memories, fingerprints, or soul that makes you YOU. You're the first of your kind. Yes, your body's genetic makeup was shaped by your birth parents' DNA, and your worldview was molded by your childhood circumstances and the people who parented you. *Of course these things are true.* But there's still no other you.

Human DNA is made up of 3 billion nucleotides, and we are 99.9 percent identical from one person to the next. The 0.1 percent variation in human DNA is what makes us different from one another. But when you consider the number of humans currently living their lives on Earth, that miniscule variation translates to *tens of millions* of possible genetic mutations. No two people are the same. Not even identical twins, it turns out.

Your life is one gigantic choose-your-own-adventure novel. There are an infinite number of subtle influences you'll have on humankind. We need your magic eventuality.

You are a unique blend of powerful individual ingredients, and your particular flavor is one that we need on this planet—desperately. You have no idea what your contribution to the universe, shared with us merely by existing, will mean for the future.

>> *"Of course a millennial is telling other millennials that they're unique because you all grew up hearing you were special, and don't you know none of you are special, and have you never heard of evolution and genetics and blah blah blah . . ."*

For all you trolls climbing out from under your bridges with the cursor blinking over the comment box, I'd like to say:

Hello, Snowflake.

I've heard it all, okay? I'm tired of the lazy pop culture trope of entitled and arrogant "millennial" (*ughh*) and "Gen-Z" (*blehhhh*) monsters (*nuh unh*) who refuse to grow up (*um, you grow up*).

According to experts, growing up in a "cushy" environment convinced us that adult life would be easy, that everything would be handed to us, and that we deserve awards for just showing up to work on Monday. We've been called "dysfunctional" adults because our parents said too many supportive things while we were growing up, things like "You can be anything you want to be" and "Girls can do anything boys can do" and "I believe in you." You know, *great things*. To top it off, we're also "narcissistic," and apparently, the so-called participation trophies our parents and teachers gave us are to blame. (Aside: Where was I when these trophies were handed out?!)

I've got two problems with this finger-pointing and editorial poop-slinging. First of all, generalizations and stereotypes are lazy.

> *"The single story creates stereotypes, and the problem with stereotypes is not that they are untrue, but that they are incomplete. They make one story become the only story."*

(Novelist and speaker Chimamanda Ngozi Adichie gets it.)

These stereotypes may be an honest representation of some, but this is only a fraction of the picture. There *are* narcissists in my generation; *they're in every generation*. Some people *did* have life handed to them on a platter, but this isn't a people-under-thirty-five thing. Some of us *did* hit the childhood jackpot with a high "standard of living" and uber-encouraging parents. But not all of us, and to assume so is reductive.

Second, all this hyperbolic pearl-clutching is just a sneaky way to distract an entire generation of young people from our most cluster-fuck-ish brain tangle:

Our righteous indignation about all the generational name-calling has made our priorities of authenticity and individuality crystal clear . . . *to the Modern Factory*.

The MF knows you don't want to work for them. But the Factory needs you to work for them, so they've already made a few adjustments in hopes of convincing you to stay: They've modified their advertising strategies by featuring "normal people" instead of models that promote Eurocentric beauty standards, and by highlighting diversity rather than whitewashing every campaign. They've diverted some of their marketing cash away from TV toward contests, quirky quizzes, and genuine-looking posts (i.e., "native ads") on social media. They've changed their policies, making a point of securing "diversity hires" (and bragging about it), hosting sexual harassment awareness trainings, and incorporating language of "inclusivity" in company-wide conference calls. The newest, wealthiest Factories have added "perks" like in-house yoga studios, coffee bars, and catered lunches. New hires can now negotiate remote work into their job descriptions (meaning we can attend online meetings with 104-degree fevers from our sick beds).

The MF is adjusting because it needs us. And disingenuous or not, *most of these changes are fuckin' fantastic.* Yes to diversity, yes to inclusivity, yes to rethinking the assembly-line style of white-collar work. Yes yes yes. But all the click-baity intergenerational critiques lobbed at millennials have the same purpose as more straightforward corporate polling, data mining, and pandering: *to compel us to tell the MF what we're willing to spend.*

How much *energy* will we spend defending our collective work ethic on social posts that are there specifically to bait us? How much *money* will we spend on subscription-based apps that promise to improve our approach to time management, our quality of sleep, or our work-life balance? How much *time* will we spend fighting to disprove the stereotype that we're lazy by clocking unpaid overtime or answering work emails at eleven at night? If we're desperate for the ultimate how-to guide because of our upbringing in Factory School, but don't trust what the MF is selling, *then what will we trust, try, or buy?*

The MF knows that to secure a steady future workforce, they'll need to convince a distrusting generation to buy what they're selling while also employing as many of us as possible. This requires that the MF collect as much data as it can about the time and money we are willing to spend, and on what. *And the MF knows they need to be subtle about these deceptions.*

Believing "we can be whoever we want to be" isn't our problem. We're not (all) lazy, entitled, arrogant pieces of shit because we received "participation trophies" or excessive support from parents. We do have a problem, though.

We fucked up on this one, BIG TIME. Are you ready to hear this? Because this might sting a little.

We've been tricked into thinking we are individual, living Brands.

4.

UNBRAND YOURSELF

You think you need to be a Brand.

I think I need to be a Brand.

We are *neck-deep* in branding ourselves.

When we use the word *brand* today, we're talking about an immaterial, floaty cloud of qualities associated with a business, idea, or person. According to BusinessDictionary.com, a brand is:

> "[Any] unique design, sign, symbol, words, or a combination of these, employed in creating an image that identifies a product and differentiates it from its competitors. Over time, this image becomes associated with a level of credibility, quality, and satisfaction in the consumer's mind. Thus brands help harried consumers in a crowded and complex marketplace, by standing for certain benefits and value."

Do you see it yet? *No?* Then watch what happens when I substitute a handful of words in that definition:

> *"[You are a] unique design, sign, symbol, words, or a combination of these, employed in creating an image that identifies* **you** *and differentiates* **you** *from* **your peers.** *Over time, this image becomes associated with a level of credibility, quality, and* **authenticity** *in an* **onlooker's** *mind. Thus* **your** *brand helps harried* **people** *in a crowded and complex* **world,** *by standing for certain benefits and value[s]."*

We think our lives need a logical, flowing storyline; a clear "Point A" to "Point B" character arc that looks great in a news feed or social media timeline; an appealing resume and consistent narrative. So, we curate a personal highlight reel, defining who the "product" [our brand] is for and what sets "it" [ourselves] apart from its competitors within the market—and we've become especially good at this online.

When social media was new, none of us knew what the hell it was for. We were all like the Little Mermaid in her cave of trinkets, collecting every single photographable moment or song we heard once and liked, putting it all up on display. *Look at this stuff, isn't it neat? Wouldn't you think my collection's complete?* (Hoarder.) We had no concept of "curating" our "content." It took a minute before we understood the "value" of "negative space" on our "grid," or realized that using a vague Nietzsche quote as the caption for a swimsuit selfie could win extra likes from followers. It took us a minute, but we eventually caught on: social media was our stage. We were no longer limited to just fifteen minutes of fame per lifetime, no longer subjected to achieving popularity among only the people we knew. We could grab the world's attention if we wanted to, and we wouldn't even have to leave the house.

We've become Internet octopi with multiple profile "arms," carefully crafting a self-image. Sorry, *self-images*. Plural, but connected, because "brand perception" is everything. How many Internet versions of You are there?

By creating a public persona with our audience in mind, we are defining who we are from the outside in.

Let's imagine that I wrote, directed, and starred in a movie about my life, and when I finally have a chance to screen it for an audience, it gets mixed reviews. I'm disappointed, but since it hasn't been released yet and this is only a screening, I still have time to act on audience feedback and tweak my movie. It's okay if my rewrites based on audience criticism end up changing the characters and the plot, because movies are made for audiences anyway—why not make something people will pay to see? I reshoot the movie and screen it again. More notes, more reshoots, more screenings. I get caught in an endless loop and never release the movie because I've become obsessed with "getting it right" by creating a product that my audience wants. Seems like a waste, doesn't it? A perfectly good creative project has slowly been corrupted, and what inspired it in the first place is eventually lost.

We've become our own audience, hovering outside our bodies, conducting thorough market research, and carefully crafting a "brand promise." We're focus-grouping our identities.

Don't worry, I'm not suggesting you delete all your accounts and move to a remote cabin in the Adirondacks without Wi-Fi. Social media is not the enemy, nor is having an "Internet presence." And yes, I'm aware many of you are wondering whether to take this chapter as an insult, considering that modern life now *requires* influencers, bloggers, entrepreneurs, and celebrities to cultivate a Personal Brand with an audience in mind. If being a public personality pays your bills, I'm happy for you. That's pretty awesome, actually.

But whether you are someone who has never posted a selfie in your lifetime or are someone who boasts a little "verified" checkmark next to your name, you *have* struggled with being a Brand. All of us have, because *all of us have internalized an abstract view of ourselves as audience members.*

Have you become a living, breathing Brand IRL? How you craft a Personal Brand online is probably obvious, but it could be entirely subconscious in real life. Maybe you've always been "the funny friend" in your crew, and you feel an unspoken pressure to never be sad around them; you can't be seen as vulnerable, because that wouldn't be "you." Maybe you've branded yourself as a "no strings attached" kind of person, so when you accidentally fall in love, your casual hookup can't take you seriously. Maybe you've branded yourself the "anything for the job" employee, arriving early, staying late, going above and beyond—except now you're burnt out, and slowing down could mean losing the respect of your bosses or, worse, losing your job.

Cultivating a Brand online has taught us how to think like an audience member in our everyday lives. We've learned to anticipate what our "audience" will think of the clothes we wear, what we say and how we say it, our social, political, and religious affiliations, our gender presentation and romantic partners, our job title and the size of our paycheck—and we've learned how to react, edit, and censor the way we present ourselves accordingly.

This self-censorship is calculated, because we despise being compartmentalized, marginalized, and misunderstood. We are a generation obsessed with *identifying* and *differentiating* ourselves; we don't

mind being "labeled," so long as *we choose* the labels (like *cisgender,*
transgender, liberal, conservative, straight, gay, and so on). We want
the power to identify ourselves *for* ourselves, to be equally and accurately represented in culture and media. Everyone does. This is not
new, *nor is it a problem.*

But commodifying ourselves is.

A "brand" is an image that identifies and differentiates something *for*
sale. This is the critical difference between expressing who we are in
a social context and believing that we are individual, living Brands:
we think our value lies in our worth to the market.

We're living like commodities, and it's fucking us up.

WORTH VERSUS VALUE

Cash seems like a concrete thing—a piece of rectangular paper or a
circular coin—but it's an abstraction (something that is only useful in
its conceptual form), because it represents the amount of work I did
that I can trade for other things. (Stick with me here, okay?)

Any money I have is a stand-in for effort, but it doesn't necessarily
have to be *my* effort; I could inherit, win, or steal money, and it still
holds its power-paper meaning. And because cash represents effort
regardless of who made an effort to get it, we can assign "worth" to
stuff that wouldn't otherwise have that worth. An avocado, for example, grows naturally on a tree somewhere, perfectly fine doing its avocado thing without a price tag. But then someone picks that avocado
(effort) and puts it in a particular building and assigns it a "worth" of
ninety-nine cents. Or maybe $2.49, if that building is a Whole Foods.
Or maybe fifty-nine cents, if you buy fifteen of the things from Costco.

Money is an abstract idea we all agreed on to make exchanging stuff easier, and it's worked really well so far. So well, actually, that we don't mind ignoring a major side effect of this abstraction:

A thing's worth (an arbitrary price) is now all tangled up with its value (its inherent usefulness, beauty, or importance).

I wanted that avocado for a salad I planned to make, but its high worth of $2.49 (*ugh, that's expensive*) lowers its value in my mind (*jeez, I don't need it that badly; I'll buy tomatoes instead*). And I'll regret it too, because avocados are my favorite food on Earth and I want to eat them every day, all the time, forever.

Here's what your abstracted experiences are telling your brain: What something is doesn't matter; what it represents matters. What I do isn't important; the meaning created by what I do is important.

What I *did* in college, for example, doesn't matter as much as what having gone to college *means*. I could have partied my ass off, cranked out a few last-minute term papers, clocked some minimal time in a lecture hall, and yet it doesn't matter if I half-assed four years of my life. What ultimately matters in the "real world" is my *degree*. The abstract meaning of this piece of paper is more important than what I did to get this piece of paper. What the degree represents—the class status that allowed me to go to college, my assumed work ethic required to complete the program, and my qualification to get paid for future work—is what matters. Oh, and because of this piece of paper, my worth on the market has gone up. I can assume getting a job will be easier than if I did not have this degree; I can also assume the job itself will require less manual labor because of what this piece of paper represents.

Abstraction makes it easier to mix up our WORTH on the market with our VALUE as a person.

Abstraction means the amount of time you spend with friends doesn't matter as much as the number of followers you have. What political activism you actually participate in doesn't matter; the appearance of it does (i.e., slacktivism, #thoughtsandprayers). What money you have in the bank doesn't matter; the money you appear to have does (so you might as well put this car payment on a credit card you can't pay off). Your current job doesn't matter, but the career you're "working toward" does. What you do day-to-day doesn't matter; how your job enhances your Personal Brand does.

In a world where your personality, skills, and hard work are a means to an end (a paycheck), and *your existence* is something of marketable worth, you'll have a much better chance of success (i.e., profit) if you market yourself as a desirable Brand, both online and in real life.

And that, right there? *That's the definition of a commodity.*

HOW THE HELL THIS HAPPENED

I think we could agree that a dream job pays you consistently (and well) for work you like, with people you like, to make a positive change in the world, right? This used to be everything we could have hoped for in our work.

And then reality TV happened. Blogging, vlogging, and social media "influencers" happened. Suddenly, posting your #ootd and consistently engaging with followers could mean "partners" and #ads. Tweeting your poetry could lead to a book deal. Applying makeup in front of your laptop camera could mean paying your rent with YouTube ad revenue. *Suddenly, you could get paid to be yourself.*

Sure, people have "made a living" without clocking in and out before; some ways seem more intrinsically satisfying than others. But this is the first time that nonaristocratic, everyday humans are being paid—in a capitalist economy—to live.

I'm not saying this new form of work isn't work. Of course it is. But this is a *new kind* of work, work that flows organically from a person's routines, habits, preferences, or ideas. Work that is essentially *self-expression* but doesn't fit under the traditional label of "Artist." Work that doesn't have a title or job description until *after* we, as a society, have started throwing our money at the people doing this new kind of work.

People can now be paid for their various forms of self-expression to do things they were going to do anyway, to say things they were going to say anyway, and to make things they were going to make anyway.

This is a new kind of career. We can't unsee this. And so, we have a new kind of "dream job" to add to our lists, one we know is so unlikely that we may never openly admit to hoping for it: The *you-do-you job*.

The problem with this ridiculous, improbable new dream is that we have no clue how anyone made the you-do-you job happen for themselves. Everyone we've heard of who makes a living doing whatever the fuck they want is doing . . . just that. There's no vocational training or degree program in "Just Be." There are no recruiters hiring for a job called "You Do You." It's obvious there's no straightforward formula for their success. We just started throwing our money at them for a weird cocktail of reasons that can't be replicated. This is *wildly frustrating* because, in case you forgot, everything worth doing has a how-to guide, every problem worth solving has a formulaic answer, and every job worth getting has a set of qualifications earned in a classroom. Or so we thought. (*Thanks, Factory School.*)

There is one thing we've noticed, though: the people who are being paid to essentially "be themselves"—influencers, content creators, solopreneurs—are good at sharing their story. Even though we don't know them, we still know *about* them—they're "putting themselves out there."

"Maybe that's the secret," you think. *"Putting myself out there. Telling my story without being narcissistic. On everyone's radar, but in nobody's face."* It's a good idea, but it's not yours.

You got this idea from Success Porn.

SUCCESS PORN

We'll always have open seats in the Hall of the Famous for actors, models, athletes, musicians, and the like, and regardless of their resumes, we consider any form of fame a type of success. But we don't model our lives after these celebrities anymore. We comment on their every move, obsess over what they wear, and watch the train wreck of their failed relationships play out on the world stage, but we don't have the same *respect* for their fame that we used to.

This is because we've lived through a massive culture shift, a time in which the Internet has ushered in a democratization of fame, storytelling, and platforms. The people we salivate over—the ones we're modeling our lives after, whose books we're buying and podcasts we're listening to—they're famous, yeah, but famous for being "successful." That is their Brand. The less dependent their success is on an organization or "big machine" (like Hollywood, a sports team, a massive company, or a trust fund, for example), the more we drool.

Entrepreneurs have the kind of fame we respect, and we're chomping at the bit to hear their personal stories: how they quit their corporate day jobs and worked day and night in their garages to launch their businesses, now funded by venture capital and valued at a billion dollars. Or how they made their YouTube channels into bonafide ways to pay the bills. We scramble to screenshot quotes about "the hustle" from interviews with them. *"They did all that before turning thirty?!"* Retweet.

Success Porn is someone's story arc without the details. Just the highlights. Inspiring and easily digestible sound bites, leaving out the boring bits of their, you know, actual lives.

Whoever this successful person is, and the countless small steps of how they really got to this moment, doesn't matter to us; it needs to fit in a podcast episode, a blog post, a magazine article, a TV interview. The individual isn't the focus, *the act is*. Their "story" is a flimsy structure for the vital message: "I did it, and you can too!" We want their streamlined life story; we don't have time for the zigzags and the hiccups (unless, of course, they are staged as plot points, because everybody loves a good underdog story). We want a mental stand-in, someone to represent the successful life we could have if we just do X, Y, and Z.

Success Porn has taught us that the details of our real lives aren't important, but the way we present ourselves is—and it seems like individuals being paid to "be themselves" have also perfected "presenting themselves," online and off. And since there's no manual on how to land the ridiculously dreamy and improbable you-do-you job, all we've been able to deduce so far is that being a living Brand seems like a nonnegotiable prerequisite. Unfortunately, this is toxic.

I've got no moral beef with celebrating hard work, just like I have no problem with how inspiring Success Porn can be. I'm only pointing out that our highlight reels *ain't the real thing.*

Being a Brand seems like a natural reaction against the slog of cookie-cutter work at the MF. We figure if we can get good at telling our story online and packaging our personality at work, we're investing in a kind of personal publicity that will inch us closer to our ridiculous, improbable new dream of being paid to express ourselves through the you-do-you job.

But this isn't our idea. *The MF gets the credit for this one.*

Self-branding gives us a false sense of individual autonomy, while not interfering with our ability to function as good Factory employees and loyal consumers.

Self-branding, especially on social media, provides the MF with a reliable, continuous stream of data on what we are willing to trust, try, and buy, and provides us with a place to get our self-expression "out of the way." We feel like creatives (momentarily) when we express our personalities and values through our purchases and carefully crafted personas, online and off—and as a bonus, we don't have to risk the raw vulnerability of sharing our fuckyeah with anyone. Being a living Brand makes us feel like we're in control of crafting "who we are," but with the comfort of knowing someone will tell us what to do when we get scared, because the MF and the market are still in charge.

You and I are so busy pouring creative energy into our Personal Brands that we don't realize our Brands are not our passion, purpose, or fuckyeah. They're distractions from our Art and a filter over our genuine selves.

While it's true that there is a new category of creative work (all varieties of the you-do-you job), it is not the only model for bringing your Art to work. Perfecting the way you present yourself, online and off, is NOT your ticket to fuckyeah—even if the #tooblessedtobestressed, hyper-happy content of paid influencers makes it look that way.

Social media can be your stage—or it can be your *community*.

If you believe you have an audience, then you will make your life an edited performance and yourself a living Brand. But if you believe you have a community, then you can connect, communicate with, and learn from a world outside yourself. You can find inspiration for your Art, share your Art, and discover the kind of community that will support and love your Art. The Internet may have made your community bigger than your grandparents (the big fish in a little pond) could have ever imagined, but it's a community nonetheless, and only *you* can decide whether you want to *perform* for the people within it—or join it.

The you-do-you job is not a problem. Neither is using social media. The problem is in thinking that *if* we behave like a commodity—a living Brand—then we will eventually be paid to "be ourselves." Treating yourself as a commodity is problematic because the market determines a commodity's value; it's only worth what other people say it's worth today—and the last time I checked, *you were not for sale.*

Abstraction is a room of fun house mirrors, distorting what's meaningful and what's not. Your success in life cannot be measured by your appearance of *worth* on the market. Your paycheck is not actually a reflection of "how well you're doing"—the number of zeros and commas on your paystub doesn't equate to how happy you are or your level of importance in the world. Your *value* as a human is an entirely different thing than the *worth* of your labor.

You are priceless.

I HAVE THIS THEORY

I have this theory that you can't know a person until you've learned their first-ever email address, screen name, or social handle. What was yours? I bet it's hilarious. I bet you've changed it since then. I bet if you had to walk around a networking event with a "Hello, My Name Is _____" name tag with your first email address instead of your real name, you'd be a ~smidge~ embarrassed. (Only at first, of course. You'd get over it, and it would end up being a killer icebreaker.)

What, mine? Yeah, my first-ever email address was godsgirlie1@kiwibox.com.

I mean, doesn't that just tell you everything you need to know about tween me?! Clearly, it's an ancient email because, honestly, *WTF is kiwibox.com*? I'm still not sure, but it was before Hotmail and Gmail established monopolies on email addresses, and I vaguely remember the logo was an emoji kiwi (before emojis existed).

Clearly, it's a young girl's email, for obvious reasons. The word *girlie* is even included in the username and spelled with an adorable "ie" instead of "y." (Cutsie spelling adjustments are key indicators of a young girl's involvement. That, and dotting the top of every letter "i" with a bubbly heart.) Clearly, it's a *pious* young girl's email, because "god" has been credited right up there in the front. HA! I feel *light-years* away from whoever made this email address. I've found my WooWoo, sure, but not within the religious orthodoxy that tween me did—and I'm fairly certain including "girlie" in an adult woman's email address today would somehow be the *opposite* of feminism.

If you ever found Myspace–me, you'd notice she uploaded seventy-eight photos with indistinguishable differences documenting just one goofy Saturday night with friends. I'm pretty sure she declared

Braveheart to be her favorite movie and that her interests included "Jesus, art, and vintage shopping." WHAT?! I don't know her.

I love these past versions of me. I look back at them fondly, smiling at their earnestness and terrible email provider choices. But they're not me. They're someone else entirely.

My point? *Life is change.* Your real story is all over the damn place. How many different versions of You have you been, online or off? The only thing that ties twelve-year-old You to present-day You are the threads of your personal history . . . and I'll bet you'll describe yourself and your story differently in fifteen years. Other than that? You are two entirely different humans. *You are change.*

The truth is, your life path will be erratic. You will pivot sharply from one thing to the next. You do not have to look good "on paper." There will be weird gaps in your resume that are difficult to explain, and awkward silences during small talk with strangers about what you "do" or how you got "here." Your life doesn't need to make for a good podcast interview. You don't have to maintain a "presence," online or off. You don't need to "delete" old versions of yourself by pretending you were never that person. You were that weirdo. I was that weirdo too. Your Personal Brand ain't the real thing. And TBH? We don't give two shits about your Brand.

We want the real you.

Here's what's first on the list of things I wish I could travel back in time to tell my seventeen-year-old self:

You don't owe a streamlined life story to anyone, not even to yourself—because you are not a Brand. You are a walking cosmic experiment, a beautiful mess. A harmonious, sloppy human. Not a Brand, not a story arc, and not a commodity.

The safest approach to finding your fuckyeah is to assume you're about to discover twelve different versions of yourself. Like the choose-your-own-adventure novels we bought at the school book fair (remember those!?), you get to decide which path you take next. You also get to be messy. You get to change your mind. You have permission to change completely, many times over, because every single living thing is in a state of continual change and transformation. Every plant and plankton and elephant and person is born, grows, lives, dies, and is reborn (at least, their atoms are). We need to be okay with unruly change. We are change. Change is sloppy. Life is a constant unfurling of inconsistent moments and unpredictable messages.

Allow yourself the room to transform, over and over, for the entirety of your life. Stop believing your paycheck reflects your inner value. Stop worrying about your inconsistent brand messaging. You're not a commodity. You're not a Brand. So . . .

Can you untangle your freedom from your paycheck? Can you unravel your search for fuckyeah from the pressure to turn a profit? Can you consciously replace your "audience" with your community, and stop trying to perform for yourself and the rest of us?

You do have a purpose, and it will bring you joy, *but it might not be saleable on the market.*

Do you still want to find out what it is?

5.

CANCEL YOUR SUBSCRIPTION TO BULLSHIT

Seriously, who ISN'T tired?

Who doesn't want to hurl their alarm at the wall on Monday morning? Who isn't sick of endlessly emailing "apologies for the late reply"? Who doesn't come home from work and immediately rip off their pants? Who doesn't feel outrage and burnout at the dangerous circus that is our current political climate?

Ain't nobody, that's who.

We're getting up before dawn, getting our asses to work (or class) on time, juggling multiple projects, managing our coworkers' emotions, and going above and beyond to prove we're promotion-worthy to our bosses. We're trying to "have a life," making plans with friends, going on dates, getting to the gym, eating three meals a day, occasionally bathing—some of us are even taking care of other living beings. We're giving it our all, each day, and somehow, it *still* doesn't feel like enough. We didn't get enough sleep, don't have enough money, can't keep up with our to-do lists, can't make that deadline. We're *Tired*™.

This is the power *scarcity* has over our daily lives.

Scarcity is an underlying principle that rules our global economy. It's the reason why we're so damn exhausted . . . It's also the reason we can't find our fuckyeah.

TIRED™

Open any economics textbook and you'll find some version of "the law of scarcity" almost immediately. At its most basic, the law of scarcity says that humans have "infinite wants" and "finite resources." In other words, *there is not enough.*

"Scarcity" is a convenient way for economists and titans of industry to explain why things cost what they do, and why some people have less than others. It's also what underpins the concept of *supply and demand* (inadequate resources raise prices). But scarcity isn't about actual abundance or lack; it's more about *perceived need.* It might be hard to find a window-mounted air conditioner in Antarctica, but we wouldn't exactly call them "scarce." Nobody needs a cooling system when they live in the coldest place in the world. But the things people universally need *are* limited; we only have one Earth, only so much crude oil, only so much food, only so much space. From this perspective, "not enough" makes sense.

Nothing epitomizes the issue of scarcity like world hunger. But according to the Food and Agriculture Organization of the United Nations, as of 2012, we were *already producing one and a half times enough food to feed everybody on the planet.* That's enough to feed nearly 10 billion people—the projected peak population of the world in 2050—*right now.* And yet, nearly a billion people still go hungry every day because people making less than two dollars a day cannot afford to buy this food, and because most of the food crops we're growing go toward industrial feedlots and biofuels (like the ethanol added to gasoline), *instead* of to the hungry.

World hunger isn't the natural consequence of limited resources, it's the result of a broken system that *we* instituted and that *we* can change. "Not enough" isn't a law of nature; it's a human invention and a way to explain away the restriction of otherwise abundant resources. Scarcity isn't "just the way things are"; it's what happens when wealth can't flow. *Scarcity is an institutionalized kink in our hose.* And when an idea like scarcity becomes a widely accepted cultural norm, it has a profound effect on our collective unconscious. Just fill in the blanks:

I'M NOT _____ ENOUGH.
Not smart enough, old enough, young enough, attractive enough, rich enough, confident enough, thin enough, strong enough, creative enough . . . you get it.

I DON'T HAVE ENOUGH _____.
Not enough sleep, time, money, energy, vacation days, money, confidence, sex, love, weekend days, friends, money, credentials . . . did I mention money?

I DON'T DO _____ ENOUGH.
We don't exercise enough, travel enough, network enough, try hard enough, or call our parents enough. We aren't political enough, friendly enough, active enough . . . you know I could go on.

There's a reason that no matter how much we buy, work, or chase, we don't get the sense of *enough* that we crave. This is because scarcity culture has sold us the idea that happiness is a limited resource, and it's running out. That *if* I just land that promotion, or find a partner, or have enough ___ (money, time, sleep, me-time, and so on), *then* I will be happy. When we continuously think in terms of "not having enough" and "if I just . . ." we're never quite satisfied.

It all makes a little more sense, doesn't it? I mean, why it was so hard for you to imagine a dream life where you could *have, do, or be anything,* back in chapter 1. Under scarcity, it seems pointless and naive to imagine a world where *there is enough* to live the life of your dreams.

In her book *The Soul of Money,* author Lynne Twist calls out scarcity as a lie, as "an unexamined and false system of assumptions, opinions, and beliefs from which we view the world as a place where we are in constant danger of having our needs unmet." Scarcity culture was instituted by the MF system and is reinforced by all the run-down employees, tired consumers, and anxious hoop-jumpers among us who, although we are lucky enough to have our basic needs of food, water, clothing, and shelter met, have still resigned ourselves to believing that *there is not enough.* For an economy powered by the MF, "not enough" represents a *useful* set of assumptions; it gets us to do things that reinforce the system. If there's not enough to go around, then we'd better hurry up and earn what we can, to spend what we can, on the stuff we think we need (*that they've just now run out of, dammit*). The scarcity mind-set has us living our lives on high alert, perpetually stressed about our dangerously half-empty glasses. It is the brain tangle keeping us from seeing the possibilities of our lives clearly—*and the most obvious reason to not share your fuckyeah.*

If we're not good enough, or our bosses aren't supportive enough, or we don't have enough money, or we don't have enough X—how could we possibly feel empowered to take risks? Why be brave if we believe it will backfire, we will fail, or we will fall short? The scarcity mind-set makes us petty, fearful, selfish, greedy, controlling, mistrusting, and hopeless, among other shitty things. Worst of all, it makes us lose belief in our ability to find happiness and succeed on a daily basis. On the hamster wheel of scarcity, we're chasing what we think we need, feeling empty, exhausted, run ragged, professionally burnt out, and—you guessed it—we join the ranks of millions of adults who are *Tired*™.

Or so we think.

YOU ARE A CREATIVE
(YOU JUST AREN'T ACTING LIKE ONE)

We think we're burnt out, but we're not.

It feels like we've given our all, but we haven't.

We're not empty, exhausted, run ragged, or even tired.

We're depressed.

I don't mean "depressed" in the clinical sense—though it's possible you've struggled with clinical depression, considering it affects millions of people each year and is one of the most common (and, thankfully) treatable mental illnesses today. I mean "depressed" in the *literal* sense of the word: *You're pressed down.* Stifled. Backed up. Smothered. Trapped. Squished. Tangled up. Censored. Life and work aren't draining you of your energy or ideas—*they're boring you to tears.*

You're not exhausted, you're bored!

It's easy to confuse the two, since "tired" feels a little like "bored" (unmotivated, sluggish, stagnant energy), but tired feelings come from the body, while bored feelings come from the brain. Your body gets tired when you've expended all your energy, burned all your calories, and you need sleep, like, *now*. Your brain gets bored when you have a kink in the creativity hose, blocked energy, and trapped fuckyeah.

> "What is depression? It is the inability to feel, it is the sense of being dead, while our body is alive. It is the inability to experience joy, as well as the inability to experience sadness. . . . Perhaps it clarifies the issue if instead of using the word 'depressed' we use the word 'bored.' Actually, there is very little difference between them, except a difference in degree, because boredom is nothing but the experience of a paralysis of our productive powers and the sense of un-aliveness."

(The brilliant social psychologist Erich Fromm got it.)

Factory School has taught you to be a *spectator* and not a *creator*, taught you that risks rarely pay off, and that someone, somewhere, must have the answers and can tell you what you should do. Your Art has long been weighted, stifled, and buried within you—*and a belief in scarcity is what keeps it there.*

In the "not enough" mind-set, you and I believe we are empty vessels that need more, more, more to be happy. Meanwhile, our fuckyeah is smothered under an avalanche of *not enough-isms* and other bullshit we don't even realize we're telling ourselves on a daily basis, leaving us scared shitless and bored out of our minds.

Yeah.

Do me a favor? Take a deep breath. *You are enough.* Come up for air, for just a second, and breathe this in: *there is enough.* You have everything you need at this moment to start sharing your Art and living your fuckyeah.

Yeah, I realize the previous sentence comes dangerously close to being one of those "vague self-help platitudes" that I warned you about in the book's introduction—and no, I'm not trying to be tone-deaf about your socioeconomic circumstances. When I say "everything you need," I'm not referring to literal art supplies, a public platform, or cash. You may or may not have those things. I mean that although you might currently discount them, you have within you *immense* inner resources of energy, creativity, and confidence—and that you already possess incredible ambition, power, and resilience—even if you're not yet aware these resources are there.

Yes, it's mysterious. Yes, you'll have to do some exploring in order to find your Art. But take a second, breathe deep, and flirt—*just flirt*—with the idea that there is enough. That you are enough.

You aren't as exhausted as you thought you were. You aren't giving everything you've got, because no one has asked you for everything you've got.

Not at the MF, anyways. They've asked for your compliance, your submission, your productivity, and the right to profit from your work, but no one has asked you for the real you, yet.

Until now. I'm asking, on behalf of all the humans who give a shit. *We need you. We want your fuckyeah.*

You are more than enough; you just aren't letting it flow.

Scarcity is a kink in the hose: When you stop creating, you start consuming. Hoarding. Panicking that you don't have enough and pressing your joy further down. If you aren't tapping into your boundless (yeah, boundless) inner resources to share your fuckyeah with us, then you're back to being crushed beneath the oppressive weight of scarcity culture. If you aren't busy being generous with your unique mash-up of sparkly universe dust, if you aren't creating, then you'll end up rejoining the "assembly line" (producing) because *Nature abhors a vacuum.* You are a Creative by nature, remember? You are driven, compelled, and motivated to create something, anything—and your Art is the fuckyeah you decide to share.

So, what will you create? Some soulless product you don't care about for the MF? Or your Art?

Okay, yes, I know you still have no idea what your Art—or fuckyeah— is. Part II of this book is all about the practical ways to find and share your Art.

But let's start with the truth: *you are a Creative,* whether you feel that way or not. You have *always* been a creative, constructing your life's reality moment by moment—you've simply censored certain expressions of that creativity in order to protect yourself and fit in. But today is a new day, and you're here, now, reading this book—which means you're tired of self-censorship out of fear. Instead of wrapping your identity up in your job, living in fear of making mistakes because of Factory School, performing for the Market as a living Bwrand, or resigning yourself to being an audience member in your life, you can choose to rebuild your reality. Rather than believe that life is "happening to you," you can begin to live with intention. You already have everything you need within you to live as a creator, rather than a spectator. All it takes is the right information (aka part I of this book) *and a willingness to change your mind.*

Ready to teach an old lizard some new tricks?

HOW TO DEAL: LIMITING BELIEFS

Want to unknot your brain, one limiting belief at a time? Yeah you do. **Grab a piece of paper and something to write with.** (Wanna stick it to Factory School? Make sure it's a glittery gel pen.) And just for solidarity, I'm going to use my real life as an example, ripped from the pages of an actual journal of mine.

STEP 1: WHAT'S OFF THE TABLE?

The first step in unraveling the mental clusterfuck that is a "limiting belief" is to *realize it's there*. What's something you want to do, be, or have? Why do you think it's just not in the cards for you? Who do you think you can't be? What will never work out? When something comes to mind, write it down. (Humor me here; research proves "reappraisal" and "emotional disclosure" via writing is more effective than just mulling things over in our minds.)

If nothing comes to mind immediately, revisit the Uncensor Your Ambitions exercise from chapter 1, look for the most unlikely, complicated, or impossible dream you scribbled down, and write it again, below.

>> *"I wish I could start my own business, but I'd never pull it off."*

STEP 2: THE INNER CYNIC TANTRUM

Okay, now write down the *opposite* of this limiting belief. Phrase it as if you're declaring you actually *can* have, do, or be the thing you know is impossible.

>> *"I am going to start my own business."*

Read this affirmative sentence out loud . . . and then wait for your Inner Cynic to throw a tantrum. It won't be long before you have a flood of *shut-the-fuck-up* reasons running through your mind; all you need to do is write them down.

List every conceivable reason "why not." Activate your lawyer brain and lay out all the "evidence" proving why this is an impossibility or a terrible idea. Do this as quickly and instinctively as you can. Your reasons don't have to make sense; just document your Inner Cynic's word vomit.

>> *"I don't know the first thing about starting my own business. I could run out of money. I'm probably just thinking this because it's trendy to be an entrepreneur and I'm bored at work. Who am I to think I could start a business? I don't even have proof anyone will like my idea . . ."*

STEP 3: BUT REALLY, WHY?

As soon as you feel a pause in the barrage of "reasons," take a breath. Now ask yourself why you *really* think this is impossible. Who from your childhood would be the first to agree with your Inner Cynic? What examples did they set for you? Do you have any proof of this "thing" going wrong from your young life? Is what you want to do or who you want to be forbidden, shameful, or embarrassing? Sometimes the truth will jump up and slap you in the face; other times nothing comes to mind. If you aren't getting any epiphanies, don't dwell on it; jump ahead to the next step. But at least give this a shot, first.

>> *"I think starting my own business, and especially quitting my job, is dangerous. I see quitting as failure, and so will others— just evidence that I couldn't hack a 'real' nine-to-five. I'll never have enough money with my own business, which will stress me out and fuck up my life. Dad was angry when I was a kid, and deeply unhappy—and he was the epitome of a 'businessman' in my childhood. I think I'm afraid of becoming as miserable and furious as he was."*

Damn. Well, there you go.

STEP 4: REVERSE LAWYERING

You and your Inner Cynic are no longer on the same side. You're consciously switching from Prosecution to *Defense*. You're going to disprove all the claims your Inner Cynic rattled off in steps 2 and 3, and you're going to do it by imagining that your "client" *isn't you*. Now you're representing someone who is even smarter, wealthier, funnier, braver, and more ambitious than you are. Prove your Inner Cynic wrong; write down your arguments.

>> *"I don't know the first thing about starting my own business."*

But you've learned things that you previously knew nothing about, right? You learned to read and write, to drive a car, and to do the job you currently have.

You learned those things because you believed you could and because you were patient enough with yourself to go through the necessary trial and error.

>> *"I could run out of money."*

Yep. But unfortunately, that could also happen if you don't start a business. There are no guarantees in life, but money can be earned back. Time, however, is not renewable, and "YA NEED CASH" isn't a reason to avoid trying something you're interested in. You might even be missing out on money because you're *not* starting this biz. Besides, your *value* is entirely separate from your *worth* on the market.

>> *"I'm probably just thinking this because it's trendy to be an entrepreneur and I'm bored at work."*

Are you the kind of person who makes drastic life decisions based on trendy things? I doubt it. If you have made that kind of impulsive decision before, what did you learn from it? Secondly, are you bored at work, or is there more to it? Do you believe there are more challenges to pursue and conquer at this job? Can you do both? Nothing occupies your attention like a full-time job and also starting your business on the side. That'll kill your boredom dead.

>> *"Who am I to think I could start a business?"*

Are you not starting your own business because you have to be an "expert" first? If all the rookies with an idea never started their businesses, we wouldn't have smartphones, or movies, or airplanes. Shame always runs the "Who do you think you are?" track on repeat; ignore it. Who "are you"? You're the only "you" in the entire known universe.

>> *I don't have proof anyone will like my idea.*

What if you're onto something with this idea? The best way to find out if your idea is sellable is to test it out with people. Why not try?

>> *"I see quitting as failure, and so will others . . . I'll never have enough money . . . I'm afraid of becoming as miserable and furious as Dad was."*

Quitting a job isn't failure; it's closing one chapter and starting another—especially since that new chapter is launching a business. You have no evidence that you won't have enough money to launch (or earn enough to maintain) this business; that's an assumption. Though your dad's behavior deeply affected you, he is by no means the only example of what a person in business "is." You are not your dad. You are totally unique, and your business will be too.

Well played. Before we complete the final step (step 5: Jedi Mind Tricks), you need to know *why* it's the most important step of all.

MY HOUSE, MY HAIR, MY ALLISONS

If what you focus on becomes your reality, then it pays to focus on the fact that you're an intelligent, kind, attractive, and wholly loved human being. Especially if you want to get shit done.

I'll bet you've heard of affirmations before. They're positive statements that can shift our focus on a subject, ultimately changing what we believe about ourselves for the better. Though affirmations are #trending in the self-help industry, the general public is pretty sure that affirmations cause dry heaving (due to the intense cheeseball factor of complimenting oneself). If you've never seen the video clip of a four-year-old girl named Jessica fist pumping on her bathroom counter, proclaiming her affirmations for the day—*drop everything* and watch it right now. I'm serious. Search for the video "Jessica's Daily Affirmation" online.

I love my house, my hair, and my Allisons too, girl. Me too.

It's adorable when a four-year-old shouts encouraging words into her hairbrush, but the Internet might not have the same viral reaction to watching a grown-up Jessica doing the same thing. Why does saying anything positive about ourselves, out loud, feel so . . . ridiculous? Why is it so easy to put ourselves down? If any of my friends talked to me the way my Inner Cynic talks to me, I'd ghost on plans/unfollow/unfriend/unsubscribe while daydreaming about punching that jerk in the throat. It's like we've all got a personal hate-speech GIF that loops over and over in our minds or something.

I have this theory that we've been *conditioned* to prefer negative self-talk because we equate it with humility; we think it's a form of "keeping ourselves in check" or "being realistic." But it does neither—and it's not humility. I define humility as having a clear, shame-free understanding of where you are in relationship to the world at this moment, knowing that you don't control much of anything, and being at peace with that, without losing your ambition to improve. *And our loud-mouthed Inner Cynic isn't helping us with any of that.* It sucks away our energy to learn, grow, and change, leaving us huddled in the mental fetal position all because we are caught up in a twisted and false understanding of humility.

This Inner Cynic thing is familiar to you, I know. You're probably not shocked to hear that researchers have found self-criticism is directly linked to *and* increases the risk of depression. But it kind of seems like anything can cause depression these days, right? Like, is the solution to combating my Inner Mean Girl to *just* "like myself more"? If I knew how, I would. Thanks for nothing, WebMD.

Good news: We don't need to instantly summon Kanye West-size self-esteem to punch our Inner Cynics in their proverbial throats. We just need some self-compassion.

Researchers have found that self-compassion—NOT self-esteem—breaks the cycle of negative self-criticism and can even prevent depression. Are you hearing this? We're not lacking self-confidence; we're lacking self-compassion! So, what's the difference between the two?

Self-esteem is our sense of self-worth when compared against external standards (*low* while trying on bathing suits under Target's oppressive fluorescent lighting; *high* while getting every single word right to "Baby Got Back" car karaoke).

Self-compassion, however, is self-kindness instead of self-judgment, a sense of common humanity instead of isolation, and mindfully questioning, instead of automatically believing, our Inner Cynics.

Self-compassion is choosing to think about yourself the way you think about your best friend.

You know they're not perfect; they're actually deeply flawed. But that doesn't change the fact that they're amazing, a motherf-in' blessing on the face of this earth, a gawtdang shining light—and you'd happily cancel/unfollow/unsubscribe/delete (and consider throat-punching) anyone who tried to tell them otherwise.

Self-compassion is rewiring your brain to be nice to you. It's reminding yourself that you don't have to be perfect because no one is, and we're all in this messy life together. And a shockingly easy way to do that? Affirmations.

———

You've heard of the fight-or-flight stress response, right?

The opposite of "fight or flight" is called the "relaxation response." The relaxation response (RR) is a way of describing what happens in your body, chemically, when you're genuinely relaxed, like in meditation or deep sleep. The term was coined in the 1970s by Harvard cardiologist Dr. Herbert Benson, whose research focused on the effects of this relaxed state on the body (all positive, in case you're wondering), as well as researching ways to "trigger" it intentionally with mindfulness, meditation, and breathing exercises. Though he didn't invent any new concepts (managing the effects of stress on the body through breathing and meditation has been done for several thousand years), he and his team did "validate" these ancient practices among scientists. Their research was among the earliest to prove that these practices *do* make people healthier, both physically and mentally. But here's what's mind blowing: *the relaxation response has recently been shown to alter gene expression.*

Lost? I was too.

WTF is "gene expression"?

I'm no expert, but I'll do my best to summarize. "Gene expression" is like the volume knob on a piece of DNA. It is the set of instructions your DNA gives to each cell for its protein production (i.e., make more of this; make less of that).

The relaxation response was found to *increase* gene expression (turn up the volume) for energy levels and metabolism, and *decrease* gene expression (turn down the volume) for inflammatory responses, stress pathways, and cell aging. Further translation: The RR is a reset button for your nervous system that doesn't just chill you out, but makes instant, lasting changes to your body's chemistry for the better. No drugs required.

Additional research has confirmed that not only can your body's natural relaxation state trigger a genetic recoding effect, improving your physical and psychological health, *but you can initiate the relaxation response with a simple meditative focus on positive thoughts and words.* In other words, "pulling a Jessica" with personal affirmations isn't hippie mumbo jumbo; it's potentially recoding your cells with increased energy and youth, and decreased inflammation and stress hormone levels.

What (*and I cannot stress this enough*) the fuck?!

If that's not a good reason to jump on your bathroom counter and get excited about your life, I don't know what is.

OKAY, BACK TO OUR REGULARLY
SCHEDULED PROGRAMMING

In steps 1–2 you explored what you want, and why your Inner Cynic thinks it's impossible. In step 3, you asked yourself where this fear might be coming from, and in step 4 you reframed the things you were freaked out about, one reason at a time. The final step, step 5, asks you to flip your excuses upside down, turning them into affirmations.

STEP 5: JEDI MIND TRICKS

Write down the opposites of your limiting beliefs, excuses, or reasons, and then read these new positive statements to yourself—aloud; you can stand the cheese. (You can.)

For example:

>> *"I don't know the first thing about starting my own business"* *becomes:*

I'm intelligent and curious; I've learned complicated things before. I can learn how to start a business.

>> *"I could run out of money" becomes:*

I have enough money right now. My creativity is not dependent on money.

>> *"I'm probably just thinking this because it's trendy to be an entrepreneur and I'm bored at work" becomes:*

I don't make life decisions based on trends. I've been dreaming about this a long time, and I can make my dreams a reality.

>> *"Who am I to think I should start a business?" becomes:*

I am creative, hardworking, and have something to share with the world.

>> *"I don't even have proof anyone will like my idea" becomes:*

All I can do is try; my best is enough. I am enough.

>> *"I see quitting as failure, and so will others"* becomes:

Quitting is not failure; it's ending one thing in order to begin another.

>> *"Dad was angry when I was a kid, and deeply unhappy—I'm afraid of becoming as miserable and furious as he was"* becomes:

There are countless more examples of "people in business" than Dad, many of them happy and successful. I am not my parents; I am unique, my experience is unique, and my business will be unique.

Read, say aloud, and reread the affirmations you create. Tape 'em up on your mirror or wall—somewhere you'll see them. Then read and reread them some more. Write them on your hand. Think about them. When you get annoyed, remember that you're not delusional or arrogant; you're trying to recode your cells.

I *promise* I wouldn't bring up affirmations if they weren't so damn effective. They're awkward, I know—but unraveling years of subconscious limiting beliefs requires something close to Jedi mind tricks. Even if you need to eye roll while reading affirmations aloud, it's *still* better than not doing it at all. That's what I had to do. (It still worked.)

What about your 1,000,004 other limiting beliefs? Lather, rinse, repeat. The "How to Deal: Limiting Beliefs" exercise has helped me more times than I can count (and I've got my own business to prove it). Use it. Reuse it. Get out of your own way.

II:

NSOR

SELF

6.

START STARTING

Have you ever caught yourself procrastinating by *overplanning*?

I have. It's kinda my thing.

It's 2011 and I'm in Houston, in my dorm room; a huge philosophy term paper is due tomorrow, but I can't work on it right now because I'm swept up in the most meticulous pros-and-cons list I've ever drafted, debating whether I should drop out of college or not. It's 2014 and I'm in West Hollywood, in my retail store's office; I should be sweating on the sales floor, dragging tables and racks around for the new season's setup, but instead, I'm hunched over a desk, erasing and redrawing the floor plan I've been trying to make painstakingly accurate for the last four days. It's 2017 and I'm in Oakland in my sun-drenched apartment; I should be sitting at my laptop, editing the travel video I've just spent two weeks creating (it's due to a major airline brand tomorrow), but instead I'm pacing the living room, staring at dozens of handwritten Post-it Notes, brainstorming a crazy book idea I have.

We, as a society, love a good plan. We admire the pros-and-cons list and celebrate a detailed brainstorm; we glorify road maps, outlines, and presentations. But you know what? Some plans are just *active avoidance*. Sometimes you don't need an exact blueprint of your future, or another list, or higher qualifications. Sometimes you know exactly what you need to do, and you're just deeply scared to do it.

If only I could travel back in time to visit past Me, briefly say hello, explain time travel, compliment her hair, and then grab her by the shoulders and yell, "Quit freaking out about being perfect, qualified, or 100 percent ready. *Just START!*"

That term paper you need to write—write it. The laundry you need to fold—fold it. The risk you've been considering taking at work—take it. The friend you've been scared to ask out on a date—ask them. This creative project of yours that could end up being rejected—make it and share it anyway. JUST DO IT.

Yes, I realize when I say "just do it," Nike's ubiquitous slogan is probably all you can think about. But do me a favor and ask yourself, honestly, *"What if I just DID IT?"* What if you tried the thing you're scared to try? What if you put your voice, work, or Art into the world? What if you just DID IT?

There are a million and one reasons to be nervous that something you want to try will backfire, or be a waste, or disappoint you. But none of those reasons should keep you from starting, because today's ceiling is tomorrow's floor.

What you learn today—by DOING—becomes a resource for tomorrow. Today's tiny step forward will bring you that much closer to finding out what you love, what you hate, and what makes your heart happy. So why not start starting?

Life has no problem handing us reasons why we shouldn't take risks—*this is scary; it could backfire; it will hurt; we will fail*—our lizard brain wants to protect us from all that. But when we're hyper-focused on avoiding the problems in our lives, we miss out on opportunities to solve the ones that will bring us joy. Yeah, you read that right: *problems are opportunities you could miss out on.*

There will always be problems in life, so what kinds of problems do you want to solve?

There will never be a clean, straightforward path to anything we want to do, be, and try—and if we wait until we're certain that we're qualified, or until we know we can "pull this off," or until we're 100 percent ready—*shit will never get done.* The fact is, "now" is better than "perfect," because perfect doesn't *exist.*

So, stop procrastinating and start starting, because some problems were *made for you* to solve, and solving them will *make you deeply happy.*

But you can't find that out if you never get started.

I AM HOW I LOOK ON PAPER

In a sub-knot of the "I Am My Paycheck" and "I Am a Living Brand" brain-tangle clusterfuck is a sneaky little gem called *"I Am How I Look on Paper."* This limiting belief has been around since our earliest report cards and has only gotten worse since we were introduced to resumes: get the right grades, rack up the extracurriculars, check all the "talent" boxes, climb the ladder, and you'll be successful (oh, and happy, rich, loved, and so on). This fear that we're only as valuable as we appear to be on paper keeps us from "getting started," learning, pivoting, or taking risks.

We seem to think the successful people, the ones who've "made it," all found this *one thing* they were good at and stuck with it. These are the One Track people—the Experts, the ones without resume gaps and with streamlined story arcs, the stars of our Success Porn.

The One Track people? They knew what they wanted to do since they were in diapers. They showed great promise at that thing in grade school, continued to be great at it in college, and got a great job in that field when they graduated. They worked their way up (which was hard, because they were pulling themselves up by their bootstraps while working their way up the ladder, *or so the story tends to go*), devoted to their One Track, until we decided they were all-knowing Experts.

What happens if you never found that One Track when you were a kid? What if school was hard for you? What if you were already on your fifth entry-level job in a new field around the same time the One Track person was deep into their bright and shiny Expert career? What do you do if you've never cared about anything enough to become an Expert in it?

You could panic. Or you could try letting go of the idea that you need to be a One Track person to be happy or successful. What if you gave yourself the permission to become an Expert *one day*? Or maybe . . . *never*?

The truth is, the people who appear to have had a straight-line career actually zigged and zagged all the way there.

People like me, for example.

In a past life, I spent over a decade climbing the corporate ladder at a huge hipster retail company, from part-time salesperson to overseeing creative visual direction for every store in the Northern California region. I oversaw eleven different locations and teams, whose combined yearly volume was in the double-digit millions (*"yeah, yeah we've already heard this, very impressive, blah blah"*). Right, right, yes—I enjoyed creative freedom through store design, styling, and social media management; I loved being a leader, boss, mentor, and teacher-trainer. I got to travel across the country multiple times a year to help a team of incredibly creative people craft the image of this gigantic brand that spanned over 190 locations. I also got to show up at work covered in tattoos, wearing whatever fashion-y thing I felt like, and still enjoyed the respect that comes with being a leader who knows her shit.

Are you getting the ladder-climbing, bootstrap-pulling, One Track vibe? Are you imagining a gigantic cushy salary, and wondering why the hell I'd leave a job like that? Of course you are—that was a sound bite. Success Porn. *I'm summarizing more than a decade of my life in five sentences.* The sound bite is true, but I left out some real-life details.

Like many so-called Experts, I worked my way up, starting twelve years earlier in part-time sales while going to school. During those twelve years I lived in ten apartments in eight cities, moving nearly every year; this meant that just as I was feeling settled and had begun to build community, I was packing again. I worked at seven different stores before being promoted to co-manage a whole district—my Expert status was far from immediate. I traveled extensively, often clocking eleven-plus-hour workdays, usually on the road by six in the morning. I was *tired*. I wish it were true that I made a cushy salary, but my take-home pay was on the low end among my peers in the industry; because the job required I live in the most expensive region of the United States, rent ate most of my paycheck. The cost of living in the Bay Area had skyrocketed so much that even with a generous budget,

I couldn't pay my teams *even close* to what I thought they deserved. I often had to give difficult feedback, talking people through tears and anger. My inbox was blowing up so regularly that I couldn't send "apologies for the delayed reply" fast enough.

The sound bite sounds like I'm bragging; the details sound like I'm complaining. I'm doing neither, just making a point: *the people who seem like One Track people are rarely One Track people.*

Everyone's public story has private details. Every job has highs and lows. We're not what we look like on paper, and the road to success is not ever what it appears. We can't compare our hustle to everyone else's, because we will never fully know their story.

On paper, it looks like I had a dream job and a straight-line career trajectory. It looks like I've always known what I wanted to do and that the "right" path to success was to climb higher and higher at one company. But off paper, in reality, I had zigged and zagged all the way to "success." I hadn't always known what I wanted to do; I simply took the appealing opportunities life presented to me. Each choice had different results; some of which I loved and some that I hated. The path that led me to "looks good on paper" was long, tiring, and jagged—and the kind of success I used to relish as an Expert eventually made me miserable. So, what did I do?

I started over.

I aggressively pivoted my career. And you know what? I survived! Pivoting careers wasn't a failure; my years spent "climbing" weren't a waste of time. I'm doing new things that I love, and *I'm okay with being a total rookie at them,* because I'm not a piece of paper, or a story line, or a Brand—and neither are you.

The founder of CreativeLive, Chase Jarvis, deftly pointed out that our parents had one career, we will have five different careers, and the next generation will have five different jobs simultaneously—and who knows how many *careers* they'll have? It might not even matter at that point. We're heading toward a world in which adaptability is a prized skill set; a world in which being a "polymath" is normal, maybe even required.

You don't have to be a One Track person to be successful; you don't have to "stick it out" if the career you once found fulfilling is now draining. Whether or not your life looks attractive on paper is not a measurement of your success and has nothing to do with your ability to enjoy it. If we want a shot at finding the ever-elusive state of *well-being* we keep hearing so much about, then we need to be okay with being amateurs, more often, in more areas of our lives.

For the record, I'm not interested in minimizing experts here. Experts are necessary. They're *awesome.* They keep the lights on and make sure the medicine gets made. They can be inspiring people with incredible self-discipline, passion, and focus; I'm definitely not trying to glorify ignorance. But I do believe that we will only find happiness in who we are and what we do when we prioritize having a *sense* of purpose over the idea that we all need to have one path, one calling, or one almighty career.

Finding fuckyeah requires the courage to try new things, to fail, and to grow—the *courage* to be a beginner and to simply start. Once you realize that your life is *more* than a streamlined story or brand messaging—*that where you are in your career is not who you are*—you can take a deep breath and finally enjoy wherever you're at, right now.

THE CARPET IS HOT LAVA

Have you ever unpacked something that came in a ridiculously gigantic box and found yourself hesitating to break down the cardboard?

Little-Kid Me would be livid at the volume of raw materials I've discarded in my lifetime. DO YOU KNOW HOW MANY FORTS YOU COULD BUILD WITH ALL THE BOXES YOU'VE THROWN AWAY? *DO YOU EVEN KNOW?*

Have you ever wondered why after working our asses off, earning promotions, and hitting our goals, many of us still feel unfulfilled? Because we don't make fun one of our priorities. It's no wonder we are burnt-the-fuck-out; we've made fun something that we do if there's time, and only after *everything else* is done. (It never is.) Along our journey to "adulting"—probably somewhere between meal-prepping and scheduling our own doctor's appointments—we forgot how to *play*.

Ever hung out with your little cousin and watched him reject a brand-new toy for the box it came in? Suddenly he's jumping from sofa to chair and climbing inside his cardboard fortress, avoiding the carpet *that has now become molten hot lava!* There's something about a kid's brain that predisposes them to imagine whole universes inside the same thing that adult brains look at as trash.

Kids are the perfect role models for play. Sure, they're a little rough around the edges. They don't pick up on our social cues, like when NOT to wail in a confined, public space; they rarely apologize for blurting out rude comments at the store or for waking you up at

2:47 a.m. They have nothing to lose. They have no concept of "the stakes." Learning things—and *life itself*—is a game they're playing.

Admit it—aren't you jealous of their mental freedom and their ability to find awe in the mundane? Don't you miss being amazed by something? *Anything?* Everything a kid touches is fascinating to them. Worms writhing out of upturned soil are awesome, not gross. That cardboard box is a *goddamn miracle.* My door-knocker hoop earrings have entranced friends' babies countless times, usually leading to said earrings being ripped out of my earlobes by adorable, chubby baby fingers. *I mean, they're so shiny!*

In their eyes, if something isn't amazing, then it's downright *oppressive.* Take a kid to the DMV or the store, and they can't stand upright under the weight of their own boredom. They melt into a puddle on the ground, unable to bear the crushing lameness of this horrible place. *How is this a real place? Am I dying? I'm so bored. MOM! I'M SO BOREDDDD! MOMMMMMMM!* Even kids understand from an early age how a place (aka life) devoid of play is totally unbearable.

We need to take a cue from the tiny humans.

We need to *play.*

The best part about Play is that we don't need to think it through very much to enjoy it. Defining it all but sucks the life out of it, but I'm going to be a little ~extra~ with a definition. Physician, play researcher, and author Dr. Stuart Brown describes Play as follows:

> *"An absorbing, apparently purposeless activity that provides enjoyment and a suspension of self-consciousness and sense of time. It is also self-motivating and makes you want to do it again."*

Why are kids so good at playing, while we bill-paying, job-holding adults are all so . . . *weird* about it?

Because Play isn't "productive."

It doesn't advance our careers, pay our bills, or put food on the table, so it's nonessential in a productive society. We try to squeeze it in when we can get away with it, but generally, we think Play is a waste of time. But if Play held no evolutionary benefit, wouldn't the playful animals (including humans) have died out, allowing for natural selection of the more serious, non-playful species? Play must have some biological benefit, right?

Yep.

Research confirms that Play is both a sign of intelligence and a form of learning, propelling the evolution of any species forward. Scientists used to think that Play was a behavior only found in "higher" thinking animals, beginning with humans, mammals, and the occasional bird, but now they've got evidence of Play all over the evolutionary chain. Dolphins play elaborate social games; octopi play with objects, as if solving puzzles. Monkeys have snowball fights. Ravens will slide down a snowy slope on their backs, head first, and then fly to the top of the hill and do it again. (Is it cute or creepy that a raven does that? I'm still undecided.) Kittens, dogs, wolves, and bears all play wrestle—and we know kids do too. Studies definitively show that Play is a crucial part of brain development in children; kids who play will grow up to be mentally healthy and socially connected people. Kids who do not play often grow up to be maladjusted, depressed, or worse—much worse. (Research on the childhood backgrounds of convicted murderers showed their childhoods were often entirely devoid of Play. *Yikes*.)

And it turns out that Play isn't purposeless for adults; it makes us smarter.

Play is a dress rehearsal for life in a safe, fear-free space; it's a way to test things out and see what works. It helps us solve problems in danger-free ways and builds new neural pathways we can use later. Playing a game of touch football with friends gets aggression out, allowing us to act the way we would when exercising real self-defense, but without really being in a dangerous situation. Teasing your kid brother lets you say what you wouldn't otherwise, in a socially safe way. Spitballing weird ideas in a work meeting relieves tension and might point us to a useful idea after the brainstorming is over. Getting lost in a movie plot or a good book isn't just a game of grown-up "make believe," it's a way for our brains to experience new scenarios from the safety of our home and to teach us empathy for the world around us.

>> *"Great, but I can't exactly quit my job and play on a jungle gym all day, you know?"*

Yeah, me neither. But I think you and I can agree there's more fun to be had in life than sending cat GIFs back and forth with a cubicle-mate or getting day-drunk on Sunday; we need to find more ways to play. You should 100 percent take that dance class your friend mentioned, bake cookies for your coworkers, join that community dodgeball league, or attend that X-rated "adults only" party you were considering. Play chess with your grandma in the park. Join a book club. Sing at the top of your lungs in the car, and keep singing when the person next to you notices and smirks. Change your office computer's screen saver to a new meme every day. Draw and write directly on your bedroom walls. (You can paint over it when you move out. It won't take that long; I've done it.) Buy bathtub finger paints meant for kids and doodle stick figures while sipping wine in the bath. Whatever. Anything. Just do something that pushes you to explore outside your creative comfort zone.

This is where fuckyeah is waiting: just past the moment you're a little embarrassed, right past the well-behaved-adults-don't-do-this signpost, just outside your comfort zone.

Little kids are bad at everything, but it's great because they're learning. Their lives are exciting because they are okay with *sloppy*. They're experts at playing and discovering things—skills we lost somewhere along the road to auto-depositing our paychecks and using expressions like "key performance indicators."

Learning to play without self-judgment or real-world adult "logic" weighing us down helps us uncensor who we are. It will be messy sometimes, but that's where fun lives—in the unexpected, exciting, fuckyeah moments of life. When learning is a game, everything starts to look like a miracle—including shiny hoop earrings and cardboard boxes.

All I'm sayin' is, that Amazon Prime box looks like it would hold the third corner of our blanket fort *perfectly*.

FIND YOUR FLOW

In the years before my district-boss-ladyness, I spent my days hustling as a store merchandiser in Los Angeles. Daily, at what I fondly refer to as the "ass-crack of dawn," my team sorted hundreds of moving-size cardboard boxes, pulled samples, organized new apparel, and then unpacked and tagged every single item with a security sensor. In the few hours we had before the gigantic store opened (three stories tall, well over ten thousand square feet in size), it was my job to make room for this new product and then make it look *magical*. Store design became a game for me. I'd lose track of time, bouncing all over the space, misplacing my coffee along the way. I'd get caught up in imagining the new concept I was pulling together, visualizing Tetris moves and killer outfitting, and then I'd actually make it happen. I partnered with a display artist to build new installations, fixtures, and window concepts that we designed from scratch, and managed to clean it all up by the time the store opened at eleven in the morning.

My guess? Maybe one in fifty people who read that paragraph thought "Fun!" Everyone else got REALLY bored midway through. My point is: *I loved that shit.*

I found Flow in something you probably wouldn't—and you may find it in something that would make me cringe. That's just how Flow works.

It kind of sounds like a yoga class or a made-up self-help thing, but Flow is an actual scientific term coined by Hungarian psychologist Mihaly Csikszentmihalyi.

Flow is that in-the-zone, no clue how much time has passed, fully blissed-out feeling you get while you're doing something equally challenging and engrossing. It happens to surgeons, tennis players, artists, musicians—and manifests in a million other ways, to a million other people. It can happen whether the thing you're doing is "important" or not. It happens to little kids on a playground, and I bet it's happened to you. In Flow we lose track of time; we work incredibly hard but feel energized afterward. Though usually fun, Flow activities have nothing to do with being *easy*. In fact, they have to be challenging to demand our full attention; it's one of the qualifications of a Flow experience. To summarize Csikszentmihalyi, Flow kicks in when we're involved in an activity that:

1. *Requires our full focus;*

2. *Is challenging for our skill level (but not too challenging);*

3. *Has rules we understand and results we can see;*

4. *Takes mental attention off our "Self."*

These details are what separates Flow from leisure or competition. Watching TV takes mental attention off ourselves, but it isn't challenging; it's passive. Running a competitive marathon requires your full focus and can be challenging, but if you're doing it for the external reward of winning, then it can't be considered Flow because it hasn't taken your mental attention off "the Self." Flow requires precise balance; all four elements of Flow need to be in harmony for us to truly experience it. (I think I just described a boy band? Flow is like a boy band.)

When an activity requires our complete attention, there's no extra "psychic energy" to direct anywhere else. We get so wrapped up in what we're doing that the activity becomes spontaneous or automatic—we lose sight of ourselves and our insecurities, focused solely on the thing we're doing. Csikszentmihalyi calls these activities "autotelic" (a Greek word that combines "self" and "goal")—an activity done for the fun of the thing itself, not for future benefits:

> *"An autotelic experience is very different from the feelings we typically have in the course of life. So much of what we ordinarily do has no value in itself, and we do it only because we have to do it, or because we expect some future benefit from it. Many people feel that the time they spend at work is essentially wasted—they are alienated from it, and the psychic energy invested in the job does*

nothing to strengthen their self. For quite a few people, free time is also wasted. Leisure provides a relaxing respite from work, but it generally consists of passively absorbing information, without using any skills or exploring new opportunities for action. As a result, life passes in a sequence of boring and anxious experiences over which a person has little control."

Did you catch that? Csikszentmihalyi identified the cycle of bouncing back and forth between stress and boredom, and how we become detached from our work. But when we take part in autotelic activities, we become fully present in whatever we are doing. We become so invested—mind, body, and *dare I say it*, soul—in the present moment that we exit the cycle of numbness and anxiety and enter Flow. Flow takes us fully into the moment, making it impossible to experience stress about the future or worry about the past (which is great, since the present moment is the only place we can experience raw joy). Think about any memory where you were utterly happy. Were you actively participating in that moment, fully present? *Yep.*

Flow is a lantern illuminating the path to your fuckyeah.

There's no one ideal activity to experience Flow in—it's dependent on your personality. One person might find it taking apart a car engine and trying to put it back together; someone else (like me) might laugh nervously at that concept while immediately googling a mechanic.

When we discover Flow, we're being introduced to the kind of problems we want to get lost in and solve.

You might find it in learning to rock climb. Your friend might find it entering data into a spreadsheet. Your neighbor might find it playing the violin. You might find it reworking a wall of T-shirts and styling mannequins, like I did. There's no one-size-fits-all. Maybe you've already experienced Flow in something you regularly do; maybe you're really into skateboarding, or slow-roasting BBQ in a smoker. Or maybe even at work; I wish on hearts, stars, and puppy dog kisses that you're lucky enough to have a job you can find Flow in. But if up to this point in life your experience with Flow has been utterly random, you *might* be wondering how in the *actual fuck* to find it. (I gotchu.)

THE TWO FASTEST WAYS TO FIND FLOW ARE:

1. *Make life, especially learning, into a game. Play.*

2. *Be willing to be bad at things that interest you for long enough to get good at those things.*

Flow requires a little kid's method of learning: approaching things with curiosity, experimentation, playfulness, and openness to failure. If you can make a game out of even a mindless task or create rules that challenge your abilities ("Let's see if I can set a personal record and flip twenty burgers in sixty seconds!"), then you might end up having fun at an otherwise boring day of work. More importantly, by *choosing* to be a rookie at something that interests you, you're giving yourself permission—and time—to figure out what problems you actually *enjoy* solving.

As part of his research on "optimal experience," Flow, and joy, Csikszentmihalyi and his graduate students decided to interview high-level professionals (aka One Track people) in the fields of art and science. They talked to hundreds of biologists, poets, dancers, psychologists, painters, novelists, physicists, and others who were living lives built around their fuckyeah. While each case was unique, Csikszentmihalyi and his colleague Jeanne Nakamura discovered a common thread in each of their interviewee's lives—something they called "vital engagement."

Each interviewee, though in completely different fields, described a similar chain of events that led them to their fuckyeah: it began with a spark of curiosity; satisfying that curiosity led to enjoyment; enjoyment led to Flow; Flow experiences led to new values, relationships, and curiosities over the years, which led to even longer stretches of Flow. In other words? *These Experts had chased down their curiosity and found their fuckyeah in the process.*

It's not that the interviewees' lives were free of problems or pain; it's not that they always knew what they wanted, or how to get what they wanted either. These professionals had spent so much time in their fields that they became experts. And the reason they spent all that time on that "one thing" in the first place? Because they were motivated to learn, play, and experience everything they could in their field. They weren't happy because they were experts; they became experts because they were happy.

Stop looking for your fuckyeah in a job title, career, or field— it's waiting in moments, experiences, and activities.

Happy, successful people are "vitally engaged" with their lives and their work. They found that "engagement" through chasing down their curiosity, *not because of their commitment to one career.*

It's time to take the pressure off, because as much as your brain would like you to believe otherwise, you can't see the future. You don't know whether today's curiosity will become a passion—and you don't need to know. That's not important. What is important is acting on that curiosity—to start something and see where it leads you. Find out if you love it or hate it and move forward from there.

Flow happens when you discover a challenge and *decide* you want to get good at that thing (even if you're bad at first), willing to power through those moments of fear, doubt, and downright sucking at it. When you come out on the other side, you not only know more about what you want (and don't want)—you're that much closer to fuckyeah.

BUT WHAT IF I HATE IT?

When I was seven years old, I wrote that I wanted to be a ballerina on my "What do you want to be when you grow up?" homework.

By age eight, things had changed. I thought "detective" was the answer, since I was obsessed with Nancy Drew and Harriet the Spy—but soon I figured out that words were more my speed. I changed my answer to "writer." By age eleven, it was "professional singer." Later that year it was "assistant to the fashion designer behind the Delia's catalog." That, or "magazine editor of *Moxie* or *YM*." Very specific, little me. (Damn, do I miss dog-earing the pages of nineties magazines.) By age fourteen, it was "an artist . . . but maybe a fashion designer?" So far, so cute.

But changing our minds gets exponentially less cute when money and time are on the line.

Like when I graduated with a degree in Fashion Design and Merchandising at age nineteen, and then changed my mind, again. *NVM, it was "artist," after all.* I had the privilege of transferring into a bachelor's program in Fine Art, and then, after one year, quit school to work as a commercial display artist. And a year after that, I went back to school, this time abroad in London, for Fine Art. (Yes, this is getting expensive.) Then I transferred to another university, in Houston, Texas, with a major in Fine Art and a minor in Philosophy, all the while working in retail to pay the bills. And then, a year later, I dropped out. *Again.*

Less cute.

Why is trying a lot of different things for short periods of time considered utter failure for adults, but not for kids? Because we think kids are *supposed* to experiment and explore; we consider that a part of learning. They need to develop their brains and to learn how to function in society; it's not the end of the world if they quit an instrument, or a sport, or change their minds about their "dream job." Their mind-changing doesn't have real-world consequences. But when we adults begin and end classes, degree programs, or jobs in multiple fields over and over again, it's considered wasteful and reckless: *"Hurry up and be a productive member of society already!"*

Kids have an excuse—they're "finding their way"—but the truth is, *we are too.* Life is a road trip that requires us to continuously ask ourselves (and sometimes people on the side of the road), "Okay, now which way?" The real reason we feel ashamed of our pit stops and pivots is the same reason we don't prioritize Play: *it's unproductive.*

"Trial and error" is fine for adults . . . so long as it doesn't cut into our time *producing.*

You had the history lesson (*eh, hmm,* chapter 2); at some point in the postindustrial era, we started valuing productivity over skill. It became more important that we *produce* than that we *grow.* Somewhere along the way, we forgot something:

Living things aren't meant to be productive all the time.

Most of us live in cities, buying our veggies in the big-box grocery store, unaware that we can only buy that avocado in December because it *probably flew here on a cargo plane.* We don't have a basic knowledge of how slowly things grow because most of us did not grow up raising crops. The nature of living things? They are only productive seasonally. SEASONALLY, PEOPLE.

You want peaches? Then you've got to plant a seed, let the seed grow, grow, grow, and then after a while, if it grows into a tree, the tree *might* bear fruit. And *if* it does, it will probably be in the summer, in the third year of growth. Don't go looking for peaches in the dead of winter of year four, or in the summer of year one. *Ain't gonna happen.*

You are a peach tree.

You cannot be productive all the time. You're a human being who grows and aches and loves and excels and fails—you're going to have an ebb and flow of productivity in your life and your work. Some months of your life will be wild; you'll be creating, working, hustling. Some months will be your own personal winter: quiet, slow, and hidden away from public view. Sometimes you'll spend more than you earn, and sometimes you'll earn more than you spend. Some days you'll feel like you could climb Mount Everest, and some days you'll feel like hiding under a blanket with a donut. Life is ebb and flow. We do not consider a peach tree "worthless" just because it can't produce during the winter. *Similarly, your value is not determined by how productive you are.* Your creative energy and Art are going to look different in every season of your life.

When we start something new, we are inevitably less productive because we are in the process of learning. *And that's okay!* All experts started out as rookies who were willing to grow.

Think you want to start your own business? Start something and find out, *right now.* Think you want to be a pilot? Sign up for an introductory flight tour in a two-seater Cessna, *right now.* Think you want to be a tattoo artist? Start drawing the "flash" you want to turn into tattoos, *right now.* Can't afford to do any of these things? Good point; a trial-run of our dreams can be expensive. It may take some time, but save what little cash you have, and then give that thing a shot.

>> *"But what if I try something and I hate it?"*

Then quit—but own it. No point beating yourself up about it. Successful people make learning into a game. They get curious about their "mistakes."

>> *"But what if it's a waste of time and money?"*

A peach tree doesn't consider the time and resources it spent growing as a waste; why should you?

If we make our goal to learn and grow, it doesn't matter if you take an app design class and never sell (or even finish) an app. It's okay if all you learned is that you have no desire to become an app designer. *You still learned something.* Who's to say we have to turn everything we learn into a money-making part of our lives, anyway? We get so worked up about starting something and becoming an expert at it that we lose out on the fun of discovering something new. Instead, find fuckyeah by following the second rule of Flow:

Give yourself permission to be bad at something long enough to find out if you want to spend time getting good at it.

And this, my friends, is how we should start anything new: with permission to be imperfect. Being bad at something naturally makes us want to quit; we want to label it a failure ("I am bad at math, playing guitar, fill in the blank"), and walk away. But in order to try new things, to maybe become an expert someday, and to reach Flow, we need to get comfortable with how it feels to be the rookie. It can be uncomfortable, challenging, and embarrassing at times. But if by working hard in fourteen different jobs across five different industries in our lives, we never really "climb that ladder," but we discover what we love (and what we don't)—*isn't that worth it!?* If we're courageous enough to change careers because we're interested in something new and not because we're running away from hard work, then more power to us, right?

Don't know what your Art is? Start by trying everything. *Just process-of-elimination that shit.* Explore. Experiment. Play. Take a class. Make something. Give something away. Wing it. Take a risk at work. Find out what problems you want to solve and which ones you'd bend over backward to avoid.

Enjoy the fact that you're not one thing, one career, one calling, one personality, one hobby, one job. You're way too multifaceted for that. You're a beautiful mess, remember?

Be someone too complicated to summarize in small talk.

Be so many different things that it confuses the extended family members you talk to at weddings.

Humans are inherently curious, but the threat of "not enough"—money, respect, time—looms large, shutting our curiosity down, keeping us from the joy of experimenting with our lives, education, and work. I'm not suggesting we abandon our responsibilities to the people we love or our obligations to the communities we live in for the sake of experimentation, okay? I'm not pretending our decisions don't have consequences. *Every decision does.* My decisions certainly did. But I can appreciate those consequences—*because the decisions behind them were mine.* If you try something and it turns out it's not your jam, be proud that you tried it, and don't mourn your decision to move on.

Let's become Experts at something because we fell in love with it, not because we're trying to impress other people or "look good on paper." Let's find out, by dancing, that we don't *want* to be ballerinas. Or writers, or professional singers, or fashion designers, or magazine editors for that matter. Let's get okay with being our best *seasonal* selves, *even if we look messy on paper.* Let's learn something. Let's grow.

NOT FAILURE; RESEARCH

Raise your hand if this sounds like you:

You swing from outraged that your time isn't your own (because you're busy "making a living") to paralyzed by your free time because you have no clue what to do with those few moments. This leaves you feeling either trapped by endless obligations or frozen in choice paralysis. You're doing everything you can to make your life more efficient and streamlined in hopes that you'll not only squeeze a few more free moments out of your day, but that you'll also have more energy, and therefore maybe fresh inspiration, for what to do with that precious free time. But no amount of "optimization" changes how you feel. When you get "meta" and realize what a cushy life you lead (*"Too many choices at my disposal and a steady job, jeeez"*), you're hit with a wave of self-loathing that's hard to come out from under. Once the self-loathing hits (*"How could I be so ungrateful? I have it so easy! Why can't I just be happy?"*), you feel renewed embarrassment at choices you've made in the past and a buzzing dread that you'll make the wrong decisions in the future. You're pretty sure if you haven't royally screwed up your life yet that you will soon. *"Why am I like this? I'm overwhelmed. Ughhh, I think I need to lay down . . ."*

How do I know this? Because I might be totally low-key psychic *but also* because I've *lived this reality.* I have an important announcement for seventeen-year-old me, and for you:

Your mistakes are answers to questions you hadn't thought to ask yet.

In 1895, Wilhelm Röntgen was experimenting with vacuum tube equipment that had been developed by another scientist (as scientists often do, to validate the hypotheses of their peers). During a routine experiment, a combination of cardboard, aluminum, and electrical discharge accidentally lit up a screen nearby with a ghostly reflection. It was too weird not to be curious about. In the following weeks, Röntgen ate and slept in his laboratory, trying to understand this mistake. *Turns out he accidentally discovered the X-ray.*

By 1928, Alexander Fleming had a reputation as a brilliant researcher—and as sort of a slob, when it came to keeping his laboratory clean (by scientist standards). He had been extensively studying staphylococcus, a type of bacteria, for years. After returning from a family vacation, he noticed that a pile of Petri dishes on the edge of a workbench in his lab looked strange. One of the dishes was contaminated by nasty fungi, while the others looked normal. *That's funny* . . . Several tests later, it was confirmed. *Alexander Fleming's lousy lab habits led to the accidental invention of penicillin.*

In 1939, Percy Spencer was one of the world's leading experts in radar tube design. His expertise helped the company he worked for gain a US Department of Defense contract to produce radar equipment for the Allies during World War II. One day, while testing an active radar set he developed, Spencer noticed the chocolate bar in his pocket had melted. *That's annoying,* he thought. People had seen this "heating effect" from the equipment before—he should have known better than to have food nearby. But . . . he was curious. He decided to run tests on other foods, and after several adaptations, he filed for a US patent in 1945. *Because he was curious about a stupid mistake that ruined his pants, Percy Spencer accidentally discovered the microwave.*

"Their mistakes worked out," you're thinking. *"Mine have not."* But here's the thing: they could have easily missed those discoveries.

Scientists are pros at treating failure like research because it's built into their jobs. Röntgen could've brushed that shadow off as a fluke. Fleming could've spent the week beating himself up for ruining an entire batch of his (expensive) research subject matter. Spencer could've spent the rest of his day with sticky pants and in a shitty mood. But they looked at their mistakes, flukes, and fuckups with *curiosity*. They discovered new questions to ask.

The choices with outcomes you weren't expecting aren't failures; they're research. Your mistakes are not failures; they're just the stuff you needed to find out to grow.

Yes, you will make mistakes. *A lot of them.* Some will have *very painful* consequences. And sometimes, even when we do everything "right," unexpected tragedies befall us. Things that are brutally unfair happen to innocent people every single day. But we humans are incredibly resilient; people survive things that are impossible to wrap our minds around, and many become stronger from their painful experiences. The problem is, we've been taught that mistakes are unacceptable failings that can be erased with hard work and that the pain caused by failure should be avoided at all costs. *Mistakes can't be erased, nor should they be.* Because they're answers to questions you hadn't thought to ask yet, mistakes help you skip ahead to the next "step."

Mistakes are research: a collection of data and wisdom necessary to discover what we really want out of life, and how to find it.

So give yourself permission to make them.

7.

UNCENSOR YOUR INTUITION

>> *"So . . . I'll find my fuckyeah by trying new stuff, right?*
By experimenting. Taking risks. Allowing myself to
be a rookie. That's great, but there's just one problem:
I have no fucking clue WHAT I want to try."

Maybe the reason you're unsure of which direction to head in this
uncharted fuckyeah territory is because as soon as *you* make a sug-
gestion, *you* shoot it down.

Remember the skittish little lizard pulling levers inside your head,
overriding logic whenever it gets nervous, filling in the blanks for
your senses, and skewing your view of reality, often leaving a trail of
limiting beliefs in its wake? Autopilot Brain believes trying something new is risky, even if that idea is as tame as taking a cooking
class, making the first move with your crush, or applying for a job.
Why do something "dangerous"? Safe is good. Safe keeps the lizard
calm. *Autopilot is the reason you feel like you have no clue what you*
want to do.

By now I've given you plenty of reasons to resent your Autopilot Brain, but it's important to realize that it isn't the enemy; it's a tool to make your life easier—if you know how to engage with it. Our goal is to learn how to fly *with* our Autopilot. To use it to our advantage. To get both of our brains working in unison, guiding us toward fuckyeah.

See, there's an easily forgotten positive side to co-piloting your life with an autopilot: *you can intuit faster than you can think.*

Your intuition IS your Autopilot Brain.

You have within you a powerfully efficient and lightning fast system to process the world, and it's operating just outside your default awareness. Call it what you want—your heart, your gut, your instincts, your spirit, your Inner Compass—Autopilot Brain *is* your intuition, and it knows *exactly* what you really want.

The trick is learning how to listen to it.

Modern science might even be able to pinpoint our intuition within the brain: just behind the forehead and between the eyebrows, in an area called the prefrontal cortex (PFC) and orbitofrontal cortex (OFC). No researcher would confidently say they know *everything* the PFC and OFC are responsible for, but they've got a strong case for a handful of things. For example, we know the OFC translates emotions into physical responses; it's to blame for your sweaty palms during public speaking and the butterflies in your stomach while talking to your crush. It's instrumental in any decision-making that requires a blend of cold logic and gut instinct (like choosing to "raise" or "fold" while playing poker), as well as in goal-driven impulse control (like switching my phone to Do Not Disturb mode so I can focus on writing this chapter). The PFC and OFC (in Pilot Brain) and limbic system (in Autopilot Brain) are deeply interconnected, and it's this tight connection between rational decision-making and instantaneous, emotional instinct that creates a perfect bridge between the conscious and subconscious mind. In other words? Intuition is *unconscious perception* that originates from within your Autopilot Brain and is expressed by your Pilot Brain.

That weird vibe you get from a stranger? That gut feeling that you should text your friend right this second? Your Autopilot Brain is picking up on something your Pilot Brain can't. It's trying to tell you something important.

In 2005, researchers figured out that if they presented a changing image to one eye and a static image to the other, people would *only* see the changing picture and *never* see the static one. This is part of a phenomenon called "binocular rivalry."

Then, in 2006, another group of scientists wanted to use binocular rivalry to test unconscious perception (science-speak for *intuition*). They decided to show a pixelated, changing kaleidoscope of color to a subject's right eye while presenting a static photograph to the left eye. Each photo included an object almost out of the frame, off to one side of the picture. Because of the binocular rivalry effect, the subjects *couldn't see* the static photo at all, but researchers asked them to blindly guess where that object was in the frame anyway. They guessed correctly about half the time with static nondescript photos—pretty standard for random guesses. The researchers hypothesized that the subjects would pick up on a static image better if it were of vital interest to their survival instincts—so they peppered in a few "highly arousing erotic images." (Porn, obviously.) When the hidden erotic image was brought into a frame, the accuracy of guesses went *waaay* up. Each subject's Autopilot Brain responded according to their sexual preference. Even though none of these subjects could *consciously* see a static X-rated image, *their subconscious minds could*. They were *intuitively* aware of it, even though they were consciously blind to it.

Your intuition is the real deal. It is instinctive, irrational You, trying to communicate with rational You.

Your intuition bypasses the pile of logical thoughts, and plugs right into your brain's emotional center; it doesn't give a flying fuck if what it's sensing is "rational" or not. It's the unfiltered part of your consciousness, your Inner Compass, your natural instincts.

But since society worships rational thought, we spend most of our lives being trained to shut this intuitive part of ourselves down entirely, or—best-case scenario—when we *do* register feelings of intuition, we tend to distrust them and don't consider them to be a valuable element of our decision-making. We start ignoring our instincts, discounting our hearts, and considering our gut feelings childish. An unexplainable gut feeling isn't as grown-up as a pros-and-cons list, so we tend to slap duct tape over intuition's "mouth" whenever possible.

Let's peel back that duct tape.

WHO DO YOU THINK YOU ARE?

A familiar, albeit bitchy, question.

According to Dr. Brené Brown, author, speaker, and research professor at the University of Houston, "Who do you think you are?" is the second of two "shame tracks" playing on an endless loop in our heads. The first? "You're not _____ enough." Sound familiar? (***achhemm, scarcity***) Shame is behind the feeling that we aren't capable of accomplishing the things we want to try and are not worthy of the good things that happen to us. It's what makes us believe the things we intrinsically like are stupid, silly, or useless. It's the duct tape silencing our intuition.

When we believe we can't have, do, or be something, that limiting belief is usually accompanied by feelings of Shame and various reasons why we "should" feel Shame and "should not" pursue what we want. For example:

>> *"I wish I could be a surgeon, but...*

I'm not smart enough to be a doctor.

Who do I think I am even entertaining this idea?
I'll never have enough money to afford school, anyways.

I should've studied harder if I wanted to get into
a decent college, let alone a prestigious medical school.

Besides, I'm not young enough to go back to school.
I should stop thinking about it—it's too late for me."

Yes, growing up with prohibitions like "You can't have that" or "You shouldn't do that" helped us develop into functioning members of society (they're why we didn't eat candy for every meal, shared our toys, and learned the importance of hard work through chores). There's just one problem with spending a lifetime abiding by the rules of "should" and "shouldn't" once we're grown:

When left unchecked, "should" and "should not" become the action verbs of the noun *Shame*. They become roadblocks and detours on your path to fuckyeah.

Let me be clear: healthy obligations are a real part of living on this planet. You won't drive your kids (or future kids) to school just because you're obligated; you'll do it because you'll love them with every fiber of your being (and they'll need an education to get a leg up in life). That's a complex obligation. And you didn't show up at work today for no reason; there are a host of reasons, one of which is that you're obligated to pay bills—and showing up at work lets you both pay bills AND buy Doritos. Also complicated. We *should* clean up after ourselves; we *should* pay taxes; we *should* take care of the people we love. There are countless things in our lives that *we absolutely should* and *should not* do.

The kind of "obligations" I'm talking about feel ... gross. *Heavy.* You'll experience an invisible magnetic repulsion from them. Sometimes it's the subtle social pressure to attend the expensive destination wedding of a close friend; sometimes it's the crushing burden of your parents' expectations for your education, career, and life. These kinds of obligations (aka "shoulds" or "should nots") are asking you to be someone you're not, or to do something you are uncomfortable with, even just momentarily; *they're expectations already loaded with Shame before any action has even been taken.*

We're freaked out by the shoulds or should nots because we feel pressure to be inauthentic, and we can intuitively sense the rules we'd have to play by if we accepted this obligation. Unfortunately, we've been socially trained (#factoryschool) to ignore our intuition, to listen to *ALL* the shoulds or should nots, and to never ever disappoint.

When people tell you what you should or should not have, do, or be, they're asking you to navigate your life using their Inner Compass.

Everyone has a different "true north." (*UGH, so cheeseball, I know.*) Your Inner Compass points toward a slightly different fuckyeah than mine, or than that of your friends, your coworkers, your family, and the people you care most for in your life. But because none of us want to let down the people we love and respect, we often struggle to redirect, attempting to navigate our lives by *their* compasses. This puts us in an unconscious cycle of feeling Shame, both when we do not stay true to our own values and whenever we disappoint others. It's a lose-lose situation. Emotion has always had the final say in our decisions—and Shame is an extremely powerful emotion.

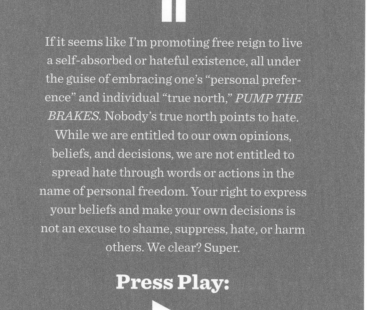

Let's press Pause here:

If it seems like I'm promoting free reign to live a self-absorbed or hateful existence, all under the guise of embracing one's "personal preference" and individual "true north," *PUMP THE BRAKES.* Nobody's true north points to hate. While we are entitled to our own opinions, beliefs, and decisions, we are not entitled to spread hate through words or actions in the name of personal freedom. Your right to express your beliefs and make your own decisions is not an excuse to shame, suppress, hate, or harm others. We clear? Super.

Press Play:

If you have no genuine motivation to do something and you do it anyway, solely out of Shame-loaded obligation, you will grow to resent the person or thing you feel obligated to. You'll also grow to resent yourself for living inauthentically.

Nobody needs resentment in their life; we need to learn to sift through the shoulds and should nots and decide which are worth it to us. The next time you feel that sticky, heavy pressure to do something you're uncomfortable with, ask yourself WHY you're so grossed out by it. If you can find a loving and healthy motivation to do it, then suck it up, buttercup. If not, look for the hidden Shame, dig it up, and deal with it. (P.S. "How to Deal" coming right up!)

SHAME'S ANSWER KEY

Shame is universal; all of us experience it, and regularly. We also all hate talking about Shame; it outranks "religion" and "politics" on the list of Topics That Make Strangers Uncomfortable at Parties. What makes Shame extra fucked-up, though, is that its control over us gets stronger the less we talk about it.

Shame is a social, fear-based emotion. According to Dr. Brené Brown, Shame is rooted in the fear of disconnection; it's an intensely painful experience of believing that when we do not meet society's expectations, we will become isolated from and rejected by others. It's the idea that we should be ashamed because we are flawed, and that those flaws make us unworthy of love and belonging. Whenever we're afraid of being isolated or rejected, we do everything in our power to censor the aspects of ourselves that might lead to that rejection; we shove down our Art, we ignore our intuition, and we willfully forget the things that are intrinsically important to us, because the little lizard does NOT want to risk going through life alone. And while it's a natural consequence of evolution to avoid rejection, Shame is standing in the way of our Art and real self-expression.

Research has revealed that although Shame is universal, men and women experience messages of Shame differently, based on gender norms (societal pressures to conform to gender-defined behaviors or "ideals"). In one American study, participants were asked to identify the values and traits they associate with both feminine and masculine gender norms. Reported feminine indicators included the following:

Nice in Relationships	Look Young
Thinness	Be Heterosexual
Modesty	Be Pleasant
Domestic	Rely on and Defer to Men
Sexual Fidelity	Be Virginal
Investment in Appearance	Be Sexy
Self as Mother	Be Dependent
Be Silent	Be Physically Attractive /
Be Married	Ornamental

In other words, women are expected to make perfection look effortless. And to shut up. And to be as small as possible. On the other hand, reported masculine indicators included the following:

Winning, Competitive	Self-Reliance
Control over Emotions	Work Comes First
Risk-Taking	Power over Women
Violence	Disdain for Homosexuality
Dominance	Pursuit of Status
Be a Playboy	

In other words, men are expected to be tough at all costs. And to maintain control. And to never express an emotion, unless it's anger.

These lists are some dark and twisty, heteronormative, deeply limiting, utterly horrendous B.U.L.L.S.H.I.T. Whenever our existence, goal, or self-expression doesn't match up with societal "norms" or the expectations of others, we experience Shame's sucker punch to the stomach.

Studies show that Shame and the "rumination" (automatic, negative thoughts on a loop) that comes with it lead to depression, while guilt does not.[1] Shame is also highly correlated with violence, addiction, bullying, eating disorders, and aggression. Shame is killing us.

———

Think of it this way: You just took a multiple-choice history exam. You did your best and submitted your Scantron test to the teacher to grade. The teacher uses a digital answer key to grade your test, but instead of using the history test answer key, they use a math test answer key. Even if there are a handful of multiple-choice answers that match up, it's purely by coincidence. Overall, that test grade will look like a massive failure because the teacher used the wrong answer key to score your test—and digital grading seems so foolproof that you're afraid to speak up about it.

Except instead of failing a history test, you think you've failed at life, somehow—and Shame's logic seems so airtight that you're afraid to fight it.

Shame is grading your life against someone else's answer key.

Shame is about performance, condemnation, and scarcity. It slams us back down in our chair, just as we're about to express ourselves; it slaps us senseless, convincing us we've failed because we've violated the rules of "the game."

---

[1] *Guilt and Shame are very different things. Guilt says, "I did something bad; I made a mistake," while Shame says, "I am a failure; I am a loser." Guilt is "I fucked up," and Shame is "I am a fuckup." So, if you just betrayed your best friend (and you're not a sociopath), you will feel guilt. And that guilt is healthy—to an extent. Guilt is the psychic pain we feel when our thoughts and actions don't align with our core beliefs and values, and sometimes that pain can help us learn from a mistake or grow as a person. Shame, however, will never help you grow, make amends, or get back up when you're down.*

SHAME'S FIRST DEMAND IS CONFORMITY

Shame expects us to be the same as everyone else, in every way, at all times. It demands homogeneity. Shame doesn't celebrate the unique differences between one person and the next; it doesn't even tolerate them. Shame wants the status quo: no risk-taking and no standing out. To play by shame's rules is to perform like everyone else at all times, or else you ought to feel like human garbage. Shame uses scarcity's "I'm not _____ enough" argument, baiting us to compare ourselves against one another. Comparison bait demands you grade yourself against someone else's life answer key, rendering you a failure *every time*.

SHAME'S SECOND DEMAND IS PERFECTION

Shame asks for perfection no matter what—rendering success totally unattainable. Normally, acknowledging that we're capable of making mistakes and learning from them doesn't trigger a full-on identity crisis. But when we take the humility bait of "Who do I think I am?" and compare ourselves to one another, we drag ourselves into a pit of self-loathing and become trapped there by our limiting beliefs.

Shame convinces us to judge ourselves by perfection and conformity because it talks to us in the first person and speaks in our voice. Shame sounds like you—and usually you can trust what you have to say. Except suddenly you've been tricked into believing these are your thoughts, your standards, and your failures. And when we're in the Shame pit, we're sure we deserve it. You don't. I don't.

Shame is expecting to be rejected, and because we want to avoid rejection at all costs, it's easy to shove down our ideas, creativity, voice, and Art. Shame is a voluntary feeling, a belief that we have to perform to be accepted, and any visible "flaws" will lead to our isolation and unhappiness. But like any belief, we have power over it: we can decide that we are worthy of love, exactly as we are, flaws and all, because we're unique DNA snowflakes.

You already intuitively know what you really want and who you truly are—you just have to give yourself permission to have, do, and be those things.

It doesn't matter if you did something genuinely mortifying, failed at something that should've been easy, or are struggling with some quality you dislike about yourself—you don't have to subject yourself to Shame's private torture. We all do embarrassing things, all drop the ball, all find ourselves the deviant off someone else's "norm." Perfection does not exist, nor does pure conformity. Shame has not and will not ever do you any good.

So let's tell Shame to fuck off, yeah?

HOW TO DEAL: SHAME

Let's use the hypothetical example from chapter 1, when the smell of grilled onions helped you realize you had a limiting belief about body image. You think you've worked through this limiting belief, but your childhood experiences left a mark on you. Every now and again Shame rears its ugly head, starting an internal dialogue about how your body "isn't good enough." Today is one of those days. Let's cancel Shame, shall we?

STEP 1: SHOULD, SHOULD NOT, OR SHAME?

Did someone (or something) make you feel ashamed of yourself, your opinions, or your choices? Think about what triggered this feeling.

>> *My jeans were tight this morning. It annoyed me I couldn't wear what I wanted; the thought of buying jeans in a bigger size pissed me off. I started thinking about how I haven't been "watching my weight," and the Shame spiral began.*

STEP 2: WHAT SHAME GIF IS ON REPEAT?

Fighting Shame is about changing your perspective. First, figure out which Shame GIF is looping loudest in your head. Is it *Who do I think I am?; I'm not _____ enough; I don't belong; I'll never _____; or I'm too _____?* What story are you telling yourself because you're ashamed? And what is Shame baiting you to do? Is it baiting you to compare yourself to someone else? Or telling you to be "humble" or "realistic," while it squashes your voice under pressure to be perfect?

>> *It's "I'm not enough" on repeat. Not skinny enough, not disciplined enough (I should work out more); not attractive enough (I'll never be my goal weight). I guess that's comparison bait— convincing me to compare my body to other bodies, and to view their size or weight as "perfection."*

STEP 3: FIND YOUR ANSWER KEY

Remind yourself of the rules you live your life by. Do you *want* to conform to societal, gender, or other so-called norms? Who's to say *perfect* looks a certain way, or exists? Isn't it good that you're unique and not the same as your peers?

>> *I only feel Shame because I agreed there was a beauty "ideal" and that my body isn't good enough. I don't need to care about gender or beauty norms (that only exist to sell me shit I don't need). Bodies come in all shapes and change all the time—that's what's normal. I don't need to conform, and perfection is a lie.*

STEP 4: TELL SHAME TO FUCK OFF (ACT AND CONNECT)

Now that you remember the rules you play by (i.e., your Inner Compass's direction), take action in the face of Shame. Do something brave; reach out to someone who you know cares about you and respects you, and tell them what you're dealing with. Next, can you forgive the person (or people) who triggered Shame in you? Can you forgive yourself for taking the bait?

"Brave" might mean calling your best friend and telling them about the Shame you're fighting, knowing they'll listen, and very likely they will remind you that they too have felt this way. Empathy is the antidote to Shame; reach out to someone you love, and trust them to remind you that you're not alone.

>> *This obsession with weight and size was my mom's emotional baggage, not mine. Every day I get closer to forgiving her for the fears that rubbed off on me—and to forgiving myself for taking the comparison bait.*

Maybe you scoffed at this example because tight jeans seem like a silly thing to get upset about, but that's an important point: Shame feels exponentially more real when it's happening to you. Do not discredit your own or others' Shame as inconsequential.

Whatever triggered the Shame vibes, fight back by loving yourself, especially when you don't think you deserve it. Let's have empathy the next time one of us is fighting the "I'm not enough" or "Who do I think I am" self-loathing hate-speech GIFs down in the Shame pit.

Maybe bring us unconditional love, snacks, and a new GIF to watch on repeat while we're down here? Maybe something with kittens?

YOU ALREADY KNOW

If the first way to uncensor your intuition is to deal with the shoulds, should nots, and Shame through radical self-acceptance, then the second is to figure out which things you choose to do when you have no obligation to do those things, aka your intrinsic motivators.

Intrinsic motivation is social psychology's way of describing your Inner Compass: your goal-oriented, guiding intuition. It's the internal motivation urging you to do something because that activity is satisfying in itself; it's doing something for the love of it. (Yeah, just like Play or Flow.) Everyone is intrinsically motivated by something. Many things, actually.

Not all motivation is internal, though. If I asked you to list ten weekly obligations you hate, you'd blurt them out in the time it would take me to sneeze. We all do shit we don't want to—and we do it because of extrinsic motivation. This is motivation created by external pressure, like chasing down rewards or avoiding punishments. Let's be real: You don't pay rent because you feel a wave of joy whenever you fork over most of your paycheck by the first of the month. You pay rent because if you don't, you get punished—and a punishment like eviction is enough to motivate you to pay rent. That's extrinsic motivation.

I have a friend who loves to run. She runs daily, whenever possible—it clears her head and makes her feel free and healthy. She used to run track in high school, back when there were external rewards for it (like trophies and college scholarships), but nowadays she runs just because she loves it. She is intrinsically motivated to run; she does it because running itself is satisfying.

Yeah, so . . . contrary to my intrinsically motivated friend, I hate running. With the fire of a thousand suns. I've tried to like it. I've tried different versions of it (on a treadmill, with friends, by a beautiful lake, a mixture of running and walking, running for a cause) . . . I just hate it. The only thing that will get me to run is an extrinsic reward, like someone telling me they'll pay me fifty bucks to run a mile. That, or actual danger (in which case it's still external motivation getting me to sprint to safety). If I started running because I thought it would help me lose weight, that would also be extrinsic; in that case, I'd be running for the "reward" of shedding pounds, not because I thought running itself was rewarding. I'm not in danger, no one has bribed me, and I like my bod . . . so I ain't runnin' any time soon.

Over the last forty years, studies about intrinsic and extrinsic motivation have helped psychologists formulate a theory ("Self-Determination Theory") about why people do what we do—and what types of motivation will best support our health and happiness. Here's what they've found: human beings have three innate psychological needs (confidence, connection, and autonomy) that must be met in order to experience well-being—and intrinsic motivators are better, hands down, at meeting those psychological needs than extrinsic motivators are.

It makes sense that something you naturally love to do would be more meaningful and satisfying than something you hate to do, right? If you're showing up to work at a soul-sucking job, Monday through Friday, it's probably for extrinsic reasons (#getpaid). Yep, money is an extrinsic motivator. Well, it turns out that working sixty-plus hours a week for thirty years—for a paycheck, promotions, glory, or other external motivators—won't satisfy your innate psychological needs. And you can't be happy if you don't satisfy those needs.

So let's talk about them.

THE THREE PSYCH NEEDS

You and I have at least three psychological needs, universal to human experience, that fuel our well-being when fulfilled: confidence, connection, and autonomy.

PSYCH NEED NO. 1. CONFIDENCE:
Not self-esteem, but competence; our need to feel equal to the task at hand or to "master" something.

We build confidence by participating in things that challenge us. When we prove to ourselves that we can overcome challenges, we reinforce confidence in our ability to overcome obstacles and in our own personal strength. But there's a happy medium—it needs to be just tough enough as a challenge that it requires us to work hard and learn in the process (**achhem, Flow**), yet not so challenging that it crushes our dreams and breaks our spirit. Confidence is feeling capable, even when we don't have all the answers.

The best way to build confidence? Take a risk, take a class, do something hard on purpose. Give yourself permission to be bad at something long enough to decide if you want to get good at that thing.

PSYCH NEED NO. 2. CONNECTION:
Our need to connect and interact with others and, most importantly, to experience caring for and being cared for by others.

Almost too obvious to mention, but yeah, humans need connection. So, be vulnerable with a good friend. Share your idea, project, smile, humanity, or Art with someone. Be generous—with your time, your money, your compliments. This isn't about being fake nice; it's about sharing what you have to offer with the world. When we filter who we are, we create fragmented connections with others. Connection requires the courage to be real with somebody.

PSYCH NEED NO. 3. AUTONOMY:
Our need for self-control and personal independence; the craving to be the boss, instigator, and director of our own lives, to feel that we're acting in line with our authentic selves.

Every day we learn more about the ever-expanding universe, all while whipping through space on a spinning ball of molten rock on an orbit that is completely out of our control; we'd like to make some of our own decisions, thank you very much. That said, autonomy isn't separateness from other people or a dictator-like control of your decisions; it's an awareness of your individual power to contribute to or make an impact on the world around you.

Looking for autonomy? Put yourself and your ideas out into the world. Start a side project, just for you. Take initiative at work; don't wait for someone to direct you. Express your weirdest, most awesome, authentic self in more ways.

———

The things you're intrinsically motivated to do naturally fulfill the three psychological needs required to experience happiness.

This is why discovering your intrinsic motivators is so important: they align your Pilot Brain's conscious plans with Autopilot Brain's subconscious desires—and we're happiest, and feel most ourselves, when our two brains work together.

You already intuitively know what you want to try, who you feel a "spark" of connection with, and what makes you feel most comfortable in your own skin. Now, you just need to trust in that intuition.

When we uncensor our intuition, we're giving ourselves permission to like what we like, to discover what intrinsically motivates us and what we intuitively want to do, whether or not someone validates it, rewards us (with money, promotions, or trophies), or recognizes us for it. This is where you'll find your Art—in the stuff you were going to say anyway, the things you were going to do anyway, the art you were going to make anyway, rewards or not. Intuition is your superpower— and it's essential to finding your fuckyeah.

The things you're intrinsically motivated to learn, earn, have, do, or be might not be obvious to you at the moment, but they exist. The trick is to dig a little deeper, beyond rattling off your favorite TV shows or top places to eat brunch, and to ask yourself what you're curious about.

You don't have to be good at something to be curious about it. The things that interest you don't need to be impressive, productive, or "worth" something on the market.

The things we're intrinsically, naturally, intuitively motivated to do are often buried under the pressure to be productive, to make us money, or to be praised by or approved of by other people. Guess what? They don't need to be any of those things. *The simple act of chasing down what makes you curious is enough to fulfill your psych needs and make you happy.*

You are *already* intrinsically motivated to create, connect, and lead, in one way or another—you just haven't given yourself permission to do those things *in your own way*. To discover your intrinsic motivators and the kind of life you want, you'll need to do more experimenting than you currently do. You'll need to play, challenge yourself, make mistakes, start things, quit things, and finish things.

You'll need to listen to your intuition.

PSA:
YOU DON'T NEED
TO TURN YOUR
HOBBIES INTO
SIDE HUSTLES
IN ORDER TO
VALIDATE THEM.
IF TURNING A
PASSION OF YOURS
INTO A BUSINESS
SOUNDS LIKE A
FUN CHALLENGE,

THEN GO FOR IT. IF NOT? THAT'S TOTALLY OKAY— JUST ENJOY THE DAMN THING AND TAKE OFF THOSE "MARKET-ABLE" OR "LOOKS GOOD ON PAPER" SEARCH FILTERS.

8.

REBUILD YOUR REALITY

So, what kind of life would you like to be living? Because you're living exactly the life you intended. Even if your Autopilot Brain is doing the intending behind the scenes, while your Pilot Brain plays catch-up— *what you intend, you are creating.*

What you focus on becomes your reality.

Want to know what your life will look like in the future? Take a look at your thoughts right now. Want to know what you were thinking about six months ago? Take a look at your life right now.

Your thoughts become your emotional state. Your emotional memories become your beliefs. Your beliefs become the framework of your reality house. Sure, you've got specific "construction materials" to build this reality house with; you have genes, life experiences, and memories like no one else's. Yes, you've poured your life's foundation in a certain environment, a particular moment in time, a specific geographical location and cultural experience. *But it's your reality.* How free, how happy, how courageous, how connected, how passionate, how fuckyeah your reality is, that's up to you. You *built* the reality you're living in, but much of it was built by accident and in the background of your mind (like with skewed memories, limiting beliefs, or smothered intuition). What would happen if you decided to reframe and rebuild your reality *on purpose*?

Automatic, negative thoughts are the mental tantrums of your Inner Cynic. Intentions are the purposeful thoughts of your Inner Compass, pointing you toward fuckyeah.

An "intention" is a thought with purpose; it's the opposite of an automatic thought. Learning to set positive intentions, both consciously and subconsciously, is how we get Pilot Brain and Autopilot Brain to end their no-holds-barred feud and *finally* learn to be friends—rebuilding our reality as creators, instead of letting life "happen to us," like spectators.

I'LL SEE IT WHEN I BELIEVE IT

Manifestation is #trending.

I mean, who *doesn't* want to make their dream life into a reality *just* by visualizing it?

Manifestation is based on the "Law of Attraction," a concept that dates back to nineteenth-century spiritualists and was later popularized by twenty-first-century TV producer and author of *The Secret*, Rhonda Byrne. The Law of Attraction is supposedly a universal law, not unlike gravity, embodying the principle that *like attracts like*.

We can summarize the Law of Attraction like this: your thoughts are energy; energy is attracted to energy of the same vibration; the energy you put out is what you will attract. So, if you think you're a piece of human garbage cursed with bad luck, then according to this law you'll have a shitty life because you *attracted* negative energy into your life. In contrast, if you believe you're a secret badass and that everything happens for a good reason, then your life will be awesome because you *attracted* positive energy into your life. It's a convenient "law," because it positions a person in complete control of their life (you attract what you put out), but it also provides an emotional, theological safety net for when things feel out of control (the universe responds according to your energy); it's spiritual without being religious.

The Internet boasts endless variations of "How to Manifest _____" guides, but believers generally agree that manifestation requires "raising your vibration" to attract what you want and an "unshakable belief" that you'll get what you want, even if you don't know when. Buzzwords around manifestation include *alignment, desire, energy, vibration, universal law, visualization,* and *intention.*

I'm already annoyed, TBH. This whole Law of Attraction thing *has* to be bullshit, right? I mean, it's obvious that health, wealth, and happiness aren't the result of fantasizing on my couch—and I'm not going to suddenly find a car in my driveway (POOF!) because I thought about it *real hard.*

But if visualization is just a money-grabbing self-help gimmick, how do I explain the results of recent scientific studies?

In a study conducted by psychologists at the Cleveland Clinic Foundation in Ohio, one group of athletes lifted weights and another only visualized weightlifting. Those in the latter group actually gained physical muscle mass even though they didn't lift any weights (about half as much muscle mass as the group that lifted weights). Researchers also found that when subjects *imagined* lifting weights, the same area of the brain that lights up when people *physically* lift weights is activated. Imagining has nothing to do with motor control; why would *visualizing* a workout, but not physically participating in a workout, build *tangible* muscle mass?

Or what about the results of a basketball experiment conducted by Australian psychologist Alan Richardson and his team? Richardson pulled together three groups of students at random. The first group practiced shooting free throws every day for twenty days. The second group only practiced on the first and last day of the experiment. The third group shot free throws on the first and last day, but also spent twenty minutes a day (on all twenty days) *visualizing* free throws. If they "missed" a shot during visualization, they'd "shoot" again. At the end of the experiment, the first group (the ones who practiced every day) improved by 24 percent. *Not bad.* The second group (the first and last day crew) didn't improve at all . . . *Uh, yeah, we kind of saw that coming.* The third group, although they physically practiced the same amount as the second group (only twice), *still improved by 23 percent.* Yes, you read that right. The players improved 24 percent and the visualizers improved 23 percent—*even though they physically practiced eighteen fewer days than the players.* Somehow, visualizing free-throw practice improved their performance as much as practicing for real, every day. Umm, *WUT*?!

>> *"Okay . . . Is this like a sports phenomenon or something?"*

Nope. Another study, led by psychologists Shelley Taylor and Lien Pham out of UCLA, found that students who visualized a positive outcome (like getting a better grade on their exams) had significantly improved grades over a control group that didn't visualize—which is pretty fucking cool, but it gets better. Students in another group visualized the *process* of achieving better results (like the act of studying) in *addition* to visualizing a positive outcome (like getting a good grade); they had *even better results* than the outcome-focused visualization group, and *way* better results than the no-visualization control group.

But wait, why would imagining step-by-step scenarios be more effective than just imagining positive results? And why in the blessed heck would imagining anything make something *materialize*?

Because our brains daydream, imagine, and visualize to rehearse real-life outcomes and prepare for them (yeah, a lot like Play). The part of your brain that activates when trying to "manifest" your dream job is the same area that pro athletes use to visualize and execute perfect aim, shot after shot. It's practice. Rehearsal. And it works.

BREAKING NEWS: Manifestation is real . . . BUT IT HAS NOTHING TO DO WITH "RAISING YOUR VIBRATION."

Let's say a goal is introduced into your conscious (Pilot Brain) thoughts. When you start visualizing what it's like to have, do, or be this goal, your brain's emotional center is activated—and when that happens, Autopilot Brain gets involved. Once Autopilot is involved, it puts that desire of yours *on autopilot* (ironic, right?), regularly checking in to determine how close or far off that goal is from being achieved. (This unconscious monitoring process is also the reason it is impossible to not think about a white polar bear after being told to not think about a white polar bear—an iconic experiment by the late American social psychologist Daniel Wegner.) With each subconscious check-in, Autopilot Brain shapes your behavior, guiding you closer to that goal you visualized. Except you're not aware this is happening. All you know is that people who can help you achieve this goal seem to materialize out of thin air, and money you never thought you'd have is suddenly pouring in. A goal that you visualized in your mind's eye is suddenly becoming real. But did you manifest it?

Yep. You did.

Manifestation happens when unconscious daydreaming meets conscious decision-making, when Autopilot Brain and Pilot Brain work together.

Here's the thing: you are ALREADY manifesting your reality WHETHER YOU'RE PAYING ATTENTION OR NOT.

Like, I didn't *mean* to manifest the end of my job-turned-twelve-year-career—but I did. Yes, really. *I accidentally manifested the elimination of my job.*

MY GETTING LAID OFF— LAW OF ATTRACTION PERSPECTIVE

In the months prior to the downsizing of the brand I worked for, I was stressed, working too much, and unsure of myself. This was a sharp contrast to the years prior, when I had been certain of my place in the company (it felt like a family) and where I wanted to go (I was gonna run the damn place one day). Things had changed. My sense of community was replaced with loneliness; my sense of ambition was stunted by a lull in company growth and personal insecurity. The year was full of highs and lows. (Fine, mostly lows.) L.o.A. (Law of Attraction) believers argue that the state of your life is a result of the energy of your thoughts, effectively drawing people, events, and circumstances toward you that match the vibration you put into the universe. If this is true, then I must've been pumping low-grade, lame-ass "please let me go" vibrations into the universe in 2016.

MY GETTING LAID OFF— SCIENTIFIC PERSPECTIVE

In the months prior to the downsizing of the brand I worked for, I was listening to podcasts about female solopreneurs who had quit their careers to start businesses of their own, and I reconnected with former coworkers who had found a way to be their own "boss." I had also planned a trip to Berlin and Amsterdam that drained my vacation days but refilled my well of inspiration, ramping up my motivation for my "side hustle"—my travel blog *Local (Tourist)*. In other words? Change was on my (subconscious) mind.

Just *three months* before my job's surprise downsizing, a subconscious goal crossed into my Pilot Brain: *"Get out of there."* I have no recollection of this, but thanks to my constant journaling, my hindsight is 20/20. There it was, scrawled in smudged ink in one of my many notebooks: *"I wish it was safe to quit my job."* In an entry a few months later, in another attempt to calm my anxious brain, I had journaled: *"What's the worst-case scenario if I lose my job? What are you freaked about?"* I answered myself with a wordy description of what life would be like if I was suddenly fired without severance or job recs; I detailed fears about losing friends and being too broke to afford rent. Finally, I asked myself, *"Is the worst-case scenario impossible to recover from? What would you do?"* My answer was a detailed daydream about a life as my own boss, free to travel, write, and do whatever I damn well pleased.

A COUPLE OF SCARY THINGS ABOUT THIS JOURNAL ENTRY:

1. *My position was eliminated just* four weeks later.

2. Every single thing *in that detailed daydream has happened, within one year of writing it. I am my own boss. I am free to travel. I have written a book. It's surreal.*

3. *I had no recollection of writing it.*

So far, it sounds like I'm proving the case for the L.o.A.—but I left something out.

When my position was eliminated, I was given a choice: take a different job with the company or take severance. *I chose severance.* When I chose to quit my job, my apartment lease was up shortly after. My landlord raised my rent. I was given a choice: move out or get roommates. *I chose roommates.* I had no control over my position being eliminated. I definitely didn't manifest being let go because of "low vibrations." But I did *choose* to quit, to move in with roommates, and to make the choices that added up to an entirely different life. In these ways, I *intentionally* manifested a different reality for myself. And I was *ready* to make those life choices because my intentions had been put on Autopilot months earlier. My intuition had been telling me the answers to what I needed all along. Do me a favor and read the following sentences twice:

Manifestation (i.e., creating your dream life) happens when your conscious goals are aligned with your subconscious desires. When Pilot Brain plans aren't censored by Autopilot with limiting beliefs, and Autopilot's dreams aren't censored by Pilot Brain through Shame or "obligation"—when both of your brains work together—you rebuild your reality around your central focus.

When you set an intention, it floats back and forth between your conscious and subconscious mind. Sometimes you set a goal you're actively working toward; sometimes you forget you wrote a detailed journal entry, accidentally stating your intentions. This is your intuition speaking to you. *And whether you're conscious of it or not, that intention is being worked on.* Whatever your intention is, your Autopilot Brain is working diligently in the background, *making micro-adjustments to your attitude, beliefs, and behavior*—to make it a reality.

As someone who has now intentionally manifested some pretty amazing shit (a book deal, a network of inspiring creatives, cash, a business of my own!), I can attest that things manifest faster *when you're paying attention.* You wanna manifest your dream life? Set a conscious intention. And then set a subconscious one.

Before we learn exactly how to *intentionally manifest* what we want in our lives, let's talk a little about the art of *subliminal manifestation.*

ME WILL TOMATO MOTIVATE SHE

Imagine you could be *subliminally primed* to do better on a test than you usually would. You wouldn't need to be smarter or study any harder, just "triggered." That's crazy, right?

A group of researchers from NYU believed it was possible and decided to test their theory on some first-year psychology students from the university. Students were (unknowingly) divided into two groups: a control group, and a "priming condition" group (aka the "triggered" group).

Researchers gave each student a ten by ten matrix of letters (your typical word search puzzle), with written instructions to find as many of the thirteen hidden words as they could, listed beneath the puzzle. Each list had the same set of neutral words: *building, turtle, green, staple, lamp,* and *plant*. The seven remaining words differed for each group. For the students in the "triggered" group, the remaining words were *win, compete, succeed, strive, attain, achieve,* and *master*. For the students in the control group, however, the remaining words were *ranch, carpet, river, shampoo, robin, hat,* and *window*. Once a student had completed the word search puzzle, they were told to set it aside and start a new set, hidden in an envelope in front of them. Unlike the first puzzle, these puzzles did *not* list the words to be found—students were instead required to find words related to a theme, like "colors," or "foods." They had ten minutes to find as many words as possible.

Guess which group performed better? *The students who were primed.* They didn't consciously realize words about "high achievement" or "performance" from the first puzzle were secret instructions to perform well on the upcoming tests, but their Autopilot Brain got the hint.

Subconscious priming is, essentially, *stealth intention setting*. It has been tested again and again, with different scenarios, subjects, and researchers and was found as effective in goal accomplishment as direct, conscious instructions. Subconscious priming has made test groups better at memorization, better cooperators, and higher achievers; in one experiment it even made them rude! Subjects who had been primed with words related to "rudeness" interrupted a researcher much earlier than people who had unscrambled word tests related to "politeness."

Subliminal priming isn't limited to language either; studies show we can be primed *just as effectively* with images. A famous movie theater experiment showed an 18.1 percent increase in Coca Cola sales and a 57.1 percent increase in popcorn sales after flashing lightning-fast subliminal images of soda and popcorn on the screen during pre-film commercials. Important note: Subliminal priming only works if you're *already motivated* to reach that goal (for example, people who were primed to buy soda only bought it if they were *already* thirsty.) So don't panic; this doesn't mean you're a brainwashed consumer zombie. *But it does mean you can be sneaky with your Autopilot Brain.*

The images, words, and ideas you surround yourself with are training your Autopilot Brain to make you behave a certain way. So, what would you like to subliminally prime yourself to do?

Make that ultra-embarrassing vision board; surround yourself with images that remind you of what you want or what you're working toward. Read books about people who've accomplished what you're trying to accomplish. Talk to people with similar goals as you; start a group text motivating each other, or join a "mastermind" group. Watch movies that inspire you. Write emails to yourself with a nonsensical subject line including words that will motivate you—then set a "delayed send" for far enough out that you'll forget you ever sent it.

No joke, I have a phone reminder that pops up every few days at different times that reads *"I am smart and creative and can do anything I set my mind to and also I look really good today."* Is that embarrassing? *Yes.* Do I care? *No.*

Do crazy, sneaky shit to motivate your Autopilot Brain. Do what's necessary to change your life.

P.S. I motivated you, didn't I? See . . . it's easy.

P.P.S. If you're confused about my P.S., read the title of this section again. *WORD SCRAMBLE, BISHHES!*

So go ahead, daydream about what you want to do and who you want to be. Know that it's not indulgent or childish because we *finally* have evidence that imagination actually helps us make things happen, whether through conscious visualization or subliminal priming. But keep something in mind: *visualization* is different than *fantasizing*.

Fantasizing is your brain's award ceremony for an achievement that hasn't been achieved yet.

Visualization is your brain's dress rehearsal for the thing you're about to accomplish in the real world.

In studies like the ones I just mentioned, research subjects who only *fantasized* about achieving their goals (and not the process to get those results) showed a measurable decrease in mental and physical energy levels afterward . . . which is kind of weird. Researchers think it has to do with the calming effect that fantasizing about our success has, by fooling our minds. It's as if our brains are saying, *"Now we can relax, we did it! We achieved our goal!"* This doesn't mean fantasizing is useless; *it actually helps reduce anxiety*.

So, if you find yourself spiraling in anxiety over a goal/intention, if you're beating yourself up for not being good enough, or if your Inner Cynic got ahold of the Shame megaphone this morning, then *fantasizing* about successfully achieving that goal will have a powerful calming effect on your brain. Fantasizing will chill you out and make visualization easier.

However, if you need physical and mental energy to make change happen, then *visualizing* will make the difference. If you are unsure how to manifest your dream life, then visualize the process, step by step, in extreme detail.

Here's my shortcut for remembering how to "manifest":

Anxious, self-loathing, or dealing with imposter syndrome? Fantasize first.

Ready for change but need a motivational kick in the ass? Visualize first.

Ready to give it a try?

HOW TO DEAL:
MANIFEST YOUR DREAM LIFE

Grab a piece of paper or open the note-taking app in your phone, and get ready to manifest your dreamiest dream life . . .

STEP 1: WHAT DO YOU WANT?

It doesn't have to be noble or trendy; this is about being *honest*. Do you want to manifest a feeling? Self-compassion? Confidence? A certain kind of lifestyle? A new job? A relationship? Do you want to manifest an object, like a car? Cash for that car payment? It's all on the table, so don't censor yourself. Let's use my business-starting dream as our example here:

>> *I want to start my own business.*

STEP 2: WHAT'S YOUR STATE OF MIND RIGHT NOW?

If you're anxious, ashamed, or dealing with imposter syndrome, *fantasize first*. Go into CRAZY DETAIL imagining what it looks like and how it feels to be 100 percent successful at your goal.

>> *You fantasize, in detail, about the* Forbes *article written about you and your business. How does it feel to be on the "40 Under 40" list? How does it feel to flip through the pages? You imagine logging in to your online banking. What number is next to the "total balance" line of your checking account? (Etc., etc. Do this for as long as you can, and in as much detail as possible.)*

STEP 3: SEE IT, HEAR IT, TASTE IT, SMELL IT, TOUCH IT

Assuming you're feeling okay but need the motivation to change your life, *it's time to visualize.* Go into CRAZY DETAIL visualizing the first steps you can take to make this goal a reality. Be practical and specific. If you have no idea where to start with this goal, then imagine the steps you'd take to find someone to ask for help or advice. Yes, really. It doesn't matter how "basic" or "baby steps" this visualization is—*you just need to be detailed.*

>> *You visualize walking into the county clerk's office and signing the permit to operate your new business. What does the building smell like, look like? (Make it up; I know you've never been there. There's probably a lot of mahogany wood or name placards on doors.) How does it feel to sign your business license? Next, visualize what your first day on the job (at YOUR company!) looks like from start to finish. (Yes, I'm aware you've never worked there before. Make it up.) Okay, now visualize the launch of your first product in detail, step by step. (Again, do this for as long as you can and in as much detail as you can.)*

STEP 4: WRITE THAT SHIT DOWN

Writing transforms an idea into something concrete that our Pilot Brain can get excited about, securing its place in both our short- and long-term memory. The daydreamy mental movies of steps 1–2 are designed to activate your Autopilot Brain (because imagining something lights up your emotional center—the limbic system—and flags that idea/dream/goal as something important to begin subconsciously working toward). Writing it down keeps your Pilot Brain engaged. Both brains need to work together, remember? Don't skip this step.

STEP 5: PRIME YOUR BRAIN

Get your Autopilot Brain and Pilot Brain collaborating by doing something that combines visual creativity *and* rational planning: Make a vision board. Yes, it's embarrassing. Do it anyway. It doesn't matter if you're on Tumblr, Pinterest, or your bedroom floor with magazines, scissors, and glue. Compile images that remind you of the thing you're working toward.

STEP 6: BONUS POINTS

Tell someone you trust about your intention/goal and what you visualized. Show them your vision board, if you can stand it. Talking about something with a friend is another way to solidify an idea's importance for your subconscious.

STEP 7: LET GO OF THE OUTCOME

This is about as close to the Law of Attraction "unshakable belief" thing I'm going to get. Once you've done steps 1–6, *trust that things will work themselves out*. I don't mean stop caring about it and actively working toward it, I mean *let go of your attachment to the outcome*. Believe things will work out the way they're supposed to because you are showing up, committing to your intentions, challenging yourself to take the steps you visualized, and being an active participant in rebuilding your own reality. Let your subconscious do some of the work.

STEP 8: TELL ME WHEN YOUR DREAM BECOMES A REALITY

Seriously, I want to jump up and down with you.

Feel free to fantasize about a confident, powerful, and successful life for yourself, especially when you feel that the opposite is true. It will increase your chances of making it a reality *and* calm you down in the process, which is a win-win in my book. More importantly, *visualize* your goals, especially the process and steps you'll take to reach them—it will exponentially increase your likelihood of making those dreams a reality.

Play make believe, daydream, make a vision board, do whatever embarrassing steps it takes to show your brain what living your fuckyeah might look like, because your mind will take that intention, rehearse it, and then help you turn it into reality.

P.S. GET READY TO HAVE YOUR MIND BLOWN

I thought I was being *so fucking witty*, you guys. When I was writing the section that reads:

"As someone who has now intentionally manifested some pretty amazing shit (a book deal, a network of inspiring creatives, cash, a business of my own!)..."

... I wrote something into the list that hadn't quite happened yet: *a book deal.*

I thought it would be really amazing if I could tell you that by the time my manuscript was finished a book deal seemed to materialize out of thin air (especially since I was self-publishing and not pitching my book to publishers). I thought it would reinforce my point about how we're already manifesting everything anyways and even the stuff that seems really far-fetched can still happen when you set intentions. *I THOUGHT IT WAS SO CUTE, LIKE, OMG!*

Yeah, well ... the day after I typed the words "a book deal," I received an email from a friend of a friend (my freelance copy editor, who had previously worked in publishing), saying she loved my book concept and *"by the way, I mentioned your book to my friend who is a Marketing Director at Chronicle, and she is asking for an introduction. I know you said you want to self-publish, but would you be open to an email intro?"*

Eight weeks later I was offered a book deal.

MANIFESTATION IS REAL, Y'ALL.

Ready to find some WooWoo in your life? Don't worry, I didn't bring crystals or tarot cards.

PSA:

MANIFESTATION,
SELF-SABOTAGE,
AND INTUITION
CAN BE BROKEN
DOWN BY SCIENCE,
BUT NOT EVERY-
THING IN LIFE CAN
BE EXPLAINED.

LET'S GET MYTHICAL

Have you noticed how obsessed the self-help world is with words like *purpose, calling,* and *passion?*

They're the kinds of words that make me squirm. I mean, they sound so . . . *final.* Permanent. Like I should be on this "one path" to complete my life's story arc—and if I would just pay a *smidge* more attention I could discover the universe's magical reason for my existence and *finally* be happy. Like I'm supposed to "follow my bliss," or "connect with my heart center," or "discover my personal legend," or something.

Isn't it a little reckless of all these self-help gurus to convince the general public we have one destiny? That the way to discover happiness is to stick with one life goal, one career, one job, one partner, one calling, one passion, one purpose? I MEAN, LIFE DOESN'T WORK LIKE THAT, YOU KNOW??

But then—you do know. You've gotten far enough in this book to know we're not all in the one-purpose or one-calling camp. And yes, the word *fuckyeah* in *Find Your Fuckyeah* could be interpreted as interchangeable with *purpose, calling,* or *passion.*

The truth is, *I do* want you to find your purpose, passion, calling, or whatever—but I'd like to point out that I'm using these words reluctantly. Why? Because your passion-purpose-calling *will continue to change.* Your fuckyeah isn't ONE BIG THING you'll stumble across at the end of this book, or on the day you turn thirty-four, or sixty-four, or at any one particular moment.

Your fuckyeah is the thread of joy woven throughout your life.

Your intuition points you toward fuckyeah, and it's magnetized by the things that bring you joy. And that will look different at different times in your life. The good news is that even if you haven't felt joy in a long time, you can tap into what brings you joy *right now*. Not when you get the bigger apartment, not when you get the next promotion, and not when you become your so-called #bestself. But to do this, you'll have to reconnect with your soul/heart/gut/intuition/Inner Compass and find your WooWoo.

Yeah, *WooWoo.*

It's fun to say, isn't it? Regardless of the language you speak, I know you've made the "Woo" sound before, whether cheering obscenely for your favorite team on the court—*"WOOOO!!!"*—or maybe a little *"Whew, that was a close one,"* when you almost drop coffee all over your white shirt. *Woo* is the sound we all make when language doesn't support the energy loaded in that particular moment.

WooWoo is the energy we often feel but can't see, moving in, around, and through everything; it's a nickname for the vibrancy, force, and spark of existence too complicated to put into words. WooWoo is the things our generation struggles to explain, things we keep trying to define with science, religion, and literature. Granted, we typically hear *WooWoo* used to mock pseudo-spiritual stuff—but I don't care; I'm going to use it in earnest.

And yes, I know I risk losing you here.

This WooWoo thing is the most convoluted concept covered in this book. Thus far I have used neuroscience to explain our self-limiting beliefs, psychology to break down our essential needs, and economics to debunk our social and political systems. But I can't even pretend to have answers to this Woo thing—I mean, *it is the unexplained by definition.* All I can tell you for sure is that the WooWoo is *real* and your connection to it is entirely *unique.* And here's the thing:

If you want to discover a life that you can't stop smiling about and an internal calm that cannot be fucked with, you need to find your personal connection to WooWoo.

REALLY THOUGH, WHAT IS THE WOO?

In my defense, an inability to explain something is not hard evidence that it doesn't exist.

Thousands of years before we could explain it, electricity *already* existed. We didn't invent electricity; all we did was name it and tap into it. Ancient peoples attempted to describe what we now call electricity as best they could; bioluminescent animals (like fireflies, glowing plankton, and deep sea fish), lightning, and thunder were attributed to the power, and often the wrath, of gods or goddesses. That's a lot of explanations that sort of . . . missed the mark.

It wasn't until the 1600s that William Gilbert's experiments led to the discovery of electricity, and it wasn't until 1752 that Benjamin Franklin gave us a story about electricity to get excited about. (You probably heard about it in grade school—Franklin flew a kite with a metal key in a thunderstorm, risking his life to prove that lightning *is* electricity . . . *Suuuuper safe, Ben.*) Then, 127 years after Benjamin Franklin's *Fear Factor* episode, our boy Tommy (Edison) and his team experimented thousands of times until they found the right elements to harness electricity, giving us a long-lasting, incandescent light bulb.

Electricity was always there; it just took us a minute to name, explain, and tap into it. So, fortunately or unfortunately, WooWoo, spirituality, and mysticism are the best ways we can describe that cosmic life-force thing right now.

>> *"Wait, I thought you weren't into that 'raise your vibration' energy shit?"*

Oh, I'm very much NOT. It's just, well—we had a bunch of thunder deities everyone was arguing about, and then a hot minute later we had designed a working light bulb. I'm just saying—can we really rule anything out completely?

FINDING YOUR WOO

Let's get one thing crystal clear: It does not matter if you believe in a version of God with a capital "G," gods, goddesses, a source energy, an afterlife, an underworld, *Underworld* the sci-fi movie franchise, heaven, enlightenment, ghosts, or Science with a capital "S."

WooWoo will find you.

If the way I threw things together on that list makes you feel defensive, know that I'm not mocking you. If something I listed makes you cringe because you don't believe in it, I get it. I'm not saying you should. What I am saying, however, is that *you won't find your fuck-yeah unless you have one foot in the transcendent*—what we, hereafter, shall call the WooWoo.

According to the Internet, the word *transcendent* means "something exceptional, mystical, outside ordinary experience," and (my personal favorite) "not subject to the limitations of the material universe." People have found transcendence in a lot of places. Back in the day, some people found it by withdrawing from society and setting out on a spiritual quest. Today, people find it in art, prayer, singing, cooking, meditation, poetry, painting, hiking, writing, running, helping others, rock climbing . . . It's everywhere and anywhere, but your connection to WooWoo is totally different than that of your seatmate's on the bus.

What about me, you ask? *My WooWoo?* Some days I plug into WooWoo with writing, occasionally it's through meditation, and on one particular day in 2016, my connection was found by sprinting into a field of millions of tulips in the Netherlands. When, without thinking, I lay down between two of several hundred rows of Dutch tulips and felt the cold sand (yes, sand!) on the back of my bare arms, I tapped into something bigger than me. While looking up at a clear blue sky, catching glimpses of magenta and crimson flowers floating in and out of my peripheral vision, I listened to the sound of billions of petals gently rustling in a crisp breeze and felt myself connect to something transcendent. *It was . . . weird.* I have no idea why that moment in the Netherlands let me connect to something bigger than myself, but it did. Just a quick feeling, reminding me that whatever WooWoo is, it's epic, alive, and addictive.

Maybe you've told yourself there is no unexplained cosmic energy or whatever—and your life experience has given you a good reason to think that's true. *I understand it because I've thought it.* I also know that underneath all that "certainty," way, way, deep down, your little human heart knows there's some kind of magic, somewhere. You just haven't found *your* magic yet, and your heart is very, very tired of looking for it and being disappointed.

Your WooWoo is *your way* of making sense of the wonderful, weird, illogical, playful, silly, transcendent, nonsensical parts of life. The stuff that hasn't been explained by science yet; the stuff that asks (and tries to answer) the question, *"What is human life for?"*

So, how do we find this cosmic woo?

If you know, believe, or connect with something with every cell in your being, then it's definitely part of your WooWoo.

Our WooWoo is hiding in the weird, surreal parts of our dreams. It's in the long-forgotten games of make believe we played as kids and tucked behind our favorite subjects in school. It's nestled underneath our *earliest* answers to the question, "What do you want to be when you grow up?" Sometimes it can be seen in something as subtle as a story line that resonates with you, or in the themes that keep repeating in your life (i.e., loyalty, sacrifice, justice, and the like).

That said, I absolutely love avocados—but it's not part of my WooWoo. Avocados are the best, but my Woo is made up of what helps me "plug in" to the transcendent, not the snacks I like. I know, for example, that *creativity* is part of my personal mythology; creativity helps me make sense of life, regardless of my changing age or roles in society (like kid, student, or employee). Creativity has been an important thread in my existence all along; it's an outlet for me to plug into my version of magic.

WooWoo is the difficult-to-explain cosmic piece of your fuck-yeah that brings you joy, peace, and growth.

Look, I'm definitely not advocating for throwing a coin into a wishing well and waiting around for your dreams to come true, okay? Just suggesting that your intuition—your connection to WooWoo—*might* have something intelligent to say, if only you'd peel back the duct tape gag for a second.

THE MAGIC OF WANDER AND WONDER

Many of the defining moments of my life have happened while traveling; most have happened while exploring. And if I've learned anything from my wandering experiences, it's this:

Go somewhere and find yourself there.

Want to get to know yourself? Want to discover a sense of wonder? Get lost somewhere new. Get outta town. Get out of the house. Beat it. You can use a traveler's mind-set just by wandering, *regardless of how far you physically go.*

Exploring is a playful act; it requires a curious mind and an openness to new experiences. When we're no longer surrounded by the familiar sights, sounds, and smells of the place we call "home," mundane details suddenly seem important. You've probably never thought about how strange the giant, distorted, white letters painted across the road that read "STOP" are until you're in a nation whose alphabet you don't understand—suddenly the characters painted on the asphalt look distinctly *surreal*. You won't realize that your neighborhood smells like cut grass and diesel fuel until *after* you come home from a place that smells like wet asphalt and pine needles.

Exploration is an essential part of finding fuckyeah because of its transformative power. We can easily live on Autopilot at home, getting ourselves from point A to point B without thought—but it's impossible to find a sense of wonder on Autopilot.

Wandering has a profound effect on us because being transplanted in an unfamiliar environment makes us completely present in that world. By intentionally placing ourselves in unfamiliar surroundings, we're activating our intuition, our Inner Compass, and inevitably, our

WooWoo. Because our minds are forced to compare and contrast this "new" world with the environment we know, the experience reveals hidden opinions and biases we would never have seen otherwise. *Travel is like self-discovery in hyperdrive.*

Wandering is active meditation; exploration is play. If you feel like you're stuck in a hamster wheel in your life, do whatever you can to make exploring into a game. Both scientists and spiritualists agree the "here, now" state is the most peaceful state we can be in, and present-state awareness is the perfect state of mind to ignite a sense of wonder and plug into WooWoo.

So get lost already.

———

My very most-favorite version of Woo in the wild? *Synchronicity*: a circumstance when everything seems to effortlessly sync up, flow, or connect the dots, leaving you with a sense of wonder.

Sometimes synchronicity feels like a cleared path. Sometimes it feels like you're turning a corner; circumstances shift suddenly, changing your perspective or plans. Sometimes synchronicity can be a sign to do (or not do) something—or it might feel like a roadblock out of nowhere, shifting your focus somewhere new.

Some people may argue that the concept of synchronicity is a symptom of our hunger for meaning in an otherwise meaningless world, that there's nothing magical about an old friend texting you out of the blue just as you are thinking of them, or finding a job the same week your severance check ran out, or dodging a car that ran a red light because you paused to tie your shoe. *I get it.* But also ... I imagine those people are sad inside, and I want to hug them. And surround them with puppies.

We would play tug-of-war with a two-month-old Frenchie I nick-named Potato, and I'd point out that in our surreal set of cosmic circumstances, life forms (including meaning-seeking human beings) somehow managed to evolve on this planet. "What if we search for meaning because we're *meant* to find it?" I'd ask. "Look at this cute puppy," I'd suggest.

Synchronicity could be a fluke; a freak set of circumstances that you're desperate to assign meaning to. Or maybe these circumstances are a conversation between you and whatever your Woo is, shaping what happens next in your life.

So, what coincidence did you recently blow off? When was the last time everything fell into place, for no apparent reason? What if synchronicity is WooWoo flowing through some kind of cosmic outlet to connect with you and tell you something?

Here's the thing about WooWoo: It's possible that the mystical things we can't yet understand will turn out to be utterly mundane and easy to explain hundreds of years from now. It's likely that the times you've experienced "miracles," "magic," or "synchronicity" had more to do with your intuition trying to communicate something important and wordless to you than anything else. None of this matters.

Life can be hard; it's made infinitely easier by living with a sense of wonder.

You and I will never have all the answers in life. As deeply satisfying as it was for me to debunk the mythology around manifestation and the Law of Attraction using scientific data, the truth is there's a lot of mystical, magical, surreal, and synchronistic things that science *cannot yet explain.* Things we may *never* be able to explain. But do we really want all the answers? Isn't life more fun with a little mystery built in?

Allow yourself the room to believe in something that brings you that deep, meaningful, hard-to-explain, magical kind of joy and connection to the world around you, even when you can't prove it, explain it, or come close to understanding it.

Let yourself have a little fun searching for WooWoo, because, I mean, WHAT IF YOU FIND IT?!

9.

GET OUT OF YOUR OWN WAY

For a long time, this chapter was alternatively titled: "How to Beyoncé, aka Make the Impossible Possible."

Maybe you've seen this phrase on the Internet: *"You have the same number of hours in a day as Beyoncé."* Fans love to post it on social media as a source of #mondaymotivation, while critics are quick to remind us she has a massive team of people at her beck and call, writing her lyrics, changing her kids' diapers, and organizing her world tours—in other words, an unfair advantage. We typically choose sides: either she's too talented and too ambitious, or too rich and too connected to model our measly life's ambitions after. Somehow, we've made a flesh-and-blood woman into an idol that, depending on which camp you're in, symbolizes either a powerful feminine queen who built her empire on flawless taste and the sweat of her brow, or a wealthy illuminati goddess who built her empire on connections and cash.

My point? Whether you love her music, hate her music, or feel indifferent, Beyoncé has become pop culture's human yardstick for impossible-to-reach #goals. And *that's* why this chapter was almost titled "How to Beyoncé": you need reminding that the life you want to live—your happiest, most ridiculously impossible, very best, praise-hands-emoji kind of life—can be yours.

You just need to take it off its pedestal.

Take your dreams off their pedestals. Take your passion, purpose, and calling off their pedestals. I don't mean stop having dreams or setting goals—I mean stop glamorizing them, because glamorizing something is a creative way of telling your Autopilot Brain that *you can never have it.*

What does your dream life look, sound, taste, smell, and feel like? Does it feel far off, blurry, and unlikely because you don't have the necessary cash, connections, skills, or experience for it to be real yet? Stop telling yourself which dreams are practical and which are unlikely, irrational, or unrealistic. Your most impossible dreams are just goals you couldn't envision a start-to-finish path to accomplish, so you elevated them to pedestal status, effectively telling your brain those goals were out of reach. *They're not.*

Do you know how Beyoncé "gets it done" today? With creative vision, the resources at her disposal, and a willingness to put her work out into the world. (And yes, she has *a lot* of resources at her disposal nowadays.) Do you know how Beyoncé "got it done" years ago? How she built the pop culture empire she now presides over? *The same way:* with creative vision, the resources at her disposal, and a willingness to put her work out into the world. When she started out, she had significantly *fewer* resources than she does now—but that didn't stop her from putting her work out there. (I'm not comparing her starting point with yours or mine—just pointing out that she wasn't a billionaire when she sang in Girls Tyme in 1993.) Over the years, her creative vision and resources have changed, but her willingness to share her Art remains constant.

You can make your most "impossible" goals into reality—with creative vision, the resources at your disposal, and a willingness to put your Art out into the world. And it all starts by taking your fuckyeah off of its pedestal.

Unless you enjoy pining over an awesome life that you'll never get to experience, stop glamorizing Future You. Take small steps to make your life amazing *starting now.*

This chapter is about setting goals that seem utterly impossible—and then crushing those goals with a huge smile on your face. BUT PLOT TWIST: The goal-setting advice I have to offer has nothing to do with achievement or productivity, and unlike most self-improvement books, this chapter is entirely "life hack"–free. There *is* a science to setting goals we can accomplish, but it's already out there, waiting for you to discover in the World Wide Webernets. This chapter is about something else that's vitally important to goal-setting; something you *won't* find on the Internet; something that nobody seems to be talking about yet:

You can make any impossible goal into a reality, but only if you get out of your own way. Not by working harder, faster, or more efficiently—but by uncensoring your strengths and weaknesses.

TO BEGIN WITH, THERE ARE FOUR
THINGS NO ONE WILL TELL YOU ABOUT GOALS:

1. *Sometimes "knowing what you want" is more like "guessing and being okay with not being 100 percent certain." You don't have to know exactly what you want or whether you can "pull it off" to benefit from setting that goal.*

2. *Your "why" doesn't need to be impressive (and neither does your goal). Your motivation could be as simple as "because it looks interesting to me." It's an honest, unfiltered admission of what you're curious about. Your "why" is also allowed to be selfish. It isn't an explanation you owe to anyone else; it's clarity you owe to yourself.*

3. *Focusing on one thing requires that you also ignore something else, if only temporarily—and there is a real possibility that something you choose to try, learn, or focus on will not come easily to you, may not be fun for you, and may not be what you expected. Don't worry about it. This isn't a waste; it is an investment in your self-education. (Mistakes aren't failures; they're research, remember?)*

4. *Never rule something out because it seems impossible. If you're sure you can pull this off, then you've set the bar way too low.*

In my opinion, number four is the most important point: **if you already know you can do it, then you're probably not dreaming big enough.**

Your brain is looking for a challenge. If you set a goal that's obviously doable, then it's not a goal—*it's a to-do list item*—and Autopilot Brain zones out when it sees a to-do list. It leaves the checklist stuff to Pilot Brain—and that's problematic, because you need both of your brains working together to achieve your dreamiest goals. Don't let the lizard in your head set the bar too low; if you want something enough to set your intentions on it, *you will rise to the occasion to make it happen.*

KNOW THYSELF

If I could boil down years of research by world-renowned psychologists from prestigious scientific institutions and hundreds of studies on personality types into *just one key takeaway*, it would be this:

Rebuild your work and life around practicing your strengths.

How many of our New Year's resolutions have been about changing our bodies? How many of our goals have been about breaking a habit? What if, instead, we built more of the things we *like* into our lives?

What is important to you? What do you love thinking, learning, and talking about? Which kinds of problems do you *want* to solve? What are you holding back from the rest of us? What are you amazing at?

>> *"Umm, 'amazing'? That's a stretch. What if . . . I'm not great at anything?"*

That's the thing—you *are* amazing at something. Not at everything, but at many things. But that can be difficult to believe, especially if you've applied a series of mental filters to your innate strengths, like "Must Be Profitable," or "Looks Good on Paper," or "Share Only When Perfect," or "Does This Help Me Conform?" Disguised as humility and realism, Shame can easily convince us that our strengths are the few and far between learned, marketable skills that can be listed on a resume, not the innate and boundless sparkly mash-up of universe dust that makes us each a unique DNA snowflake.

Stop wasting time by filtering, minimizing, and suffocating your innate strengths—and watch how fast your dream life becomes reality.

Studies show that people who practice their strengths have higher job satisfaction, are more productive at work, experience a protective buffering effect against depression and anxiety, have stronger, happier relationships, including romantic ones, and experience high levels of "thriving" (yes, this is something that scientists can measure with a battery of tests).

>> *"So how do I figure out what my strengths are?!"*

In one of positive psychology's early endeavors, the founder of the theory, Martin Seligman, and his colleagues Katherine Dahlsgaard and Chris Peterson were determined to find out if a kind of "handbook of health" could exist. They started by sifting through thousands of cross-cultural "virtues" in an attempt to figure out which were consistent across all humankind. They found at least twenty-four unique "character strengths" consistent across all cultures that, when practiced, were clinically proven to increase happiness and well-being. After further research, they formulated a 120-question test that measured and quantified those strengths.

Fast-forward more than a decade later, and their test (called the VIA Character Strengths Survey) has been taken by over 6.5 million people and validated in over two hundred rigorous scientific studies. (And frankly, if a bunch of bickering scientists can agree that something is useful, then it's good enough for me.)

The research identifies twenty-four strengths; see if you can pick out your top three to five core strengths from the following list. Hint: They're probably the values most important to you or the qualities that come most naturally to you.

Creativity	Fairness
Curiosity	Leadership
Judgment (i.e., seeing all sides, critical thinking)	Prudence (i.e., thoughtful, careful decision-making)
Love of Learning	Teamwork
Bravery	Forgiveness
Honesty	Humility
Perseverance	Self-Regulation (i.e., discipline, self-control)
Zest (i.e., enthusiasm, lust for life)	
Kindness	Appreciation of Beauty and Excellence
Love	Gratitude
Social Intelligence	Hope
Perspective (i.e., "big-picture thinking," "street smarts")	Humor
	Spirituality

If you're anything like me, you're probably weirded out by the old-fashioned terminology. I mean, *Prudence??* *Zest??* You're likely also wondering how you "practice" something like "Hope." Maybe a few quick examples will help clarify things.

>> *If one of your top strengths is Appreciation of Beauty and Excellence, then you could practice it by making a list of as many places or activities as you can think of that celebrate curation or stir up a sense of wonder— like visiting an art museum or hiking to a waterfall— and then plan one activity focused on appreciating beauty or excellence each week.*

>> *If one of your top strengths is Perspective, then you can practice it by taking opportunities to help others "see the big picture." At work, you could compile a project or report that unifies statistical data on how the company is performing, customer perspectives, and your creative vision for the future. (Imagine dropping that on your boss's desk—major points for you!) Or in your personal life, you could carve out time to listen to a friend who is going through tough circumstances and offer your perspective and advice.*

What if we capitalized on what we're *naturally* good at? Instead of killing ourselves trying to change who we are, why not lean in to what comes naturally to us? For detailed explanations of each character strength and ways to practice them, check out the free VIA Character Strengths test (www.viacharacter.org). We'll cover more ways to practice your strengths before the end of this chapter, but first, I need to break some bad news to you. (Gently, I promise.)

EMBRACE YOUR WEAKNESS

You are inherently bad at a lot of things, some of which you will *never* be good at, regardless of how hard you work. You are going to make some *painful* mistakes in your life—and you have some serious weaknesses that could put you at risk of never reaching your highest goals or living your most praise hands-emoji, fuckyeah-filled life.

So what.

Most people let their weaknesses get in the way of what they want to accomplish—either by ignoring them or by defending them. But you're not most people.

You've got no reason to be scared of your imperfections; you're working on accepting them, rather than being ashamed of them. But have you ever approached learning about your weaknesses with the same open-minded curiosity as learning about your strengths? I mean, really—how many "Discover Your Greatest Weakness!" quizzes have you taken? How much dread do you feel before a performance review at work? Can you be *specific* about what your natural weaknesses are, without becoming defensive, anxious, or depressed?

It's not easy. Because we were taught that imperfection was failure (#factoryschool), and that failure meant rejection (#shame), we've spent most of our lives being trained to disguise and minimize our weaknesses from others. We practice answering job interview questions like, "What's your greatest weakness?" with *fake* weaknesses meant to appeal to the MF's agenda: "Oh, I just care too much; I'm a workaholic; I'm a perfectionist." We crop, filter, and edit the ever-loving hell out of every selfie. We "un-tag" ourselves from unflattering photos on social media, hoping to present a pore-less, flawless image of ourselves to the world. We censor what we're honestly looking for in our dating profiles, afraid that we'd never find a match if we were vulnerable or real. "Please, please, will somebody just swipe right already??"

If we want a shot at finding fuckyeah, however, we'll have to get good at acknowledging and accepting our weaknesses for what they are. *Why*, you ask?

Because the people who know their weaknesses as intimately as their strengths, who accept those weaknesses without shame, and who refuse to tolerate any obstacles in the way of their goals, including themselves—ARE FUCKING INVINCIBLE.

Did you notice that I wrote "accepting" your weaknesses and not "eradicating" them? Acknowledging our flaws requires self-compassion, *and a lot of it*—especially since we can't eliminate our weaknesses. But what would happen if you not only admitted your imperfections, but embraced them? Made friends with them? Learned how to work with them and around them? You'd be *untouchable*. No one could hold the threat of exposing your weaknesses to the world over your head, because you already decided to be transparent about them. Total self-awareness is POWER, and it's yours to step into.

Let me guess: you're wondering what your weaknesses are. Well, that's easy. *They're your strengths.*

Your weaknesses are your strengths, either overamplified or underused.

Think about the little ways that your strengths have shown up as weaknesses in your life: if you're a naturally curious person, you've probably also been called "nosy"; if one of your core strengths is perseverance, then you're probably irritatingly stubborn too. Think about all the famous creatives in history who were also considered "erratic" (Salvador Dalí, Nikola Tesla) or the famously courageous people we'd also call "reckless" for putting themselves in harm's way (Amelia Earhart, Nelson Mandela).

Research has found that overuse of one's strengths can create unnecessary stress and interpersonal conflict. The good news? You can *prevent* overuse of your core strengths by intentionally practicing your *other* strengths, the ones that fall lower on your list.

Interestingly, researchers have also found that *underuse* of strengths is more closely tied to serious problems (like depression and social anxiety disorder, for example) than overuse—because underuse creates a "mindless state of languishing—a void, hollow, empty state."

Overusing your strengths creates conflict, frustration, and self-sabotage; underusing your strengths leaves a vacuum that boredom and stress will rush in to fill.

You know that irritated feeling you get when you hear people say, "Just be yourself!" and you're thinking, "Who or what else could I *possibly fucking be*!?" Well, what they're really pointing out is that you might be *less yourself* by censoring your innate strengths. In other words, *underusing our strengths is a form of inauthenticity.*

If you find yourself in constant conflict with people in your life, chances are you've leaned too hard on a core strength, expecting others to minimize theirs to go along with whatever it is you want or need. But that's not nearly as common as *underusing* your strengths—censoring yourself and shrinking from what you're best at for fear you won't fit in. When we underuse our strengths, we're *stifling* our Art and shoving down our joy, leaving an inner void where feelings of both apathy and anxiety will immediately flood in and fill.

The solution? Stop editing your strengths; give yourself permission to be *fucking amazing* at what comes naturally to you. Experiment, explore, and take risks to discover what other innate strengths you never knew you had. But also, quit filtering your weaknesses! **By trying to hide them from others, you're hiding them from yourself, creating your own roadblocks to trip over.** You're not perfect, and that's fine. Own it.

Studies show that the happiest people *intentionally* practice their strengths, acknowledge their weaknesses, and refuse to tolerate the obstacles in the way of their goals. Of course, "refusing to tolerate obstacles" doesn't mean "assuming that everything should go exactly the way they hope, expect, or plan." It means they know that no problem is impossible; they just need to find a way *through*:

OPTION 1: EVOLVE.
Learn and practice the necessary skills to overcome your weakness.

OPTION 2: GO AROUND YOUR WEAKNESS.
Instead of struggling to do something you're naturally bad at, change the path you're taking to get to your goal. This usually involves creatively practicing your core strengths.

OPTION 3: RECRUIT OTHERS.
Ask for help! Enlist someone who is naturally strong where you are naturally weak, and/or utilize tools that help compensate for your weaknesses.

Your weaknesses aren't a problem; they're a natural part of being a human. Instead of being ashamed of them or defending them, discover the tools you need to counterbalance them and MAKE PROGRESS. People who know their "why," who practice their strengths and accept their weaknesses, and who know, deep down, that no obstacle is insurmountable—are *invincible*.

YOU, UNCENSORED

It's time to stop glamorizing your "best life" and to make it amazing *right now*. Time to chase down your curiosity. Time to start experimenting, exploring, and taking risks. Time to uncensor your intuition and admit to yourself what it is you instinctively want and what you're naturally drawn to. Time to practice being your unique, flawed self without shame. Time to set intentions, subliminally and consciously, and to manifest your fuckyeah in the process.

Using the following blank space (or the back of a napkin, your phone, whatever you can find), complete the exercise. After reading the prompt, write what comes to mind as quickly as you can. Make an orderly list or scribble randomly all over the place, whatever comes naturally to you.

RULE NO. 1.	*Be honest, even if it's embarrassing. Nobody sees this but you. I promise.*
RULE NO. 2.	*Do not edit, censor, or tweak your answers. Do not rationalize with yourself; do not disqualify anything.*
RULE NO. 3.	*Set a timer for five minutes, read the prompt, and then start the clock.*

If you could have anything, go anywhere, try anything, start anything, be a rookie at anything, become an expert at anything, or play at anything—knowing that ALL the money and time you need for the life you want is available, because you no longer live under scarcity—and knowing that your creativity is endlessly regenerative, that it is impossible for you to fuck your life up, that you are wholly loved, that you are more than *enough*, and that we desperately need your Art to be expressed in the world, no matter how many forms it takes or how many ways it changes over time...

What would your Uncensored Self create, try, build, have, do, or be?

GO.

ALL OF THAT IS YOURS, IF YOU WANT IT.

Your fuckyeah is right here, waiting for you. Go get it!

Wait, wait, wait; did you think I'd abandon you here? I mean, fair enough—most books of this genre hold our hands along the "journey" to happiness, fulfillment, and self-improvement, right up to the door of change—and then, POOF! They ghost on us. It's just *"Deuces! You've got it from here, right? K, baaaaaiiiiiiii."*

I just can't bring myself to do that to you.

Though it's unlikely that you've "found your fuckyeah" at this point, you definitely know where to go looking for it. That's a big deal, and I'm really proud of you for making it this far—there was a lot of heavy work to get to this moment. Problem is—you will find your fuckyeah, *and then you'll lose it.*

You will share your Art with us,
and then we will reject you.

You will express your uncensored,
genuine self at work, in a relationship, anywhere in public really, *and
we will freak the fuck out about it.*

It's not enough for me to show you
where to go looking for your fuckyeah—I have to show you how to find
it and *how to KEEP finding it*; how
to *exercise* your happiness; how to
maintain your joy; how to *fan the
spark* of your fuckyeah into a wildfire of joy.

Ready? I brought matches and
lighter fluid.

10.

IS SHIT HITTING THE FAN? YOU'RE (PROBABLY) DOING IT RIGHT

Raise a hand if this sounds like you:

You finally had the courage to try something you've been dreaming about doing for years, and it turns out you hate it. *"Ummm . . . what the hell do I do now?"*

You uncovered something that makes you little-kid-eating-first-ever-ice-cream-cone happy—and as soon as you told us about it, we made you feel like a pile of human garbage. *"This is what I get for 'uncensoring' myself? UGHhhh."*

You found your actual, for-real, deeply fulfilling fuckyeah, and it turns out you are terrible at it. Just really, really, really bad. *"Do I follow common sense and quit flailing, or stick with it and embarrass myself some more?"*

You're genuinely frustrated because you haven't even *come close* to finding your fuckyeah yet. Not even a hint; not even a little. *"Seriously, is there something wrong with me?!"*

Take a deep breath—this is NORMAL. It's good, actually. Healthy.

This idea that once we know "when to experiment in our career," or "where to go looking for happiness," we'll be set for life in the Modern Enlightenment Department is just a side effect of buying into the health and wellness industry's version of "self-care." Nothing is permanent. Happiness is not a destination; it's a process (kind of like exercise). Life is change, and you are a walking cosmic experiment, a beautiful mess. Your fuckyeah will change, over and over, for the entirety of your life—and that's perfectly fine—especially since you're not a story arc, brand, or commodity.

Whether you think you found it, hate it, or lost it, your fuckyeah is the thread of joy woven *throughout* your life. It is ever-changing, disappearing, reappearing, and multiplying, because you are change. Joy isn't a one-time fix. We have to *exercise* our happiness to create an "upward spiral." It takes *practice* to hang onto the momentum created by moments of fuckyeah—and to chill the hell out when you've temporarily lost it.

If you haven't noticed, the world is a mess. To hold on to your joy, you will need to fight and stand for the things you love. On a regular basis. You'll need to be your genuine self *in defiance of us*, occasionally. You'll need to continuously remind yourself to uncensor who you are, your dreams, your relationships, and your work.

That's what part III of this book is all about: crafting our own road maps to an inner happiness "well." It will never run dry; there will always be enough. When we figure out how to take care of ourselves by *our* standards, understand how to live on purpose, know which people to carefully surround ourselves with, and how we can help others find their fuckyeah and share their Art, we'll know where to locate our joy, every time, without fail. *Even when shit is hitting the fan.*

And so, I'd like to dedicate this chapter to Alanis Morissette and the third CD I ever bought, *Jagged Little Pill*. If you've ever sung karaoke to "Isn't It Ironic," you're familiar with this "shit hitting the fan" concept.

>> *You finally end a long-running, toxic relationship— a painful, but much-needed decision. The same week you begin to feel waves of relief instead of heartache, your apartment is flooded. Now you feel waves of toilet water around your ankles.*

>> *You get paid for your first-ever freelance job as a professional photographer. Awesome. While depositing the check at the bank, your car is broken into, and all your camera gear is stolen. Not awesome.*

When you're changing your life, your brain is actively looking for a sign that what you're doing is a good idea. It's easy to take a bad day, painful rejection, or sudden obstacle as a sign to "quit while you're ahead," but this resistance isn't some warning from the WooWoo; it's your little lizard struggling with *fear*.

When we're in the middle of changing our lives and things go awry, every negative event seems to symbolize a personal failure—even if these circumstances were far outside our control.

This is because your Autopilot Brain is *looking for meaning* in all these new, big, scary changes, and with big change comes big resistance. Fear is a hard-wired emotion, and it doesn't disappear (POOF!) the moment we discover our fuckyeah.

Fear remains; courage is deciding that this idea, Art, or change you're about to make is worth making in the face of fear.

The only way to resist this fear is to "show up," to make the incredible effort necessary to be your authentic self, every day. Finding fuckyeah doesn't mean your life won't have hurdles, hiccups, or problems—it means you'll have the inner resources to know which problems are the *worth-it problems*.

Did you "show up" to life today? Set intentions? Work through your automatic thoughts? Share your authentic self, humanity, and Art with the rest of us? Then you're doing the work. Don't quit yet.

GOING HARD

Raise your hand if you found out about a healthy diet that sounded like a miracle, so you bought vegetables you'd never heard of to try "juicing" for the first time (after throwing away most of your pantry, since it was full of junk food and expired spices). Did I mention you don't have money for a juicer, but you thought your fifteen dollar blender would probably work the same way and its motor *may or may not* have just gone out in a blaze of glory, celery sticks, and apple skins? You went hard. (That's what she said.)

When you become passionate about new ways to chase down your fuckyeah, you go hard after big change. But if something comes up that scares you in the process, you also ~might~ pause and panic.

>> *"Wait, wait, wait, wait, did I just quit my job, sell all my clothes, and start an online business in the same week? What the HELL was I thinking!?"*

Does it feel like shit is hitting the fan? Good. That means you're doing it right.

This is a new, transitional moment in your life. The awkward feelings, growing pains, and flashes of fear resulting from the decisions you make during this transition won't last forever, but neither will this wave of momentum to change your life for the better. Which is why we need to take it. **Nothing is permanent; no decision, no mood, no mistake, and no achievement lasts forever. Fuckyeah is not permanent. It is ever changing, just as we are.** That's why it's crucial not to panic right now: each tiny step, brave attempt, and huge risk is propelling you forward, edging you closer to your fuckyeah. Can it be terrifying to realize you're not in full control of this momentum? Yep. But it's getting you somewhere you want to go.

Be patient with yourself if you're turning your life upside down. Change is exciting when we want it and terrifying when we don't.

Human beings avoid change like the plague, unless they're ready. *And you are* ready, because right now you're taking steps to unfilter who you really are so you can find the joy of living the life you *actually* want.

Take comfort in the fact that you have everything you need within you to handle what comes next, even if you don't know exactly what "next" is. You've learned new things before, haven't you? Try to accept that you can't predict the future, and trust that things will turn out *far* better than your lizard brain is claiming they will. Do your best to listen to the joy that drives you whenever fear attempts to shift your course. Take a deep breath and remember you are enough; you have enough; there is enough. YOU ARE GOING TO BE OKAY.

But wait, are *you* the one throwing shit at the fan?

SHIT THROWER

Hello self-sabotage, my old friend.

Autopilot is the perpetually skittish part of you that hates risk. Imagine the scale of your little lizard's freak-out when your Pilot Brain decides, *"I want to live differently now! I'm okay with taking risks, and I don't need you to protect me anymore. I'm taking over from here!"*

Autopilot seeks revenge. (Band name, I called it.)

When we aren't confident that our choices, risks, and experiments are going to make us happy, we can subconsciously *create* diversions and roadblocks for ourselves.

An idea pops into your head to group-text friends you haven't seen in ages—the crew you used to go out with all the time. By some miracle, everyone is free, and you meet up at a bar downtown. You're having a fantastic time, but around your fifth shot of tequila, you get this weird, sad feeling—almost like something terrible has happened.

Your tequila-soaked Pilot Brain has no idea that you're setting yourself up to oversleep, wake up painfully hungover, and miss tomorrow morning's interview for your dream job.

Autopilot saw an opportunity to throw shit directly at the fan.

If you miss an important job interview, you also miss the opportunity to be *rejected* by your potential dream employer. Somehow, your primal lizard brain thinks that sabotaging your interview outweighs the benefits of landing the job, because if you don't try, you can't fail. *The crazy part? Your Autopilot Brain is just trying to protect you from "the unknown" at all costs.*

Success can be as scary as failure because it guarantees your life will change—creating an unknown future.

Autopilot doesn't *mean* to sabotage your progress toward fuckyeah; it honestly thinks it's helping you to escape a very real danger: pain.

PAIN IS NOT THE PROBLEM

But I know why you think it is.

Scientists have hypothesized that our "mental time travel" abilities (remembering the past, imagining the future) evolved because predicting danger was useful, and avoiding pain meant the survival of our species. The avoid-pain pathways in your Autopilot Brain are deeply entrenched, as if evolution were a cartoon character running in circles, digging the pain-hating track deeper with every turn. Since Pilot Brain stepped onto the evolutionary scene, however, it's made some upgrades.

Pilot Brain has helped us push through plenty of physical pain (like exercise) because we knew the future outcome (a healthy and strong body) would be worth it. We've endured psychic pain too (like the grief of losing a loved one), because even though Autopilot can't always see beyond the pain in that moment, our conscious mind can (*this will pass; my heart will heal*).

Well, except when it comes to ego.

Our ego—our sense of self—lives smack in the middle of Pilot Brain, in the prefrontal cortex. Faced with any pain that relates to our weaknesses, lack of skill or talent, humiliation or embarrassment, or any criticism or attack on who we are, Pilot Brain quickly taps out, unwilling to endure the indignity. Our focus instantly switches from *"Let's accomplish this goal"* to *"Let's defend ourselves."*

Caught between Autopilot's panic mode and Pilot Brain's ego tantrum, we are distracted from realizing that *pain is trying to tell us something.*

And yeah, I know how obvious that sounds. If you broke your ankle, pain is trying to tell you, "HEY!!! WE JUST BROKE OUR ANKLE—DO NOT ATTEMPT WALKING RIGHT NOW—YOU'LL ONLY MAKE IT WORSE!" Physical pain is there to tell you that the path you're currently taking isn't working and you need to make some changes, ASAP. Well, psychic pain is trying to do that too.

Psychic pain—like disappointment, anguish, confusion, or frustration—is there as a signal. It is an opportunity to change, pivot, stretch, or grow.

Most of us will do everything in our power to avoid being criticized, embarrassed, or viewed as failures. We dial back our ambitions, we censor ourselves, we avoid risks, we refuse to be vulnerable with others. Pain can be a signal to quit to prevent further damage (broken ankle), but too often it is used as the perfect excuse to stop experimenting. Our first instinct is to dodge the pain those risks might cause (flight); our second instinct is to transfer that pain somewhere else or onto someone else (fight). Successful people, on the other hand, know something most of us don't: *Pain is not a problem. Pain is an opportunity.*

Successful people have learned not to waste time in a negative spiral over the pain they experience. They make the negative emotions created by failure, criticism, rejection, and embarrassment useful, by treating them as a signal: *"What opportunity—for change, perseverance, or growth—is pain trying to make me aware of?"*

Self-sabotage sneaks into our lives when fear has blinded us to something; when Autopilot has hijacked control of our behavior because it would rather avoid being hurt now than see the big picture. If we want to overcome self-sabotage, we have to get our Pilot Brain to look past our ego and see pain for what it is—an opportunity.[1]

You won't be good at everything. Your Art will not make sense to everyone. Some leaps of faith will have amazing rewards, and some will leave you with bruises. But do you want to be resilient? Meet all your goals? Bounce back faster from the shit that life loves to hurl at the fan? *Then let pain speak to you.* Before jumping to solve a "problem," sit with it. Let it burn, just for a second; find out what the pain is *signaling*—so you can solve the problems that matter. And most importantly,

When you catch yourself acting in self-sabotage, be glad you noticed, forgive yourself, and refocus your attention, because what you focus on becomes your reality.

The real question is, which problems are the worth-it problems?

"I DON'T KNOW, YOU'VE JUST . . . CHANGED"

We've established that when we change our *minds*, it means we change our *lives*, one way or another.

Well, if you spent years believing you were unworthy of love and needed to perform for others to keep them from abandoning you, *chances are there are a handful of people in your life who got used to*

---

[1] *It is not my intent to trivialize chronic pain, especially the immense psychic pain experienced in all forms of mental illness, including depression. When I say "pain is an opportunity," I mean an opportunity to change our perspective (and in the case of mental illness, it is a crucial opportunity to seek help).*

you behaving that way. If you decide to stop censoring who you are around your family, or bending over backward to impress people at work, the people who got used to the "old you" might be a little . . . *ticked off.*

If you're serious about making changes in your life, don't be shocked when people respond by treating you differently.

Hopefully they'll celebrate these changes, but sometimes that's not how the cookie crumbles. Someone's inappropriate reaction to your life choices is no reason to revert back to a limiting belief that squashes your joy; it's no reason to shrink your ambitions to avoid being shamed either. But living your "new" life may feel a little *uncomfortable* around other humans at first. It might even feel like shit is hitting the fan. Change does that.

The good news is, the people who care about **you**—the real, raw, you-as-you-are-right-now you—will not only adjust to these changes in your life, but will *celebrate* your uncensored self-expression. Loudly. Publicly. Joyfully.

On the other hand, the people who try to shame you for your decisions and experiments, who want you to "perform" a certain way, who do not encourage you to explore what makes you curious—those people will begin to backpedal out of your life, leaving you room to breathe and be yourself. And although it can be deeply painful to discover that you've grown apart from someone you care about, creating space to be you is crucial for your mental health—and for theirs too.

So how do we get comfortable with knowing some people will not approve of the direction that fuckyeah is taking our lives? By learning the value of rejection.

THE VALUE OF REJECTION

Our default response to the pain of rejection—whether being dumped, fired, criticized, left out, or worse—is to lash out in anger or withdraw into self-judgment. But these aren't our only options.

The value of rejection is the opportunity it gives us to change direction or stay the course with renewed clarity.

If you're thinking about your life like a scientist, then mistakes, rejection, failure, and all the various forms of "No" will make you *curious about your options.* Curiosity can change a negative situation into a positive one. In this mind-set, it's not failure; it's research, right? *It's not rejection; it's a new direction.*

When you're trying something new or sharing your fuckyeah with the rest of us, there is a *real* possibility some of us won't be ready for it. And we may tell you, loudly. Obnoxiously. Maybe to your face. Maybe in an anonymous tweet. Maybe in a catty email. Even worse? Some of us might make you feel utterly ignored. *But do you believe in this risk you're taking, this Art you're sharing? Then take it, share it, let it grow.*

If you share something authentic, something fresh, something still "in process," with us—chances are someone will tell you that they don't want or need it; someone else will sincerely appreciate and support it (but may never take the time to tell you), and a handful of us will lose our minds telling every soul we know about how *totally epically amazing you and your Art are.* But guess what? YOU AREN'T LIVING YOUR FUCKYEAH FOR US. It's for you; it's the thread of joy woven throughout *your* life.

Your Art needs to be shared—not for our sake, but for yours.
Because whatever it is—an idea, a project, a gesture, something

physical, something immaterial—if you don't share it, then it will be stifled, smothered, and shoved down within you again and again, making you increasingly miserable, restless, and numb to your life. Share your Art for *you*.

> >> *"But what if I'm not ready to share it? What if . . . my Art isn't any good?"*

Maybe you found your fuckyeah, but you're running into issues. Maybe your Art looks funky or isn't working, or you're thinking "I suck at this." The thing is, "awkward" is one of the key stages of beginning literally *anything*. Keep showing up, keep creating, because creating something special and authentic takes time, patience, and hard work.

A peach tree isn't valueless just because it doesn't have ripe peaches on it—it's just not the season for peaches right now. Keep growing, because peaches are on their way. Grow them for you, because your fuckyeah *isn't about us.*

THE STATUS QUO HATES CHANGE

Sometimes your fuckyeah is a bulldozer.

Except for the occasional stop-and-stare moment on the sidewalk, we don't really celebrate the bulldozer. The whole process of tearing down old structures is loud, messy, and really, *"Why does it take so long? Haven't they been tearing down this building for years???"* We don't want to look at the breakdown process; we put up fences with forest-green mesh to block out our view of the partially annihilated site of destruction. We want a new, shiny building to go up, *like now.* Sometimes people aren't ready for your fuckyeah bulldozer to knock the old structure down; sometimes they'll protest, put up signs, or tell you how awful you are for tearing down this historic building.

You know the question: "What would you do if you knew you could not fail?" I think it's misleading. I think we should ask the question differently:

Since you're inevitably going to fail and make mistakes in your lifetime, what's important enough for you to do anyway? And since, at some point, your Art will be met with significant resistance, what is important enough to you to create anyway?

Good ideas are always met with a ridiculous amount of resistance; *criticism means someone took notice.* Art is change; change ruins the status quo; our entire economic system is founded on the status quo—so the chances that someone will feel threatened by your fuck-yeah at some point? *Pretty high.*

Maybe it's the final nail in the coffin of an outdated idea or way of thinking—without you plowing through the old structure, an entire generation of new creators and thinkers wouldn't have the space to build. Activists and revolutionary thinkers set trends, create movements, and amaze us for good reason. They have the courage to make change, often being the first to do so. Someone has to be first, so why not you?

Sometimes your fuckyeah is a bulldozer—and we need you to ignore the haters (no matter how loud they are). Remember that the people hungry for your Art will eventually find you, support you, and upset the status quo with you, on purpose.

Rejection is an inevitable part of life. Not everyone is going to like you. That's okay, *because some of us will love you.* Not everyone will understand you. That's okay, *because some of us will truly see you. Life* would not be *life* if it didn't occasionally feel like shit was really hitting that proverbial fan. So what can you do? Keep moving. Keep looking for your ever-changing fuckyeah. Keep sharing today's version of your Art with the rest of us. It's worth it, I promise.

11.

REAL SELF-CARE

We've flirted with self-care for a while now, making self-care a New Year's resolution and reading books written by acne-free celebrities on the topic. Yoga and bubble baths, bee pollen shots and cold-pressed juice, setting boundaries with coworkers and Gwyneth Paltrow's skin-care regimen . . . Self-care is a de facto life goal at this point.

I have the luxury of joking about self-care being all these bougie, commercial things because I'm not . . . *uncared for.* I'm not starving, or in danger. I am privileged. Comfortable. I have time to joke about meaning, wellness, and the fountain of youth (which I'm pretty sure I found in a moisturizer). *But why* are we suddenly obsessed with this concept of self-care as a society?

Because we live in an era (and in a place, especially if you live in North America) that values the "self" above "the collective whole," and "personal choice" above "the greater good." Wealth and power used to be passed down through family name or inheritance—the powerful held land, titles, and property. Nowadays, however, power is slippery; it's liquid. "Wealth" is now a combination of cash, reputation, and exerting your power as an individual by *choosing what you buy.* Capitalism guarantees that there are thousands of ways for us to *buy* self-care (subscription boxes, apps, face masks, and the like) and thousands of purchases that can represent who we are as unique individuals. "The self" is all-powerful; we express ourselves by buying stuff and with online personas built around the "lives" we buy.

Don't worry, I'm not about to go on a rant about minimalism or anything. I just want us to be clear on where this self-care trend came from: *the market.*

At its worst, self-care is a marketing gimmick, invented to sell people like us all kinds of shit we don't need.

And it's not just "stuff," like organic charcoal whitening tooth powder, CBD tea for a better night's sleep, or a watermelon face serum (all shit I've bought, BTW)—it's *experiences* too. Everyday we're streaming, scrolling, and internalizing images of the self-care ideal: a satisfying career of your choosing, punctuated by photographable vacations, a ride-or-die squad of fun friends, and Zen weekends set aside for "me-time." We're being pitched a new version of the "American Dream"—*and many of us are totally unaware of it.*

What if you don't need a dreamy beach vacation to keep you from working too much, because you enforce healthy work boundaries naturally? What if you don't need a squad of lifelong friends, because your life affords you rotating but deep friendships that flex every year? What if you don't need a whole weekend of private "me-time" at some mountain retreat, because your twenty-minute nap gave you peace and relaxation?

For the record, taking better care of ourselves is a *great* idea; any one of the psychologists, neuroscientists, or researchers cited in this book would 100 percent agree that practicing real self-care will *vastly* improve our health and happiness.

But the market isn't interested in improving our health and happiness. The market exists to sell us things—more things than we'll ever need—and in order to create demand for this stuff, the market has to convince us we have secret, unmet needs and problems that need solving.

Self-care is just a crafty repackaging of work-life balance by the market.

Your life isn't a scale that needs balancing—and it definitely can't be broken down into compartments. Work, life, relationships, hobbies, friendships, physical health, mental health . . . these things are *too intertwined to be compartmentalized.*

Real self-care is an individual assessment of what nourishes you specifically—not your dentist, not the influencers you follow on Instagram, not your best friends—YOU.

Have you ever asked yourself what those things *really* are? Or *why* you think you need the life you think you need?

Let's be clear: I *like* that watermelon face serum I bought. We can take care of ourselves in a lot of different ways, and occasionally, that self-care can look like buying stuff. But what we're really looking for, and what we really need to ground ourselves, to sustain our joy, is *space.*

Freedom to take up space.

To feel embodied.

Room to breathe.

Mental quietness.

An inner reserve of energy.

Real self-care can be a revolutionary act of embodiment, a reclaiming of our bodies and lives as our own.

"Revolutionary act" may sound dramatic, but by that I mean that reclaiming your body, time, and boundaries can feel like you are standing up against centuries of oppressive social norms (especially if you identify as a woman, LGBTQ+, or person of color). Real self-care can be a courageous assertion of your value as a unique individual. It is prioritizing your mental health over pleasing other people and prioritizing your time over the frantic timeline of the market, the MF (and a culture that glorifies both). It is practicing self-compassion when you would normally sit in self-judgment, and honoring your personal boundaries rather than minimizing them for someone else.

Real self-care is practicing self-awareness (i.e., recognizing your boundaries), while the market's version of self-care is practicing self-centeredness (i.e., assuming the world revolves around you and your comfort level).

Practicing *real* self-care creates a deep sense of contentment, joy, and present-state awareness—an inner resource, filled moment by moment, that we can draw on as needed. It gives us the tools we need to bounce back faster from the shit that life loves to hurl our way; it's a spark of joy that can't be snuffed out.

So . . . if you can stomach the buzzwordiness of "self-care," then know that I'm talking about the *real* thing and not the market's gimmicky version—and remember that self-care is individualized, so you'll need to experiment to figure out what works for you.

We *could* start by talking about real self-care for your body. I could tell you about the science behind why you should exercise, eat whole, minimally processed foods, and drink what would probably feel like your body weight in water; how to get necessary vitamin D from your time spent in the sun; or ways to get deep, restorative, uninterrupted sleep—but you already see the common sense behind those suggestions. Thankfully, there's plenty of accessible scientific research available on why, and how, we can take better care of our bodies, and you don't need my help to discover it.

You may, however, appreciate some help understanding how to take care of your *mind*—and especially, what to do with all your ever-present and uber-complicated emotions. I know I did.

Real self-care begins by *dealing* with *feeling*.

"THE FEELS"

Did you know that every emotion—that you've ever experienced—was produced by a chemical? A CHEMICAL, YOU GUYS.

Love, fear, guilt, anger, lust, disappointment, courage, jealousy, interest, pride, excitement, trust, and everything else—all the result of chemical reactions generating our moods, forming our life experiences, and coloring our memories.

There are dozens of hormones and neurotransmitters involved in creating our emotions, but we can boil it all down to just a handful of key players: the feelings that contribute to what we'd call happiness are run by four primary chemicals (*serotonin, dopamine, oxytocin, endorphins*), while most of our negative emotions are run by three (*adrenaline, noradrenaline,* and *cortisol*—along with any imbalance of the "happy" chemicals).

Our emotions are automatic; they're the body's way of saying, "YO! This is important." They're the chemical equivalents of little red flags for our brains, an evolutionary fail-safe, motivating us to do things in our species's best interest (you know, eating, sleeping, makin' babies, avoiding death, and so on). They're primitive and lightning fast because they originate from deep within our subconscious Autopilot Brains.

While your body prefers to communicate with the chemical language of "emotion," your brain communicates using the language of "thought." In fact, a feeling is always the chemical *translation* of a thought:

Your thoughts are chemical reactions that create your emotions.

Autopilot Brain translates thoughts into emotions, transmitting that message throughout our bodies. This can feel positive (like noticing how clear and blue the sky looks today; that's translated into the relaxation response and the emotion of *awe*)—or this can feel negative (like noticing how blisteringly hot the stove top is on your fingertips; that's translated into the fight-or-flight response and the emotion of *fear*). And since we can't be aware of all of our thoughts (*cool, thanks, Autopilot*), some of our emotions and moods will feel like they came out of nowhere.

But they didn't. *A thought came before a feeling, every time.*

**If you're wondering where your mood came from, ask your-
self, "What's the last thought I remember having?"**

Real self-care requires self-awareness, but our emotions can be
annoyingly opaque to understand. *Am I just bored or truly depressed?
Why am I suddenly overwhelmed and distracted? How can I hang on to
the peace of mind I felt on my last vacation?*

Getting answers to these questions starts with an understanding of
how your positive and negative emotions work, and once you realize
you have the power to *change* these emotions and moods, waking up
each morning and thinking, *"Fuck yeah!"* won't sound so outrageous
(or so cheesy).

Let's start by learning about how to ramp up the good vibes,
shall we?

GOOD VIBES ONLY

Negative emotions like anxiety or rage *narrow* our focus and prepare
us to behave in a certain way (like flee the scene or throw a punch).
They give us tunnel vision, making them great for emergencies and
horrible for literally any other situation.

On the other hand, *pos-emotions* (aka positive emotions, I feel like
abbreviating) like joy or contentment *broaden* our focus, giving us
clearer thoughts and more mental resources to draw from in the
moment. Research shows that people experiencing positive emotions have thought patterns that are diverse, flexible, creative, inclu-
sive, efficient, and receptive to information; that kind of openness
builds their physical, mental, and social resources, ultimately making them more resilient.

Dr. Barbara L. Fredrickson, who coined the "broaden and build" theory of positive emotions in the late 1990s—and who was named the thirteenth most influential psychologist alive today—helped prove that fleeting pos-emotions don't just make us temporarily happy; they also multiply and create inner resources that improve our health *in the long term*.

I mean, yeah, IT'S KIND OF OBVIOUS that *neg-emotions* (again, I'm abbreviating) would have negative effects on your health and happiness, while pos-emotions would have positive effects. But you might not know this:

Pos-emotions actually undo the damaging physical and psychological effects caused by neg-emotions.

Studies show that people who focus on something positive during a stressful experience can immediately undo the racing heart rate, elevated cortisol, and other FOF (fight-or-flight) side effects that wreak havoc on the body. Pos-emotions also undo the narrowed attention and tunnel vision caused by neg-emotions, restoring flexible thinking and creativity.

That means that emotions like playfulness, interest, love, and tranquility can actually *erase the damage* caused by emotions like fear, anger, jealousy, and disappointment.

>> *"Great, but . . . how am I supposed to suddenly feel positive about everything all the time?"*

You're not.

This is important: feeling happy about everything all the time is unrealistic. **Happiness is an ongoing process**, just like exercise is an ongoing process. We can't just exercise once and be healthy the rest of our lives, although I desperately wish that were the case (*hates the gym with a burning passion*). Nobody is suggesting you detach from reality or fake your way into happiness. While it's impossible to be "happy about everything all the time," we do know, thanks to extensive research, that it is possible to *learn* optimism—meaning we don't have to be naturally cheerful to turn our moods around. That's a huge deal.

But you should know, pos-emotions are different from pleasure. The good feelings you get from a cold drink of water, an uninterrupted night's sleep, or a blissful orgasm come from satisfying a physical need, *not from a pos-emotion.*

Why would this distinction matter? Because if we want the health benefits of pos-emotions, we don't want to go looking for them in the wrong place. And we often do; when we don't know how to deal with the neg-emotions stirred up in our lives, it's easy to confuse pleasure with happiness. This is why we might binge-drink with friends after a stressful week at work, "eat our feelings" after a tough breakup, or lose ourselves scrolling through our social media feed—distractions temporarily numb our negative feelings. But, unchecked, these kinds of behaviors can lead to a buildup of unresolved neg-emotions (and in some cases, mental and physical illness, even addiction). The solution? Chase pos-emotions instead of pleasure.

THE TOP TEN
POS-EMOTIONS TO SEEK OUT

1. JOY

Happiness is spontaneous. The easiest way to get it? Play. Goof off. Give yourself permission to enjoy the stuff you think you're too old for. Experiment, explore, and wander. Do things that have a surprise element, because discovering something new can trigger joy.

2. GRATITUDE

Think of gratitude as *savoring life*. You know when you take a bite of something, and it's so delicious that it stops you in your tracks? You're like, "Holy shit—this is SO good—this is the best sandwich I've ever had!" That's savoring. Next time you're doing something fun, treat it like that sandwich. Stop and think about how great the moment is, even if it doesn't last forever. Bonus points for writing it down; your head and heart will thank you.

Multiple studies confirm that people who expressed gratitude in writing on a daily basis (by listing "three good things" that happened each day for a week, for example) scored significantly higher in measurements of well-being—including improved mood, physical health, and positive outlook on their lives—in comparison with neutral control groups and groups assigned to document their life's hassles. Plus, the subjects' well-being *continued* to climb, and depression levels continued to decrease the longer they practiced documenting those "three good things."

3. SERENITY

Aka *calm, tranquility, peace*. This is the pos-emotion I feel on a sunny, obligation-free Saturday, laying on a picnic blanket by the lake with an ice-cold beer in one hand and a really good book in the other. It's the thing that makes you sigh really deeply because you're happy doing nothing at all. Serenity can be found any time you relish the present moment you're in, and it's easier to find if you aren't filling every waking second of your day with multitasking and distractions.

4. CURIOSITY

Aka *interest*, curiosity is the excited feeling you get about digging in, learning more, or trying something new. Adults are trained to shoot down our curiosity unless the thing we're interested in will pay the bills or make us look good on paper. How well has that strategy served you so far? Ramp up your good vibes by getting curious about as much as possible, including your mistakes—because *mistakes aren't failure; they're research*, remember? Learn as much as you can, on purpose. It will make you happier.

5. HOPE

This underrated emotion is special because it's one of two pos-emotions you can access even when shit is *aggressively* hitting the proverbial fan. Hope is stirred up whenever you see new perspectives on a situation that would otherwise bum you out, bringing together your Pilot Brain (with a conscious focus on gratitude and how "things could be worse") and your Autopilot Brain (activating its emotional center by imagining better, future scenarios); once you open that mental door, hope builds your resilience and helps you problem-solve with a clear head.

6. PRIDE

Think of pride as a surge of satisfaction and sense of possibility created by the good mood chemical, serotonin, whenever you celebrate your accomplishments or the accomplishments of others. It's the feeling behind "because I pulled this off, I can do anything!" Perfectionism works directly against this emotion, so if you're struggling to acknowledge your accomplishment, check to see if you're feeling ashamed (and then follow the steps in "How to Deal: Shame" in chapter 7 to tell Shame to go fuck itself). If you want to experience more pride, celebrate the little wins in your own life, and encourage and champion others as often as you can.

7. AMUSEMENT

Aka *laughter*. Like gratitude, amusement can't work its magic if you fake it (studies show the brain can *instantly* distinguish a fake smile from a real one and fake laughter from real laughter). It's simple: find things to *really* laugh about, especially with other people, because we laugh more often with others than by ourselves. Play will help you with this one too.

8. INSPIRATION

This is a sense of wonder combined with motivation. Inspiration introduces us to something we didn't know was possible, like some epic feat of human engineering, art, or an idea that changes our perspective. The best way to get inspired? Experiment and explore.

9. AWE

A lot like inspiration, awe is a sense of wonder, but it makes us feel *closer* to others or to our environment. It's a willingness to accept that we can't know or understand everything, and it's the capacity to *enjoy* the sense of smallness we experience when something awe-inspiring happens—like when watching a massive wave crash on the shore, or a baby being born. Awe is a be-here-now emotion. When we are willing to look for our form of WooWoo, awe is within reach.

10. LOVE

This is the most common of the pos-emotions, since all of them can be wrapped up in and reinforced by love. It's also the second of the two pos-emotions you can access even when shit is hitting the proverbial fan—circumstances don't have to go your way for you to experience love for yourself, for someone else, and from others. There are many kinds of love—friendship, passionate love, respect—and all forms make us healthier and happier. Remember that love is more than a noun—it's also a verb—so seek out ways to love yourself and others, rather than waiting for love to "happen to you." And accept help, kindness, and love from others.

And these are just the top ten! There are countless variations of pos-emotions, and all of them build on each other to multiply our inner resources and make us resilient in the long term.

THE UPWARD SPIRAL

As I said earlier, you don't have to be naturally cheerful or genetically predisposed to optimism to turn your moods around. Here's why: *upward spirals*.

This will all make more sense if I start by describing something you're much more familiar with: *the downward spiral*.

We all know negativity is a self-propelling cycle. There's no clearer example of that than the procrastination brought on by depression. This involuntary negative spiral starts with thoughts like *"I don't feel like it. I won't feel better if I try. I shouldn't force myself to do something I don't want to do. I'll just lie here awhile. Distracting myself with TV will help me forget about the stress. Sleep will help me calm down."* These kinds of thoughts can create emotions of boredom, guilt, apathy, self-hatred, discouragement, and worthlessness, which then lead to more negativity and inaction. Over time, the repetitive choice to avoid social activities, people, work, and challenges whenever possible has consequences: you can become isolated from your friends (which may convince you that no one likes you) and disconnected from your work (which could leave you feeling that you're not enough), dragging you deeper into negative thoughts and paralysis. THAT, my friends, is a downward spiral.

An upward spiral is the exact opposite: it pulls you up and out of the negativity pit, empowers you, energizes you, and fuels your creativity. And the reason this upward spiral thing is a big deal?

Because for a long time, scientists didn't think it was possible.

See, up until the 1980s, researchers thought that positive emotions were just the *absence* of negative emotions. If negativity was subtraction, draining a person's inner resources, then positivity must be like addition, adding to their inner resources. You can't really blame them; up until that point, most emotion-based research had been done on neg-emotions like fear and anger. The breakthrough came with Dr. Fredrickson's research, when she and her colleagues realized that positivity is *nonlinear*; it's not one cause leading to one effect—it's one cause with many effects, spiraling out in all directions. In other words,

Negative emotions are like subtraction—but positive emotions are more like multiplication.

An upward spiral is simple, really. Let's say I engage in a positive behavior like exercising in yoga class. This feeds my three psych needs, and that experience creates pos-emotions that build my unconscious motivation to go to yoga again. Here's the weird part: In addition to convincing me that yoga class is fun, pos-emotions are opening my mind (making my thoughts more creative and flexible) and building my inner resources (like motivation and resilience). All the good vibes that got me to go to yoga in the first place get stronger and stronger, making me want to go again—**and** also motivate me to try new things, **and** meet new people, **and** smile for no reason. And THAT my friends, is an upward spiral.

No matter how big or how small, any form of positivity *multiplies* upon itself.

> >> *"But what if your life is just an endless parade of unfortunate, frustrating circumstances? And what if you're a natural-born pessimist?"*

Life will always have frustrating and tough circumstances. The good news? You don't need to avoid pain at all costs or change your personality to be happier; you just need to get the positivity ball *rolling*.

By experimenting more, you'll discover new things that make you happy and give you moments to savor. The best part? Even if you try something and realize you hate it, you're still left with the pos-emotion of *empowerment*, because choosing to experiment or explore is an exercise in autonomy, and by proving to ourselves that we can take risks or learn something new, we build our confidence.

You don't have to be cheerful to find fuckyeah; you only need to practice experimentation and appreciate what makes you happy. And then do more of it, because this will trigger an upward spiral.

Because pos-emotions multiply once you put the upward spiral in motion, they create an inner well of perspective and resilience that we can draw on whenever life gets difficult, helping us bounce back faster.

That said, there will always be a little lizard in your head, and sometimes that primal side of you can get "triggered" by the difficult parts of life—enough to hijack your rational thoughts and override your focus, flooding your mind and body with neg-emotions like anxiety, frustration, rage, or sadness. Though pursuing pos-emotions will transform your life, Autopilot will *still* find reasons to throw shit directly at the fan—so it helps to know how to deal with those dark and twisty "feels."

Let's calm your lizard brain.

THE THING ABOUT AUTOPILOT MOVIES

Your mind is a movie theater, and there's always something playing.

If your surroundings are familiar and there's nothing survival-based to occupy your attention, Autopilot Brain will start remembering, imagining, visualizing, or worrying. And sometimes those films spiral into some dark alternate endings—M. Night Shyamalan twist endings. This sends confusing messages to your body, starting and stopping the cortisol stress response in tiny doses, slowly rising in severity. These upsetting mental movies on a loop create the slow-burn neg-emotions that we know as *worry, anxiety, stress, nervousness, frustration, irritation, tension, disappointment*, and the like.

All our negative feelings are created by a mental movie about a past or present experience that we believe will lead to future unhappiness.

For example, losing a job might make you feel instantly afraid that you won't have enough money to eat or pay rent. That fear leads Autopilot to compress and shortcut "losing job" to mean "future threat to my survival and happiness," played out in a negative mental movie. It's at this moment that adrenaline and cortisol step in—*"Hey! Is that a threat? We know what to do!"*—and suddenly your brain is soaked in the fight-or-flight (FOF) chemicals, even though there was no *immediate* danger. By temporarily paralyzing your prefrontal cortex (in Pilot Brain) with FOF chemicals, cortisol and adrenaline override your "happy" chemicals, making you experience projected neg-emotions from the future *right now.*

But in reality, you can't be *certain* that you won't find another job or that you won't be able to pay your rent. I mean, can you *predict the future*? Of course not. But your lizard thinks it can. This becomes a self-fulfilling cycle: the unhappiness we're afraid *might* be waiting for us rushes in to meet us, and the disappointment we're worried we *might* feel if we fail in the future rushes into "the now" *before we ever try to do anything.* Here's why these mental movies can be dangerous:

Your Autopilot Brain will filter your present moment with the "color code" (emotional tone) of whatever your last mental movie was.

Say you were running late to work this morning, so Autopilot sent a low-key FOF response through your body. Not life-or-death level, just a feeling of *"HURRY!"* You had to make a quick decision on which route to work would be faster, so you visualized your options, creating a mental movie of various traffic routes to do so. Because of the chemical emotions moving through your body while Autopilot directed this movie, a *"HURRY!"* filter was applied to every traffic scenario you envisioned.

A few hours into your workday, the adrenaline (from being late) will have worn off, but *"HURRY"* was the last filter applied to the last mental movie Autopilot ran. So, when you envision yourself presenting at the mid-morning meeting, the *"HURRY"* filter is applied—leaving you convinced that you're not prepared to lead the meeting. And later, during your lunch break, the *"HURRY"* filter is applied, leaving you with feelings of resentment over your job because your lunch break "felt too short." Even though your rushed morning is totally unrelated to your preparedness for the meeting or the length of your lunch break, you can't help but *feel* stressed, rushed, and frustrated.

Does it seem ridiculous that running a little late could stress you out for the remainder of your day? It is. But Autopilot Brain can't help but create drama. *Autopilot Brain thinks the HURRY color code is helping you.*

Unfortunately, if you're not careful, Pilot Brain can make Autopilot Brain's drama worse.

Instead of noticing that this HURRY-colored alarm has unnecessarily stressed you out, Pilot Brain might join the negativity party with a *conscious* self-defeating, negative, or helpless thought like *"I'm always running behind for some stupid reason . . . I'll never get my shit together."* That thought will then be translated into the language of emotion, hitting your body with a wave of chemical negativity (adrenaline and cortisol). Your brain, in turn, will respond with escalated emotions and darker thoughts, creating a downward spiral of negativity.

The good news? This downward spiral isn't a given. By engaging both our conscious and subconscious minds, we can flip the script and create an upward spiral instead. But to do that, we first need to recognize a bad mood for what it truly is: Autopilot's unnecessary, end-of-the-world-as-we-know-it, sometimes Oscar-bait and sometimes MTV's *Jersey Shore*, hyper-exaggerated *drama*.

THE LOST-IN-TRANSLATION LIST

Things can get easily lost in translation between the languages of thought and emotion, giving us a false impression of ourselves, our lives, and the world. These false impressions lead us to misinterpret our reality (creating what psychologists call *cognitive distortions*). These distortions are a normal part of being human, but they're also why a life lived solely on Autopilot makes you miserable.

Here's what it feels like when reality gets lost in translation:

THE APOCALYPSE

You blow things way out of proportion; a single negative thought, event, or moment feels like a *catastrophe*. Your mistakes, or someone else's accomplishments, are Godzilla-size. This is the end as you know it.

THE BLIP

You *shrink* things way out of proportion; a single thought, event, or moment feels meaningless or microscopic. Your positive qualities and skills, or someone else's mistakes, are barely a blip on your radar. You (and your accomplishments) feel insignificant, valueless, or worthless, especially in comparison to other people (and their achievements).

THE HARD EVIDENCE

You overgeneralize something; a single negative example feels like hard evidence of an endless pattern of shittiness. For example, a bad grade on a test is evidence that you're "stupid" and "bad at school"; a painful breakup is proof that you'll "never find the one."

THE DISQUALIFIER

Your positive traits, thoughts, moments, and experiences "don't count." Good things are an exception to the negative rule; you apply this to yourself or other people. For example, your boss praises your hard work on a project, and instead of receiving the compliment, you deflect, saying, "It wasn't me; it was all so-and-so's work/idea." Everything good comes with a catch; someone's kind gesture must mean they want something from you.

THE PSYCHIC

You jump to conclusions; you're sure you know what other people are thinking (like, "Everyone knows I'm a fraud"). You also think you can predict the future: Things will turn out badly. They always do. It's a fact.

THE LABELER

A thought, moment, or behavior seems to require a label (like, "I've always been a fuckup" or "He's just an asshole"). This one comes loaded with shame either about yourself or directed at someone else.

THE SHIT-COLORED GLASSES

The opposite of rose-colored glasses, where a single negative trait or event takes over your focus, coloring your view of the world and your whole day—Autopilot's mental movies gone rogue. An intense emotion filters into the rest of your reality ("I feel X; therefore, Y must be true too").

THE PERFECTIONIST

It's all or nothing. Black or white. Always or never. Negative events feel permanent; positive ones seem fleeting.

THE SHOULDS AND SHOULD NOTS

You bury yourself under a sense of obligation: shoulds, musts, can'ts, and so on. Since you can't always follow these rules, you feel like you deserve punishment; guilt and shame tag along with this distortion. You often think about all the things other people should and should not have, do, or be, creating resentment, anger, and frustration toward them.

THE MARTYR

You believe you are somehow the cause of an external event that you could not have been the primary cause of. Guilt, worthlessness, and shame follow. Worst case: You believe yourself omnipresent when it comes to causing harm, but helpless when it comes to doing good.

Familiar, right? Whether you're aware of them or not, *your thoughts are creating your emotions*, and your emotions can create these distortions of reality. Anger, fear, disappointment, frustration, envy, anxiety—whether justifiable or not, *the suffering caused by these emotions is rarely necessary.*

Bad moods are not something you have to accept; they're a symptom of thinking something negative and choosing to believe it.[1]

Don't worry, I'm not about to tell you to plaster a fake smile on your face and act like life is never difficult. Learning to manage our dark and twisty mental movies has nothing to do with fake cheerfulness.

---

[1] *The negative thought patterns and emotions that accompany any mental illness, including depression, are never "a choice." No one chooses a mental disorder, and I want it to be abundantly clear that mental illness is never a personal failure. Though we don't choose our brain chemistry, thankfully, all disorders are treatable, and most professional treatment includes training patients in "cognitive reappraisal," or learning to reassess their automatic, destructive thoughts.*

Our skewed, negative views of reality don't need to be permanent, but to change our perspective and mood, we have to get our Pilot Brains involved, via what cognitive behavioral psychologists call "reappraisal": *consciously and intentionally changing our thoughts.*

The positive side effects of reappraisal include a boost in energy, self-esteem, and mental health; it's been used by therapists and psychologists all over the world to help millions of people overcome everything from bad moods to full-blown clinical depression. It also completely changed my life. Wanna give it a shot?

HOW TO DEAL: "THE FEELS"

If it feels like you've just been bitch-slapped by your neg-emotions, start by trying "third person self-talk." This is a strategy that puts distance between ourselves and our thoughts, making it easier to deal with both. Honestly, whenever I'm freaking out about something, I try this first, because I almost always end up laughing off my whole inner freak-out. So, what are the magical steps?

There's just one: talk about your mood and automatic Inner Cynic thoughts, with yourself, in the third person. *It's mortifying.*

>> *"Alexis is irritated and tense. Alexis can't understand why her boss thinks it's fine to continue to reschedule their quarterly meetings, or to show up to today's meeting late. They obviously don't care about Alexis, or value her hard work. They must think they're better than Alexis and her team . . . Okay, no, there's probably a good reason for this, but Alexis is frustrated . . ."*

HAHAHAHAHAHA! Apparently, I think I'm a mind reader. I have no evidence of any of this; unexpected circumstances have nothing to do with my value. Let's enjoy the day.

We rarely talk to ourselves in complete sentences—and never in the third person. But that's why psychologists recommend this strategy, including for people who have suffered extreme psychological trauma—even PTSD—because creating mental distance between yourself and your emotions helps you deal with them. So . . . get ready to laugh at your internal freak-outs.

If you're still genuinely pissed, despondent, or stressed after using the third person self-talk strategy, you probably just went through something truly stressful and should follow the upcoming steps.

STEP 1: HOW DO YOU FEEL?

Can't figure out why you're in a bad mood? Ask yourself, *"What's the last thought I remember having?"* You might not be able to remember the exact thought that triggered an emotional reaction in your body, but I bet you can figure out the *vibe* your most recent mental (horror) movie had and work backward from there. What scenarios were running in your mind? Were you worrying, planning, or imagining something negative recently?

>> **Current Mood:** *Tense. Irritated. Snippy.*

>> **Last Thoughts:** *"This meeting will never end. I'll never get out of here on time. Traffic is always shitty; I'm going to be late to dinner tonight with my friends. They're going to think I don't care about them. Why do I always do this?"*

STEP 2: AUTOMATIC THOUGHTS AND THE INNER CYNIC

Now that you know how you feel and what triggered it, we're going to practice "reappraisal" by acknowledging our automatic thoughts; checking to see if any of them have fallen prey to those cognitive distortions (aka the Lost-in-Translation List) that happen whenever Autopilot applies a neg-emotion filter to one of our mental movies; and finally, engaging Pilot Brain by consciously arguing against those distorted, dark, and twisty thoughts we have, changing our mood in the process.

Take a piece of paper (yep, we're writing again!) and make three columns. Label the first column *Automatic Thoughts*; label the second column *Lost in Translation*; and label the third *Self-Defense*.

AUTOMATIC THOUGHTS	LOST IN TRANSLATION	SELF-DEFENSE
"This meeting will never end. I'll never get out of here on time. Traffic is always shitty; I'm going to be late to dinner tonight with my friends. They're going to think I don't care about them. Why do I always do this?"	The Apocalypse	"This meeting will end. It's not the apocalypse if it ends late or if I leave late."
	The Hard Evidence	"Sometimes traffic is rough; sometimes it's smooth sailing. I have no proof I'll be late to dinner, and if it looks like I will, I can just text my friends and give them a heads-up, apologizing. No big deal."
	The Psychic	"They know I care about them; this planned dinner is proof! I'm not a mind reader. If I'm worried I hurt their feelings I can straight-up ask them."
	The Perfectionist	"I don't always do this. Sometimes I'm late because of circumstances out of my control. I've done nothing wrong, and even if I had, I could forgive myself. I'm human."

Automatic Thoughts: In this column, write the thoughts you remember having around the time you started feeling shitty. In step 1 you were focused on how you *feel*, but now, in this step, you're writing any *automatic thoughts* you recall having *before* you started feeling this way. Your emotional state is real and valid, but arguing against how you *feel* is pointless. Instead, we need to deal with the *thoughts* that created this garbage mood by uncovering if you have a distorted reality.

Lost in Translation: Now run through the Lost-in-Translation List, and see if you recognize any "cognitive distortions" (i.e., The Apocalypse, The Blip, The Hard Evidence, The Disqualifier, The Psychic, The Labeler, The Shit-Colored Glasses, The Perfectionist, The Shoulds and Should Nots, The Martyr) in the automatic thoughts you just wrote down. List any reality distortions that apply in the Lost in Translation column.

Blowing things a ~smidge~ out of proportion, right? "This meeting will *never* end" (The Apocalypse). Lots of *always* and *nevers* in those thoughts: "I'll *never* get out of here on time," "Traffic is *always* shitty," and "Why do I *always* do this?" (The Perfectionist and The Hard Evidence). Some attempts at mind-reading and future-telling: "*They're going* to think I don't care about them," and "*I'm going* to be late to dinner tonight" (The Psychic). There's also shame behind that last thought; "Why do I always do this?" (The Perfectionist).

Self-Defense: Just like when dealing with limiting beliefs, you and your Inner Cynic are not on the same team anymore—time to represent yourself fairly and shoot down some of this "evidence" with rational thought. Remember, it's not about countering an automatic thought like "I never do anything right" with glitter and rainbows. If you're feeling dark and twisty, you're not going to believe statements like "I am a magical sunbeam of perfection." Write something *practical* in the third column; think like an attorney who wants to win the case.

After completing all three columns, check in again with how you feel—you'll be surprised by how quickly the intensity of your neg-emotions fades.

Does this exercise seem excessive and embarrassing? I AGREE.

But this strategy is *exactly* aggressive enough to combat the dark and twisty neg-emotions that can accidentally ruin your day, self-esteem, or *life*. Reappraisal is Pilot Brain's way of pumping the emotional brakes when Autopilot Brain has mistranslated a thought into a bout of "The Feels"—and I guarantee being this methodical about your blown-out-of-proportion thoughts will help with chilling the hell out.

This wordy, in-depth, borderline excessive "How to Deal" strategy is a powerful tool to wake up your Pilot Brain and get Autopilot's mental horror movies in check, but the most reliable way to deal with your *feels* is by shifting your mind into a neutral space, *bringing yourself back to the NOW.*

Neg-emotions are created by some kind of movie looping in your head—leaving you stuck recalling and rehashing the past, or lost trying to imagine the future. But when we're in the present, we're incapable of fearing the future or regretting the past, because we're forced to see our world *as it is* in this very moment. Feeling *here, now* can not only have an extremely calming effect on you both mentally and physically, but it can also change the direction of your mood *spiral*—bringing you back from the negativity pit, up to neutral and calm in the present, and finally forward into an upward spiral of good vibes.

Can human beings eradicate shit moods and dark thoughts forever? Nope. But as a former living, breathing Mood Swing (I mean, my astrological sign is Cancer), I can tell you that the following strategy is basically *magic.*

Borderline WooWoo, even.

BE HERE, NOW

Think of a moment in your life when you felt totally aware of *being alive.*

Maybe it was walking along the beach, feeling the breeze on your face, realizing that you're standing on the edge of a continent. Maybe it was bouncing your beautiful baby boy to sleep, looking at his ridiculously long eyelashes, and feeling his tiny and powerful heart beating. Maybe it was standing on a sidewalk corner, eating a scalding hot slice of greasy perfection (aka New York pizza), while people-watching in absolute peace. Or maybe you hate the beach, will never reproduce, and are disgusted by pizza.

Even so, I bet you've experienced some kind of "cue" that shifted your focus from the past or future to the *here and now.* What if you could cultivate these moments intentionally, instead of needing life to hand them to you at random?

You can. Scientists call this *mindfulness.*

Mindfulness is a type of mental exercise that puts distance between yourself and your automatic thoughts, creating clarity, calm, and space in your otherwise noisy brain.

It's intentionally taking your mind out of Autopilot's mind-wandering, drama-filled mental movie mode and back into the conscious and present moment (a mode overseen by Pilot Brain)—and in case you're wondering, *yes*, this is like 90 percent of what meditation is.

Extensive studies have been done on both the long- and short-term effects of mindfulness practice, and it's borderline MAGIC, guys. Mindfulness significantly improves mood, attention, thinking, memory, creativity, test scores (yes, really), and even glucose regulation for people with diabetes. Mindfulness *substantially reduces* mind-wandering, stress, blood pressure, fatigue, anxiety, depression, the risk for depression, and the likelihood of becoming depressed again; it also reduces the risk factors for cardiovascular disease and obesity. It reduces activation of the amygdala (the source of all our scared-shitless emotions, a part of Autopilot Brain), increases activation of the prefrontal cortex (the intuitive, intentional part of your Pilot Brain), and even increases hippocampal gray matter density (translation: it makes a piece of your brain *smarter*).

Studies show that any mindfulness technique, whether thought of as a spiritual practice or not, will improve your physical health and mental state—because all forms of mindfulness can elicit the body's relaxation response (RR).

You'll recall the RR is the *opposite* of the FOF response; it's a state of deep relaxation that "turns up the volume" on energy, healthy metabolism, and youthfulness, and "turns down the volume" on stress pathways and inflammation (the cause of most diseases). Just as pos-emotions cancel out the damaging effects of neg-emotions, the RR cancels out the residual effects of stress by relaxing muscles, lowering heart and breathing rates, reducing blood pressure, and decreasing activity in the sympathetic nervous system (the one pumping high levels of adrenaline and cortisol into your bloodstream). So how do we initiate this magical relaxation response? With a meditative focus on positive thoughts and words (like the affirmations we talked about in chapter 5)—or by practicing mindfulness.

Practicing mindfulness is simple: zoom in or zoom out.

Washing the dishes? Stop daydreaming, planning, remembering, or worrying for a second, and *zoom waaay in.*

What does the sloshy water *sound* like? How does it *feel* to pop the bubbles clinging to your hands? How *heavy* is the plate you're holding? What does the dish soap *smell* like? By *zooming in* on physical, experiential details of the moment you're in, you are teaching your Autopilot to create and hold mental space, rather than flood your mind with automatic thoughts.

Mindfulness as a mental exercise is simple, but not easy. It's hard to stay zoomed in on the present moment for long—and you'll *always* start daydreaming again. The trick is to zoom out from your automatic thoughts and start again.

Have you ever gotten lost in an amazing film, totally absorbed in the story? It's not until someone's phone starts buzzing obnoxiously that you're brought back to reality and become consciously aware again that you're in a movie theater. *Zooming out* is recognizing that your automatic thoughts have taken over and pulled you out of the present moment and into a mental movie.

Mindfulness is practicing zooming out from your future- or past-focused thoughts in order to zoom in on the physical world around you.

Here's an example:

>> *You're walking to the grocery store.*

Zoom In: "The air feels cold on my face. I hear a lot of birds singing different kinds of songs; three so far. The diesel fuel from this bus smells sweet and bitter—"

(**gets caught up in automatic thoughts and pulled out of the present**)

"What do we need from the store? TP, bread . . . should get stuff to prep lunch, don't want to think about cooking this week, need to finish that term paper . . . ugh, I'm never going to finish on time . . ."

Zoom Out: "Oops. Okay, let's try this again . . ."

There's no point in being pissed about your automatic thoughts; just come back to the present moment when you realize you're having them. This takes practice. But the important thing to remember about mindfulness? It's a *nonjudgmental* act.

When a camera zooms in or zooms out, it doesn't judge what it's looking at; it just observes it. When practicing mindfulness, you are the camera.

By intentionally zooming *out* from Autopilot's automatic thoughts and zooming *in* on Pilot Brain's here and now experience of the world, you can create—and hold—mental space, a practice that has the power to transform your life.

If we want to hang on to the happiness we find, we have to *practice* getting our Autopilot and Pilot Brains to work together. When it comes to our moods and emotions, it's important to remember that they're not an automatic consequence of things that "happen to us"; they're created by our subconscious Autopilot thoughts. They're temporary, and we *create* how we feel. By engaging our Pilot Brain by chasing down pos-emotions through experimentation and savoring them, exercising conscious reappraisal (like the "How to Deal" exercise from earlier), and practicing mindfulness by actively zooming in on the present moment, we're training ourselves how to be, and stay, happy.

And that's the thing: happiness is learning how to be alive *on purpose.*

12.

LIFE ON PURPOSE

"Thirty spokes join one hub.
The wheel's use comes from emptiness.
Clay is fired to make a pot,
The pot's use comes from emptiness.
Windows and doors are cut to make a room.
The room's use comes from emptiness.
Therefore,
Having leads to profit,
Not having leads to use."

(Ancient Chinese philosopher and poet Lao Tzu got it.)

You can't drink from a glass of water unless you have an empty glass to pour the water in; you need *empty* space before you can *fill* a space. What Lao and I are trying to say is,

You have to create and hold space for the life you want to lead.

Fullness begins with a kind of emptiness; if we want to live our lives *fulfilled*, then we need to *make room*. But nature abhors a void, right? Whenever there's space, something wants to rush in to fill it. Whether it's space in the cosmic vacuum or space in your schedule, *something will rush in to fill it*. That's the reality of our universe, and why "holding space" is so important to our well-being; if we aren't careful, we won't have any say in what rushes in to fill our lives.

Unfortunately, the market has convinced us that the *space* we crave—feeling comfortable in our own skin, mental quietness, an inner reserve of energy—can't be created; it must be *bought*.

The market offers us instant spirituality, fully optimized free time, and perfectly packaged "life hacks"—and we're throwing our money at these meditation apps, morning journals, vitamin packs, and productivity software because most of the time, *these tools work*. These kinds of products can help us create the habit of truly taking care of ourselves, and that's important in a culture that has, until very recently, idolized working ourselves to death.

But there's an important difference between self-care *habits* and self-care *products*.

Like anything else in our lives, routines, books, classes, bubble baths, and superfoods will rush in to grab our attention and fill our schedules—unless we learn how to *create* and *hold* space for our fuckyeah.

So how do you make room for the life you want to lead? With *intention*. You try to live the entirety of your life *on purpose*. This doesn't mean pretending you have all the answers; it means, in addition to consciously practicing awareness of your thoughts and feels (mindfulness) and setting lofty goals, you can explore, play, and bring wonder into your life *deliberately*.

You don't have "a" purpose—but you can live on purpose.

If we want to design our dream lives and make room for them, we can't just *go through the motions*, living fully on Autopilot. We can't go on believing that our life circumstances or emotions *happen to us* or that we have as little control as a plastic bag blowing in the wind (my post-Internet brain is glitching on which reference to make: Katy Perry's song lyric or that scene in *American Beauty*!?). *We're* building our reality. We have to live intentionally—as creators, not spectators—because finding fuckyeah is something we'll do over and over, and *that's a good thing.* What brings us joy will change because *we* are change.

If you want to know how to find fuckyeah—whether for the first time or for the millionth time—start by living with intention.

But you can't set an *intention* unless you know what's occupying your *attention.*

SHINY OBJECTS

Imagine you're sitting at a desk, working at your computer. You've got what, four or five browser tabs open? Maybe a news tab, an incognito Twitter window, a random link you opened from a previous email, a Google Docs tab, plus your inbox, along with an email window (drafted in reply to someone who insisted it was "urgent"). In addition, you might have a couple of documents open to occasionally reference, as well as a running Slack chat or IM convo with coworkers.

Suddenly, a text message lights up your phone screen, pulling your eyes down from the computer. You shoot back a quick reply, also noticing an Instagram notification hovering over the app's icon; you open the app and read it. You scroll through your feed and eventually remember where you are. Your eyes dart back to the computer screen and your inbox: *"What was I doing again? Oh. Right…"*

There are plenty of things competing for our attention—11 million bits of information *per second*, as you know. But on our best *second*, you and I can only handle 120 bits at a time. Sure, Autopilot Brain works hard to bridge the 10 million–plus bit-size gap by filling in the blanks—and it does a damn fine job of it too. But no matter how fast and automatic this network in your brain is, *it is not a computer.* It's a brain.

It gets tired.

The neurons responsible for constantly monitoring your environment and helping you decide what to focus on are *living* cells that need oxygen and glucose to function. They burn energy, just like the rest of your body. You know what costs a lot of energy? *Paying attention.* That's why we call it "paying" attention; it costs us both energy and time to focus.

Your attention is your only limited inner resource.

The question is, do you have any left to spend? We spend most of our lives jumping from one task to the next: we're answering emails during work meetings, texting while across the table from friends at dinner, and watching TV while working on complex homework assignments. But rather than admit the downsides of this reality (missing important details, distancing ourselves from others, not being able to retain the information we learn), we glorify this perpetual state of interruption, calling it *multitasking.*

Because the MF profits from our productivity, the market offers us countless tools to optimize, streamline, and juggle multiple tasks at once. It takes pains to convince us that multitasking is not only an attainable, admirable goal for any hardworking person—but that the resulting mental exhaustion and distractibility are *personal failures* that we must overcome.

Trouble is, science has proved that we are *incapable* of multitasking. According to neuroscientist and author Dr. Daniel J. Levitin,

> *"It's as though our brains are configured to make a certain number of decisions per day, and once we reach that limit, we can't make any more, regardless of how important they are. One of the most useful findings in recent neuroscience could be summed up as* the decision-making network in our brain doesn't prioritize."

The modern world is a crowded, overwhelming, distracting place— and for better or worse, your brain evolved to attend to *one thing at a time.* Your prefrontal cortex (the squiggly bit of Pilot Brain behind your eyebrows) has what neuroscientists call a "novelty bias." While this part of your brain helps you remember birthdays, achieve goals, and focus on the task at hand, it's also hardwired to prioritize change, or "newness."

When deciding what to focus on, your brain's attention system uses two filters, in this order: **urgent** and then **important**. If you're walking down the street and a snarling dog starts charging at you, teeth bared, that's an *urgent*, dangerous change in your environment that your brain will notice. Similarly, if you're sound asleep and your newborn baby starts crying, that's a new, loud, urgent sound that your brain will prioritize, waking you up in the process. (*Why is a baby crying? Is someone in danger?*) The sound creates the *urgency* to wake you up, but what gets you out of bed is when your brain recognizes the *importance* of getting up to take care of your kid. (First, *is someone in danger?* Then, *oh, that's my baby! I need to check on her.*)

Pilot Brain struggles to prioritize important over new because Autopilot Brain evolved with the belief that new = survival (and Autopilot is in charge of your attention, by default).

You know how Autopilot Brain can't tell the difference between a cyberbully's cruel comment and a saber-toothed tiger leaping out of the bushes, flooding your body with fight-or-flight chemicals either way? Same deal. Except in this case, your *Pilot Brain* can't prioritize between opening an unread email and opening a 401k. Or between replying to a text and noticing the car ahead of you, merging into your lane. Or between deciding which candidate to hire at work or catching up on your Twitter feed.

Given the option, your Pilot Brain will automatically prioritize the *newer* thing (a new tweet, new text, or new email) over the *important* thing (deciding who to hire, focusing on the road, or saving money for retirement), because it has evolved to take a back seat to Autopilot's priorities (new = survival). This is one of the reasons we get in our own way; we prioritize "shiny objects" over valuable goals.

Rebuilding our reality doesn't just require choosing what we focus on, directing our intentions—we have to remove the distractions hijacking those intentions too.

How many times a day would you guess you're being interrupted by notifications, texts, emails, reminders, alerts, alarms, and other people?

About 89 percent of us look at our phones *immediately* after waking; around 81 percent of us are still on our phones within an hour of going to sleep. Studies conducted in 2013 and 2017 showed we pick up our phones *between 86 and 150 times a day*. We spend more than 40 percent of our productive time per day multitasking with digital communication tools (like email, IM, texting, and social apps), and we are interrupted an average of four times *per hour* by them.

A recent study of one hundred Stanford students confirmed that people who regularly "media multitask" *can't pay attention, switch tasks, or control their memory* nearly as well as people who choose to do one thing at a time. Another study found that the mere presence of one's smartphone dramatically reduced attention span and task performance, even when the phone was screen-side down. Actually, face down, notifications off, on silent, or turned off—it didn't matter. The fact that people unconsciously knew their phones were in reach *reduced their working intelligence.* WTF?!

This constant barrage of digital interruptions—called *media multitasking*—isn't just zapping our productivity, leaving us with the attention span of a goldfish; it's also messing with our mental health, raising our cortisol and adrenaline levels, leaving us overwhelmed and anxious.

Abruptly switching our focus from one thing to another feels easy, but it's expensive: it costs us physical energy and mental clarity, resulting in exhaustion and, often, wasted time.

Look, don't panic, okay? I'm not about to recommend you live the life of an off-the-grid hermit or revert to T9 texting on a paleolithic-era flip phone. Smartphones are not necessarily making us stupid; technology is not inherently evil. *They're just shiny objects taking up more mental real estate than necessary.*

Your attention is your only limited inner resource. It's just as drained by the shiny objects you struggle to *ignore* as the things you intentionally devote your attention to. Rather than fall prey to the MF's multitasking myths, productivity hacks, and "work harder, be better, do more!" marketing, inadvertently draining yourself of your ability to focus and exhausting your inner resources, take a beat and ask yourself:

What do I want to leave room (i.e., attention) for in my life?

What you focus on becomes your reality, *so what would you like to be able to focus on? And what are you giving too much attention and energy to?* If you allow your attentional resources to be stolen by fake productivity and digital distractions, you'll spend the rest of your life trying desperately to catch up with your just-out-of-reach goals, breathless and bitter.

Instead, actively create and *hold* space for the life you want. That might mean turning off push notifications, instituting "batch" emailing (responding to emails during designated times of the day and notifying your coworkers, bosses, and customers of it), having a phone "valet" spot during dinner with friends, switching to a 1980s-era alarm clock and sleeping with your phone in another room . . .

Honor your attention, because it's the most powerful inner resource you have.

THE LIFE-CHANGING MAGIC OF SMALL CHANGES AND BABY BANGS

I don't know about you, but whenever I know things are about to shift in one area of my life, change manifests itself in weird ways in *other* areas of my life. I'll get a wild urge to rearrange the furniture in my apartment until 1:00 a.m., for no apparent reason, until a few days later when I remember that my lease is up in three months. *"Ohh, right. That explains the interior decorator that possessed me the other night."*

See, Autopilot Brain is very opinionated, but entirely *nonverbal*. Whether we're fighting to make a positive change (quitting smoking), afraid of a change that's coming whether we like it or not (graduating high school), adjusting to a change that just happened (a breakup), or hesitating to make a change we know we should (accepting a job offer), the only way Autopilot Brain knows how to cope is with *action*.

We act out change, almost symbolically—before we even know why we're acting.

If you need to make a difficult decision and you feel overwhelmed by that choice—like whether to break up with the person you've been dating for over a year, for example—your Autopilot Brain will suddenly come up with a dozen little changes "worth making," like painting your apartment or impulse-buying new shoes. Why? Because Autopilot wants you to be happy, safe, and autonomous (psych need no. 3)—and it's a lot easier to predict the emotional outcome of painting your walls the color Raspberry Beret than the emotional outcome of a big breakup.

We impulsively act out small changes that we can have some element of control over, because Autopilot Brain is trying to help us cope with a major change we're afraid of. (Personally, this has led to some weird hair choices, aka "baby bangs," a sudden urge to collect vinyl records, and multiple impulse orders from Glossier.) The good news? We can use this automatic habit to our advantage.

We can subconsciously prime ourselves to make the big, important, positive change we're afraid to make—by intentionally making small, positive changes in our lives.

Prior to what I now affectionately call "The Great Closet Purge of 2014," my bosses had been teasing me with a potentially huge job promotion and relocation for over six months. This would've driven me crazy, had I not also been *deeply* unsure of what I actually wanted. As expected, my Autopilot Brain was freaking out over the potential life change; I had already chopped off all my hair, painted my kitchen, and ordered shoes I didn't need at two in the morning. (Yeah, those examples from earlier were real.) I also impulse-purchased Marie Kondo's book, *The Life-Changing Magic of Tidying Up*.

It wasn't until I was knee-deep in vintage sweaters and plastic storage bins of college art supplies that I got the inner clarity I needed: "Actually, YES. I want this promotion. I want to move for this job. I'm ready. LET'S FUCKIN' DO THIS." After I had wrangled my apartment inside out, I told my partner about my epiphany. As always, he was supportive and ready to go with me. That is, if my bosses decided to offer me the position.

Guess what happened a few weeks later? I was offered a promotion *above* the job I thought I was up for. More creativity, more team members, higher salary, paid relocation. *Whoa, WTF?! Wooooo!*

Listen—*I am aware that organizing my apartment didn't get me a job offer, okay?*

Being *intentional* about my environment and belongings, however, cleared the mental space necessary to be able to answer a major life question with confidence and personal clarity. Being intentional with my *stuff* got my Pilot Brain and Autopilot Brain working together— and when life handed me an opportunity, *I knew what I wanted to do with it.*

Purging your junk drawer is not the path to finding your purpose in life (unless you are Marie Kondo; that's her fuckyeah), and buying expensive new shoes or getting a new haircut won't transform you into the badass version of yourself you've been searching for. *We can't commodify internal change.* But when you consciously choose details in your life, right down to how many pens you want in your desk drawer—you've found a form of *living on purpose.*

Being intentional about the small, everyday decisions in your life helps prime your Autopilot Brain to unconsciously monitor for—and welcome—a new goal: change.

If you're stuck, hesitating, or afraid of a change, it's time to make tiny, positive changes. Purge your stuff. Dye your hair. Take that meeting. I wish I could guarantee that you won't also impulsively cut heinous baby bangs in the process like I did, but I can't.

None of us are safe from the possibility of baby bangs.

HABITS: THE STICKIEST INTENTIONS

Ever been driving somewhere you've been a thousand times, arrive at your destination, and suddenly snap back into reality like, *"Wait, how did I get here?!"* It's a little scary when you realize you've been driving on autopilot and an entire stretch of highway is wiped from your memory. (Commuters—y'all know what I'm talking about.)

Your brain *automates* habits like driving the same route home every day because if you don't have to pay close attention to something and can *still* get it done, you've saved psychic energy. Habits are "sticky" because *shortcuts are Autopilot Brain's jam.*

Thanks to the time-saving power of Autopilot, our lives are made up of micro-habits and little routines we follow without thinking. But if we want to wake up in the morning and feel psyched about our work and comfortable in our own skin, then it's important to create new habits that maintain our joy, *both consciously and subconsciously.*

HOW TO DEAL: GOOD HABITS

Want to make a one-time thing into a good habit? Like, instead of taking that one class at the gym and never going back, do you want to use your membership every week? Or maybe instead of falling asleep to the TV, do you want to switch to reading a good book every night? The trick is to create mental shortcuts with something psychologists call *implementation intentions,* or *"if this, then that"* logic.

Rather than simply setting a goal, like "I want to finish writing my screenplay," implementation intentions give both of your brains a job: "**If** it is a weekday, **then** I will wake up one hour early and work on my screenplay." With this exercise, Pilot Brain has a job: you've consciously declared a goal you want to work toward. Then by offering a recurring trigger, or signal of *when* to work on this goal, the lizard then can do what it does best: create an automated habit. Researchers have found that people who use *"If, then"* intentions are much more likely to accomplish their goals than people who simply set their goals—so let's give it a shot.

STEP 1: WHAT HABIT ARE YOU TRYING TO FORM?
>> *"I want to exercise consistently."*

STEP 2: "IF _____ , THEN _____."
Make your intention more specific by breaking it into two parts. *"If X happens, then I'll do Y."* This sets up a cue (*If*) and a routine (*then*) for both your brains to follow through on.

>> *"If it's a weekday,*

>> *then I will take my dog for a walk or run right after I get home from work."*

STEP 3: ADD A LINK TO THE CHAIN.

This is the most important step, IMO. It's not enough to create a trigger for your goal; you have to create a detailed, clear-cut system for your Autopilot Brain to act out.

To do this, piggyback your If/then onto an activity that's already part of your routine (like brushing your teeth or grabbing your keys before you leave the house). Research on the brain's method of saving information tells us that your brain would rather add "links" to an existing action chain (i.e., routine) than form a new one.

>> *"If it's a weekday,*

>> *then I will take my dog for a walk or run right after I get home from work."*

>> *New link: "This is easy because I hung Potato's leash on the same hook as my house keys; I will just swap them out when I walk in the door."*

By tacking a new intention onto a routine that's already been automated by your Autopilot Brain, you're creating a mental shortcut and getting your conscious mind to work together with your subconscious.

This method has gotten me to floss regularly, pay my rent on time, and finally accept compliments (instead of deflecting them, as women are socialized to do), so—yeah, five stars, thumbs up, would recommend.

———

"Creating and holding space" will look different for each of us: It might mean setting aside protected, open-ended time in our schedule; it might mean creating communication boundaries with our friends, coworkers, or bosses; it might mean valuing our mental health through something as significant as therapy or as simple as deleting Facebook from our phones. Living with intention might mean practicing mindfulness while staring at the dishes; it might mean priming ourselves with a vision board about our highest goals; it might mean reorganizing our apartments at three in the morning.

Whatever forms it may take, living *on purpose*—actively rebuilding our reality and holding space for the life we want to lead—gets our Autopilot and Pilot Brains working *together*, bringing us that much closer to fuckyeah.

13.

PICK THE PYROS

We've just spent twelve chapters talking about ourselves: challenging, exploring, and uncensoring who we are.

But the world doesn't revolve around us.

Finding fuckyeah is the process of rediscovering a raw joy that has been buried, stifled, and smashed under the self-censorship we all experience as we make our way through the world. It is the clearing away of a dense fog of limiting beliefs, shame, and insecurity we've grown accustomed to and accepted as "adulthood," so that we can finally see, with clarity, what we want out of our lives and how to make it a reality.

And it's a process we can't go through *alone*.

While we can't control how other people receive our uncensored selves or our Art, we can choose to surround ourselves with people who will support and challenge us. We *create* every one of our relationships. And when we are *intentional* about the relationships in our lives—from social media followers to coworkers to romantic partners—we're building in a joy-sustaining, fuckyeah-finding fail-safe.

If you want to fan the spark of your fuckyeah into a wildfire of joy, it helps if you aren't smothered by a bunch of wet blankets. You have to pick the pyros.

Which is why, in love, in our friendships, at work, with family, the trick is to carefully surround yourself with the pyromaniacs who will keep the fire of your fuckyeah ablaze.

> >> *"But where is this '#squad' everyone keeps bragging about? And how do I cancel toxic relationships without being an asshole or ending up totally alone in the world?"*

#SQUADGOALS (*EYE ROLL*)

Brace yourself for an earth-shatteringly astute sports analogy:

In sports, the only people allowed on the field, arena, or court are *players* and *coaches*. But not the fans—no matter how die-hard they are. Fans can cheer, boo, or scrutinize every play, aggressively defend their favorite players to other fans, or just passively observe the game—*but only from a distance.* If fans storm onto the field, they're carted off by security. My question is,

Who is on the field with you right now?

The field isn't just the inner circle of relationships in your life—it's your inner world, your headspace. *Who have you invited into your thoughts?* Whose opinions are you valuing? Who are you inspired by, afraid of, or accountable to? Because your thoughts are your focus, and what you focus on becomes your reality . . . you see where I'm going with this.

You become what you surround yourself with: the books, the music, the people; everything has an influence.

Just for this moment, give yourself permission to privately assess the effect of the people you've invited into your life—partners, friends, family, coworkers, social media friends, one-night stands, Internet commenters. Who is *actually* helping, and who is holding this team back?

THE TEAM

On this field, **your team is made up of people whose fate is presently tangled up with yours.** If something is good for you, it's good for your team (and vice versa.) You celebrate each other's wins; you mourn each other's losses. Players on your team experience pieces of your life in *real time*. In other words, if they know the rough patch you and your partner are going through, it's because *you chose to be vulnerable with them*, not because they heard about it on your social feed. Your team could be family members, coworkers, friends, partners—and those team members may change. But whoever your team is, *you chose them.*

>> *"Hold up. I didn't get to pick my family."*

True, but you can *absolutely* choose how far inside your inner circle they are. You are under no obligation to invite a toxic person onto your team just because they're a blood relative—or because you've known them your whole life, or because they asked you nicely. Family doesn't get a free pass here. And what about your significant other?

Are they the pyromaniac that your little spark of fuckyeah needs, or are they a wet blanket? Either way, *you get to choose your team—so be intentional.*

THE COACHES

A coach is anyone who guides, mentors, and challenges you; someone who has your best interests at heart. Coaches are great at zooming out, seeing the big picture, and giving fresh perspective.

We aren't limited to just one coach per lifetime; coaches flow in and out of our lives, challenging us to be our *real* selves. We only allow coaches to hold us to such high standards because they're "in it" with us—they're at every practice, putting in overtime to help us see the necessary "play." They've earned our trust.

But I think I have a better name for the coaches in your life: accountabilibuddies.

The accountabilibuddy picks you back up when you've failed; they're who you call when you're clawing your way out of the Shame pit. "Yeah, that sucked as much as you thought it did," they'll admit. "But I'm pushing you back in the ring, cheering for you . . . Here we go, round two. You got this." They're so totally 100 percent on your side that they'll cheer you on even as you attempt something that may or may not blow up in your face—*and will be just as ready to call your bluff when you're avoiding a necessary risk.*

Although awareness of your Autopilot's fear, hesitation, and self-sabotage will help you untangle your limiting beliefs, *old habits die hard.* When you're exploring, experimenting, and taking risks, it helps to have a trustworthy squad of people aligned with your *highest* goals and challenging you to raise your *lowest* bar.

Accountabilibuddies call you on your bullshit.

Three years ago, when I was (unknowingly) scared to take my business seriously (*hello, limiting beliefs!*), I was lucky enough to have multiple accountabilibuddies in my life.

While talking through my website ideas for the millionth time, my mum listened patiently, gave her verbal support, and *then called me on my bullshit.* She told me it was time to get my website off the ground, like *now.* And then she offered to help. While complaining to my sister that I didn't know enough about recording a podcast, making videos, or web design to launch something I could be proud of, she listened patiently . . . *and then called me out on being chickenshit.* "Have you seen anything on the Internet?" she asked. "Most of it is really, really bad. Stop being so hard on yourself and put it out there!" So, I did. I launched a website, learned to record and edit video, and started my podcast, "Call Me When You Get This"—because they held me accountable.

And when I admitted to my good friend, a successful entrepreneur, that I was afraid of releasing my book into the world because it would require being seen or having an audience, she reminded me of everything that qualified me for my new platform—*and then called me out.* She then recruited me to lead my first ever workshop for women in business at her retreat, placing me in front of a real-life audience to share the contents of my book (and soul, tbh). And you know what? I loved it. Clearly, these are the kinds of people I want on my team.

You can make this accountabilibuddy thing as formal or informal as you want. You could simply ask a trustworthy friend (or two) to hold you accountable to an intention, goal, or habit. Or you could form a group meet-up to share ideas, progress, freak-outs, and accountability with each other online or IRL. However you do it and whoever they are, there's only one mandatory ingredient: *trust*.

And speaking of trust...

THE FANS

Of course you want to have fans in the stands—watching you, cheering for you, wearing your jersey. Everybody does. But you don't need them telling you how to do your job, and you definitely don't need them rushing out on the field, mid-game.

The fans in your life are the people temporarily caught in your orbit, whose first loyalty is to the game, not you.

An easy example is social media friends—people who often don't know you, who follow along with your life story and only see as much detail as they can from *the stands* (aka your newsfeed). Fans could also be people in your periphery—bosses, coworkers, friends, family—anyone with an invested curiosity in how things turn out for you. If things are looking good for you, they might consume your story like Success Porn; if you're having a tough (or embarrassing) time, they might change loyalties and comment from the stands on your failing performance as a player, and so on.

Fans don't have to be loyal; they've got opinions, because they feel involved—but they're only there to watch the game unfold, not to help you play better. *Fans cheer you on, but they're also allowed to talk shit on your game.*

Fans aren't on your team, so why keep inviting them onto the field? Why trust the belligerent spectators of your life, slurring drunk opinions about how you should have made that last play?! They're not out here on the field; *you are.*

Your team, your cheerleaders, your coaches, your account-abilibuddies: you get to hand-pick us, so be choosy. Pick the pyromaniacs who will help fan the spark of your fuckyeah into a wildfire of joy.

This isn't to say that no one should be allowed to criticize you—we should *definitely* accept feedback from our coaches and teammates, even if what they have to say hurts at first. Their constructive criticism can help us get where we want to go, and they're *allowed* to call us out because they earned the right to an opinion. But you don't need to tolerate toxic people in your life, and especially not in your inner circle.

WAIT, WHAT IS TOXIC?

Well, if this were pop culture *Jeopardy*, I would answer: "What is a 2003 Britney Spears classic?" But this is not *Jeopardy*. It's your life. What you're probably asking is: *What relationships qualify as toxic?*

Any relationship slowly sucking the life out of you.

Got one or two in mind? Maybe someone in your family, a coworker, a significant other? I thought so. But before you go ape-shit, blocking them on social media or cutting them entirely out of your real life, let's narrow down that toxic definition a little further.

Think of someone you're close to—a friend, a partner, a family member, anyone who you care a lot about—and rate that person by circling one of the three options in each line that follows.

The person I have in mind is typically:

intuitive	analytical	depends on the situation
energetic	relaxed	depends on the situation
committed	free-spirited	depends on the situation
outgoing	reserved	depends on the situation
resolute	flexible	depends on the situation
playful	serious	depends on the situation
realistic	idealistic	depends on the situation

Okay, now rate yourself on the same things.

You probably chose to describe yourself *situationally* most of the time (the last column), and you probably described your friend with *traits* most of the time (the first two columns). I mean, of course you did—you're not a mind reader. You have access to *your* inner thoughts and memories, but you can't see the inner thoughts of others.

We assume people behave the way they do because it's who they are, while we explain our own behavior in terms of the circumstances.

I might label myself an "introvert," but I know that label only applies in certain situations: I'm deeply shy in front of an audience, but confident and outgoing in a small group of people. I might be totally comfortable at a friend's party (one of the last people to leave) and also be socially anxious enough at a coworker's event to "ghost" before even an hour has passed. How I behave depends on the situation.

We tend to think of other people, however, in terms of *permanent traits*—as introverts or extroverts, as intelligent or stupid, as understanding or cruel. We quickly forget the power that circumstances have to affect how someone behaves, because we only have access to *our* inner world, and no one else's.

So, when someone pisses us off, it's a lot easier to believe we're being taken advantage of by someone inherently careless or selfish than by someone momentarily influenced by their circumstances. We want to explain their failure with a characteristic; we want to generalize, **because it's easier to distance ourselves from someone we've labeled**. When someone takes us for granted, lets us down, or lets themselves down (by acting in self-sabotage), we don't realize that the person was trying their best and just momentarily fucked up.

Think about it: With the exception of flat-out sabotage or spite, when are you *not* doing the best you can at this whole life thing? When you're deep in an argument with your partner, are you deliberately saying things to confuse and frustrate them? Or are you trying to express yourself as best you know how, and it's just not coming out as clearly as it sounds in your head?

Most of the time, people are doing the best they can with what they know and what they have in that moment.

Sometimes someone else's "best" will be enough for you. Sometimes it won't. Does that mean it's time to lower your expectations? Give up on mutual respect and honesty? Stop asking for what you need in your relationships?

Nope. *But it is time to set boundaries.*

BOUNDARIES = FREEDOM

Setting boundaries doesn't have to be complicated; it's about knowing what you're willing to have, do, or be—and what you're not willing to have, do, or be.

It's being able to say, "No, I can't," or "Sorry, I'm not available," or "I'm not comfortable with that," without being a dismissive jerk. In fact, research has shown that the more compassionate a person is, the clearer they communicate their personal boundaries. Compassionate people are clear on what they will do, won't do, and why—and they practice communicating that with others.

Compassion helps us remember that everyone else is doing the best they can—and that sometimes, someone else's "best" won't meet our expressed needs. Instead of believing this person is taking advantage of us, we can set boundaries with them—sparing them unnecessary judgment and us unnecessary future frustration.

Will taking on a project overwhelm you? Then say no. Will answering someone's "quick question," or letting someone "pick your brain," or doing someone a "huge favor" leave you feeling disgruntled and strapped for time? Then don't agree to it. Will adjusting how you look or act because your partner asked you to eventually build resentment in you? Then don't do it. Setting boundaries requires the courage to say no often, and prioritizing what you need.

If you have no genuine motivation to do something, and you do it anyway, solely out of shame-loaded obligation, you will grow to resent the person or thing you feel obligated to. You'll also grow to resent yourself for living inauthentically.

We say "yes" to things we're not comfortable with and take on projects that will overwhelm us—all because we're afraid of what someone will think if we say no. We're afraid of being shamed. Unfortunately, life without boundaries creates festering internal resentment, poisons our relationships, and takes up our valuable mental space and attention. So saying "yes" when we mean "no" is not a trade-off worth making.

Are you feeling overwhelmed? Set boundaries with yourself.

Are you feeling resentment? Set boundaries with other people.

Of course, there's always the possibility that our personal boundaries will surprise, disappoint, or frustrate someone else. I follow a personal rule: the degree of explanation I owe about my boundary is determined by how close or how far they are from my inner circle. Is this person an Internet commenter? No explanation needed. My desk-mate at work? A simple explanation will usually do. My partner of over a decade? He deserves a vulnerable and transparent conversation.

Before giving up on any strained relationship, check to see if you've set your boundaries first.

EXIT STAGE LEFT

We can't expect everyone to do things the way we think they should be done; everyone lives differently and has a right to.

But are there people in your life who continually ignore what you have to say, or otherwise disrespect your existence? Do they shame, belittle, and judge you on a regular basis? Do they drain you of your energy and undermine your self-esteem? Then you may have a toxic relationship on your hands. And if that's the case, *it's time to get out of there.* If you're not being heard, being louder won't work. If your boundaries are continually being violated, pointing them out again and again won't work either. As Maya Angelou famously said, "When someone shows you who they are, *believe them the first time.*"

How you distance yourself from a toxic relationship is obviously dependent on the situation; maybe you unsubscribe, unfollow, unfriend, and block because they're an Internet troll and that's all it takes. Or maybe you pack your bags and stay with a friend for a while, because it's safer than living with this person just one minute longer.

A toxic relationship is one that continues to slowly suck the life and joy out of you, even after you've done everything in your power to be compassionate, to set your boundaries, and to have empathy.

You get to decide how close or far someone is from your inner circle and headspace, so show yourself some real self-care and walk away from truly toxic relationships—and walk toward a team of people who value you, your boundaries, and your fuckyeah.

KIND IS THE NEW COOL

We all want to be seen, heard, and loved by others, but the truth is, we can't be seen, heard, and loved by *everyone*. Your perspective, voice, and fuckyeah will inspire many of us—but not all of us. Your Art isn't meant for everyone. *And that's okay!* Don't waste your precious energy chasing the approval of people who don't see what makes you and your Art amazing—seek out the people destined to be raving fans of your work and champions of your fuckyeah. Whether in life or in love, *pick the pyros*. We're here, waiting.

But I'd like to offer you a quick reality check:

Fanning the flames of someone else's fuckyeah is also *your responsibility*.

Technology has tied us all together; we're a global culture, connected with strangers and ideas we never knew before. There is no room, or reason, for hate—hate is choking the life out of humankind.

What are you and I *actively doing* to put love, inclusion, acceptance, and kindness into the world? If we spend all our time screaming in ALL CAPS at the belly-button-gazing, wounded people with spiteful things to say on Twitter, we're only yelling into a void. Yes, let's speak out against bigotry, racism, closed-mindedness, and any form of hate, online and off. Let's also *do* some tangible, real-time acts of kindness to counter the hate that people seem so comfortable spewing into the cosmos. Whatever your platform is (school, job, blog, social media, an actual platform outside on the sidewalk), use it to start a new conversation rooted in kindness.

It's time to champion someone else's Art and fuckyeah.

It's time to take the focus off ourselves and start caring for other people *on purpose*. Opportunities for kindness are easy to ignore—but if you're willing to pay attention, you could help someone else find *their* fuckyeah.

Contribute to someone's lifelong dream project on a crowdfunding website, even if you don't know them personally. Offer to babysit for your sleep-deprived friends who are new parents. Go out of your way to remind someone you care that they exist. Pay the bridge toll for the person in line behind you along your commute to work. Bring snacks to share into work on Monday. Signal-boost an activist's work online. But beyond practicing intentional acts of kindness, practice *cheerleading for fuckyeah.*

Did someone bring their Art to work today? Applaud them. Is someone's authenticity showing? Thank them for being real. Is someone you know living their fuckyeah? Are they experimenting, exploring, playing, taking risks, uncensoring who they really are? Your job is to make as much noise as possible reminding them that they are seen, that they are loved, and that *the fuckyeah in you recognizes the fuckyeah in them.*

While we (your fellow human beings) aren't always the easiest to live with, we're doing the best we can while finding, losing, and rediscovering our fuckyeah. And honestly? Finding yours and sharing it with the rest of us is *exactly* what we need.

So please hurry, because we're a goddamn mess, and we really need that Art of yours to help us turn the tide.

WTF DO I DO NOW?

You know the weird feeling you get when you can't find the right words to describe something? The almost desperate feeling of mentally combining different words, struggling to describe an experience, feeling, or thought because the words available to you in the language(s) you speak don't quite . . . fit?

Some words are just lost in translation; there are many emotions that can't be described in English that have been aptly named in other languages. The feeling of pleasure we get from someone else's pain (like watching "wipeout" clips on the Internet): *schadenfreude*, a German word. The euphoria you experience when you begin to fall in love: *forelsket*, a Norwegian expression. The witty comeback you think of only after it's too late to use: *trepverter*, a Yiddish term that literally means "staircase words."

Sometimes, there just aren't words to describe something, or we can't seem to find them. And sometimes we have to invent an expression to describe a complicated state of being or feeling—until we can crowd-source a better word for it.

Thus, the MVP of this book: *"fuckyeah."*

Fuckyeah is too many things to squeeze into one word; it's more than just *joy, purpose, meaning,* or *happiness.* It's all those things at once—and contrary to the limiting beliefs many of us have loaded in those individual words, fuckyeah is real, attainable, and enduring.

It's having a clear sense of purpose without needing all the answers. And a persistent, raw joy without being delusional or afraid of the pain that life can cause. It is your genuine, uncensored self-expression and the thrill that comes from sharing your Art with the rest of us. It's clarity. Feeling like you can *breathe.* Like you have something incredible to look forward to, without knowing exactly what that thing is.

It's freedom.

Unlike everything you've been told about joy, purpose, meaning, and happiness, you *do not* have to optimize every minute of your time, streamline your life, or edit yourself to deserve, or find, your fuckyeah.

Fuckyeah isn't the kind of happiness you spend your life chasing down; it's a gift you unwrap.

The meaning and happiness that we've been looking for in self-care products, Success Porn, and external validation is actually already within us, hiding under layer after layer of social programming and biological defaults—and all we have to do is peel back the wrapping.

Unearth your limiting beliefs and have the courage to dethrone them. Question your methods, habits, and assumptions about the way the world works. Challenge your Inner Cynic: try something new despite how "qualified" you think you are. Set goals no matter how "impractical" your dreams may seem. Stop shaming yourself for where you're "at" in life, and celebrate how far you've come. Instead of concealing your weaknesses from us, take ownership of them; work with them and around them. And rather than tell yourself that how you *actually* look, sound, or feel today isn't "_____ enough" to share with us, give yourself permission to show up, in public and on social media, as you *are*, truly unfiltered. Quit editing yourself, not just in photos, but by taking active, creative risks and listening to your intuition in every decision, whether big or small. Instead of frantically trying to erase your past mistakes and "write" the rest of your life in pencil, let those failures lie, learn from them, and *write the whole damn thing in pen.* Experiment, explore, and get curious about your life. Uncensor who you are. *Find* fuckyeah.

Most of us have idealized "finding our passion" as the final-sounding *solution* to our ravenous appetite for transformation. We are obsessed with change (*Be better! Work smarter! Do more!*), because we're not taught to celebrate the *process* of transformation—we're taught to idolize the final results. We're obsessed with self-improvement—but ashamed of the experimentation that goes hand-in-hand with it.

We've told ourselves that our infatuation with self-optimization, efficiency, and productivity, although exhausting, is necessary and only temporary, because once we improve enough, or learn enough, we'll finally find our "thing" (aka what to "do with our lives") and we won't feel like we're scrambling anymore. And once we find our "calling," get the promotion, have the perfect body, buy the big house, *fill in the blank*, we will at last be unequivocally happy.

We don't realize that transformation is our natural state.

You'll never be able to "pin down" your Art or your fuckyeah as just one particular thing, because *you are perpetually changing.* You will be an entirely new being—over and over and over again—in your lifetime. This means your fuckyeah will continually change, and you will need to find it over and over again—*and this is actually a good thing.*

See, the word *find* in *Find Your Fuckyeah* doesn't mean *chase*, like you're on some kind of long, exhausting quest, and that you'll never be satisfied because it's just out of reach. By *find*, I mean to *uncover.* To unfilter, dig up, reveal, uncensor, peel back, unwrap.

The happiness you're looking for isn't gated behind your next accomplishment. The meaning you crave in your career, relationships, and life isn't missing because you're "not _____ enough." They're both waiting within you, ready for you to notice them.

When you suddenly feel pissed off, or exhausted with something about yourself or your life, realize those emotions are *potential energy.* Your life isn't something broken that "needs fixing"; you've simply noticed that something about you has changed, *and you get to decide what you want to do next.* The negative feelings that often precede change aren't meant for you to "sit with" for long—they're momentum to help you transform.

In other words, if our fuckyeah is a spark, then we have to do everything in our power to fan that flame. Instead of trying to stifle the emotions that flare up at a "fork in the road," take them as a sign that there's something new to find. Some new Art to make. Some new joy to unwrap.

We don't always need to fix something about ourselves to be happy—we need to wake up to our lives. Finding fuckyeah is making a daily decision to participate in being alive, rather than allowing life to happen to us.

It is taking steps to change our perspectives, rewire our brains, and rebuild our realities by realizing we were never meant to be spectators; we've *always* been creators, whether we were paying attention before or not. When we simultaneously *accept* that we can't control everything in the universe (okay, much of anything) and also *refuse* to live passive, reactionary lives, we're finally waking up, taking our lives off autopilot. Finally unwrapping our Art.

Let's fight the popular panic over being smart enough, interesting enough, experienced enough, rich enough, happy enough, attractive enough, well-rounded enough, or any other *Not Enough*. Let's decide to have fun being ourselves—our real, right now, authentic selves—because *we are enough*.

So, no more bullshit. No more apathy. No more beating yourself up, tearing yourself down, stalling, stressing, or shrinking. It's time to live an uncensored life. It's time to live a life of your making.

Ready? Don't forget the snacks.

NOTES

I referenced *hundreds* and *hundreds* of scientific studies to make this book possible—and my publisher insists there just isn't enough room to list them all here. But there's plenty of room on the Internet! Please visit http://www.alexisrockley.com/findyourfuckyeahresources for an unabridged list of the research sources that went into this book.

1: The Brain Tangle

37:   *"Phantom words" experiment:* Deutsch, Diana, *Phantom Words and Other Curiosities* (La Jolla, CA: Philomel Records, 2003). See also Deutsch, Diana, "Phantom Words" [website], http://bit.ly/2NnnaSz.

38:   *Experiment . . .* Mlodinow, L., *Subliminal: How Your Unconscious Mind Rules Your Behavior* (New York: Vintage, 2012), 65–66. See also Roediger, H. L., and K. B. McDermott, "Creating False Memories: Remembering Words Not Presented in Lists," *Journal of Experimental Psychology: Learning, Memory, and Cognition 21*, no. 4 (1995): 803–814, http://dx.doi.org/10.1037/0278-7393.21.4.803.

39:   *Frederic Bartlett:* Bartlett, F. C., *Remembering: A Study in Experimental and Social Psychology* (New York: Cambridge University Press, 1997; originally published 1932).

39:   *Split-brain patients:* Gazzaniga, M. S., "The Split-Brain: Rooting Consciousness in Biology," *Proceedings of the National Academy of Sciences 111*, no. 51 (2014) 18093–18094, http://doi.org/10.1073/pnas.1417892111.

40:   *Even if those explanations aren't true:* Gazzaniga, M. S., "The Split Brain Revisited," *Scientific American 279*, no. 1 (1998): 50–55. See also LeDoux, J., *The Emotional Brain: The Mysterious Underpinnings of Emotional Life* (New York: Simon and Schuster, 1996).

46: *Thoughts . . . changing the function and physical structure of the brain:* Lumma, A., et al., "Change in Emotional Self Concept following Socio Cognitive Training Relates to Structural Plasticity of the Prefrontal Cortex," *Brain and Behavior 8*, no. 4 (2018): e00940, http://doi.org/10.1002/brb3.940.

46: *Thoughts . . . and cure diseases:* Doidge, N., *The Brain That Changes Itself: Stories of Personal Triumph from the Frontiers of Brain Science* (New York: Penguin Books, 2007).

2: I'm Only as Free as My Last Paycheck

53: *Before the Industrial Revolution . . . Machines changed:* Bowles, S., and H. Gintis, *Schooling in Capitalist America: Educational Reform and the Contradictions of Economic Life* (New York: Basic Books, 1976), 52–84. See also Fromm, Erich, *The Sane Society* (Greenwich, CT: Fawcett, 1955), 76–170.

57: *MF . . . come enjoy being told what to do:* Godin, Seth, *Tribes: We Need You to Lead Us* (New York: Penguin, 2008), 96–99.

58: *In* Linchpin *. . . Seth Godin:* Godin, S., *Linchpin: Are You Indispensable?* (New York: Portfolio, 2010), 9–10.

3: Someone Will Tell Me What I Need to Do

70: *As President Woodrow Wilson put it:* Wilson, W., "The Meaning of a Liberal Education," a speech to the New York High School Teachers Association, January 9, 1909, http://bit.ly/2xirqso.

75: *Not even identical twins, it turns out:* Bruder, C. E. G., et al., "Phenotypically Concordant and Discordant Monozygotic Twins Display Different DNA Copy-Number-Variation Profiles," *American Journal of Human Genetics 82*, no. 3 (2008): 763–771, http://doi.org/10.1016/j.ajhg.2007.12.011.

76: *Chimamanda Ngozi Adichie . . . gets it:* Adichie, Chimamanda Ngozi, "The Danger of a Single Story," TED [online video], July 2009, http://bit.ly/2NQxy4O.

4: Unbrand Yourself

81: *According to BusinessDictionary.com:* "Brand" (n.d.), BusinessDictionary.com, March 29, 2018, http://bit.ly/2MEpBeh.

5: Cancel Your Subscription to Bullshit

98: *According to the Food and Agriculture Organization of the United Nations:* "1.02 Billion People Hungry," Food and Agriculture Organization of the United Nations, June 19, 2009, http://bit.ly/2OAxrHC. See also Holt-Giménez, E., et al., "We Already Grow Enough Food for 10 Billion People . . . and Still Can't End Hunger," *Journal of Sustainable Agriculture 36*, no. 6 (2012) 595–598, https://doi.org/10.1080/10440046.2012.695331.

100: *Lynne Twist . . . danger of having our needs unmet:* Twist, Lynne, *The Soul of Money: Reclaiming the Wealth of Our Inner Resources* (New York: W. W. Norton, 2006), 47.

102: *Erich Fromm got it:* Fromm, *The Sane Society,* 179.

105: *"Reappraisal" and "emotional disclosure" via writing:* Pennebaker, J., and C. K. Chung, "Expressive Writing: Connections to Physical and Mental Health," in *Oxford Handbook of Health Psychology,* edited by Howard S. Friedman (New York: Oxford University Press, 2011), http://doi.org/10.1093/oxfordhb/9780195342819.013.0018.

109: *Self-criticism . . . risk of depression:* Körner, A., et al., "The Role of Self-Compassion in Buffering Symptoms of Depression in the General Population," *PLoS ONE 10*, no. 10 (2015): e0136598, http://doi.org/10.1371/journal.pone.0136598.

109: *Self-compassion . . . breaks the cycle of negative self-criticism:* Zhang, H., et al., "Self-Criticism and Depressive Symptoms: Mediating Role of Self-Compassion," *Omega: Journal of Death and Dying 1* (September 2017), http://doi.org/10.1177/0030222817729609.

110: *Relaxation response (RR) . . . Dr. Herbert Benson:* Benson, H., J. F. Beary, and M. P. Carol, "The Relaxation Response," *Psychiatry 37,* no. 1 (1974): 37–46, http://doi.org/10.1080/003327 47.1974.11023785.

111: *Decrease gene expression:* Bhasin, M. K., et al., "Relaxation Response Induces Temporal Transcriptome Changes in Energy Metabolism, Insulin Secretion, and Inflammatory Pathways," *PLoS ONE 8,* no. 5 (2013): e62817, http://doi.org/10.1371/journal.pone.0062817. See also Dusek, J. A., et al., "Genomic Counter-Stress Changes Induced by the Relaxation Response," *PLoS ONE 3,* no. 7 (2008): e2576, http://bit.ly/2NRflUC.

111: *Trigger . . . focus on positive thoughts and words:* Newberg, A., and M. R. Waldman, *Words Can Change Your Brain: 12 Conversation Strategies to Build Trust, Resolve Conflict, and Increase Intimacy* (New York: Penguin, 2013), 32. See also Longe, O., et al., "Having a Word with Yourself: Neural Correlates of Self-Criticism and Self-Reassurance," *Neuro-Image 49,* no. 2 (2010): 1849–1856, http://doi .org/10.1016/j.neuroimage.2009.09.019.

6: Start Starting

119: *What kinds of problems do you want to solve?:* I think I heard this phrasing on a "Being Boss" podcast episode, hosted by Kathleen Shannon and Emily Thompson—unfortunately, I can't remember which episode, or in what context. Check out https://beingboss .club/podcast.

123: *The founder of CreativeLive, Chase Jarvis:* Unfortunately, that class recording is no longer live. Check out https://www.creativelive.com/.

125: *Dr. Stuart Brown, defines Play as:* Brown, Stuart L., *Play: How It Shapes the Brain, Opens the Imagination, and Invigorates the Soul* (New York: Penguin, 2009).

126: *Play . . . crucial part of brain development in children:* Hedges, J. H., et al., "Play, Attention, and Learning: How Do Play and Timing Shape the Development of Attention and Influence Classroom Learning?" *Annals of the New York Academy of Sciences 1292,* no. 1 (2013): 1–20, http://doi.org/10.1111/nyas.12154; Wang, S., and S. Aamodt, "Play, Stress, and the Learning Brain," *Cerebrum 2012,* no. 12 (2012), https://www.ncbi.nlm.nih.gov/pmc/articles /PMC3574776/.

129: *Flow . . . psychologist Mihaly Csikszentmihalyi:* Csikszentmihalyi, Mihaly. *Flow: The Psychology of Optimal Experience* (New York: Harper Collins, 2009).

130: *Calls these activities "autotelic":* Csikszentmihalyi, *Flow.*

132: *Csikszentmihalyi . . . interview high-level professionals:* Nakamura, J., and M. Csikszentmihalyi, "The Construction of Meaning through Vital Engagement," in *Flourishing: Positive Psychology and the Life Well-Lived,* edited by C. L. M. Keys and J. Haidt (Washington, DC: American Psychological Association, 2013), 83–104.

7: Uncensor Your Intuition

145: *Binocular rivalry:* Jiang, Y., et al., "A Gender- and Sexual Orientation-Dependent Spatial Attentional Effect of Invisible Images," *Proceedings of the National Academy of Sciences 103,* no. 45 (2006): 17048–17052, http: //doi.org/10.1073/pnas.0605678103.

145: *Changing image to one eye and a static image to the other:* Tsuchiya, N., and C. Koch, "Continuous Flash Suppression Reduces Negative Afterimages," *Nature Neuroscience 8,* no. 8 (2005): 1096–1101, http://doi.org/10.1038 /nn1500.

140: *In 1895, Wilhelm Röntgen:* "Wilhelm Conrad Röntgen, Biographical," NobelPrize .org, http://bit.ly/2NRg7ku.

140: *By 1928, Alexander Fleming:* Fleming, A., "On the Antibacterial Action of Cultures of a Penicillium, with Special Reference to Their Use in the Isolation of B. influenzæ," *British Journal of Experimental Pathology 10*, no. 3 (1929): 226–236, http://bit.ly/2QGKdFK. See also Eickhoff, T. C., "Penicillin: An Accidental Discovery That Changed the Course of Medicine," Healio [website], August 10, 2008, http://bit.ly/2pk9kSD.

140: *In 1939, Percy Spencer:* Blitz, Matt, "The Amazing True Story of How the Microwave Was Invented by Accident," *Popular Mechanics*, February 23, 2016, http://bit.ly/2MJcit6.

146: *According to Dr. Brené Brown:* Brown, Brené, *Daring Greatly: How the Courage to Be Vulnerable Transforms the Way We Live, Love, Parent, and Lead* (New York: Penguin Random House, 2013): 24–25, 68.

151: *Reported feminine indicators:* Mahalik, J. R., et al., "Development of the Conformity to Feminine Norms Inventory," *Sex Roles 52*, nos. 7–8 (2005), http://bit.ly/2MKsbiF.

151: *Reported masculine indicators:* Mahalik, J. R., et al., "Development of the Conformity to Masculine Norms Inventory," *Psychology of Men & Masculinity 4*, no. 1 (2003): 3–25, http://bit.ly/2xmEcGp.

152: *Shame and the "rumination" . . . lead to depression, while guilt does not:* Zhu R., et al., "Early Distinction between Shame and Guilt Processing in an Interpersonal Context," *Social Neuroscience 17* (2017): 1–14, http://doi.org/10.1080/17470919.2017.1391119.

158: *Three psychological needs:* Paraphrased from Ryan, R. M., and E. L. Deci, "Self-Determination Theory and the Facilitation of Intrinsic Motivation, Social Development, and Well-Being," *American Psychologist 55*, no. 1 (2010): 68–78, http://dx.doi.org/10.1037/0003-066X.55.1.68. I changed "competence" to "confidence" and "relatedness" to "connection" for the sake of clarity for the reader.

8: Rebuild Your Reality

167: *Study . . . Cleveland Clinic Foundation in Ohio:* Yue, G., and K. J. Cole, "Strength Increases from the Motor Program: Comparison of Training with Maximal Voluntary and Imagined Muscle Contractions," *Journal of Neurophysiology 67*, no. 5 (1992): 1114–1123, https://doi.org/10.1152/jn.1992.67.5.1114. See also Ranganathan, V. K., et al., "From Mental Power to Muscle Power—Gaining Strength by Using the Mind," *Neuropsychologia 42*, no. 7 (2004): 944–956, https://doi.org/10.1016/j.neuropsychologia.2003.11.018.

168: *Basketball experiment . . . Alan Richardson:* Morrisett, L. N., "The Role of Implicit Practice in Learning," in *Mental Practice: A Review and Discussion, Parts I and II, Research Quarterly 38*, no. 2 (1967): 95–107, 263–273.

168: *Study . . . Shelley Taylor and Lien Pham out of UCLA:* Pham, L. B., and S. Taylor, "From Thought to Action: Effects of Process- versus Outcome-Based Mental Simulations on Performance," *Personality and Social Psychology Bulletin 25* (1999): 250–260, https://doi.org/10.1177/0146167299025002010.

169: *Brain that activates when trying to "manifest":* Stephan, K. M., et al., "Functional Anatomy of the Mental Representation of Upper Extremity Movements in Healthy Subjects," *Journal of Neurophysiology 73*, no. 1 (1995): 373–386, https://doi.org/10.1152/jn.1995.73.1.373.

173: *Researchers from NYU:* Bargh, J. A., et al., "The Automated Will: Nonconscious Activation and Pursuit of Behavioral Goals," *Journal of Personality and Social Psychology 81*, no. 6 (2001): 1014–1027, https://www.ncbi.nlm.nih.gov/pmc/articles/PMC3005626/#R83.

174: *Subconscious priming ... found as effective:* Légal, J. B., et al., "Don't You Know That You Want to Trust Me? Subliminal Goal Priming and Persuasion," *Journal of Experimental Social Psychology 48*, no. 1 (2012): 358–360, https://doi.org/10.1016/j.jesp.2011.06.006.

174: *Subconscious priming ... memorization, better cooperators, and higher achievers:* Bargh, et al., "The Automated Will."

174: *"Rudeness" ... unscrambled word tests related to "politeness":* Bargh, J. A., M. Chen, and L. Burrows, "Automaticity of Social Behavior: Direct Effects of Trait Construct and Stereotype-Activation on Action," *Journal of Personality and Social Psychology 71*, no. 2 (1996): 230–244, https://www.ncbi.nlm.nih .gov/pubmed/8765481.

174: *Primed just as effectively with images:* Ruch, S., M. A. Züst, and K. Henke, "Subliminal Messages Exert Long-Term Effects on Decision-Making," *Neuroscience of Consciousness* 2016, no. 1 (2016): niw013, https://doi .org/10.1093/nc/niw013.

174: *Movie theater experiment:* Karremans, J., W. Stroebe, and J. Claus, "Beyond Vicary's Fantasies: The Impact of Subliminal Priming and Brand Choice," *Journal of Experimental Social Psychology 42*, no. 6 (2006): 792–798, http://doi.org/10.1016/j.jesp.2005.12.002.

9: Get Out of Your Own Way

197: *Rebuild your work and life around practicing your strengths:* There are WAY too many studies to cite here; see https://www.viacharacter .org/www/Research/Research-Findings.

198: *Practice their strengths have higher:* Niemiec, R. M., "VIA Character Strengths: Research and Practice (The First 10 Years)," in *Well-Being and Cultures: Perspectives on Positive Psychology*, edited by H. H. Knoop and A. Delle Fave (New York: Springer, 2013), 11–30, http://bit.ly/2xk2xg8.

199: *Research identifies twenty-four strengths:* Peterson, C. F., and M. E. P. Seligman, *Character Strengths and Virtues: A Handbook of Classification* (Oxford: Oxford University Press, 2004).

202: *Overuse ... underuse of strengths can create:* Freidlin, P., H. Littman-Ovadia, and R. M. Niemiec, "Positive Psychopathology: Social Anxiety via Character Strengths Underuse and Overuse," *Personality and Individual Differences 108* (2017): 50–54, http:// doi.org/10.1016/j.paid.2016.12.003. See also Niemiec, R. M., "The Overuse of Strengths: Ten Principles," *PsycCRITIQUES 59*, no. 33 (2014), http://bit.ly/2xsEHOo.

204: *"Refusing to tolerate obstacles":* I owe this phrasing to Ray Dalio's excellent book: Dalio, Ray, *Principles* (New York: Simon and Schuster, 2017), 175.

11: Real Self-Care

235: *Thought patterns that are diverse, flexible:* Cohn, M. A., et al., "Happiness Unpacked: Positive Emotions Increase Life Satisfaction by Building Resilience," *Emotion 9*, no. 3 (2009): 361–368, http://doi.org/10.1037 /a0015952.

236: *Positive ... undo ... side effects:* Fredrickson, B. L., et al., "The Undoing Effect of Positive Emotions," *Motivation and Emotion 24*, no. 4 (2000): 237–258, https://www.ncbi.nlm.nih .gov/pmc/articles/PMC3128334/.

237: *Possible to learn optimism:* Seligman, M. E. P., *Learned Optimism: How to Change Your Mind and Your Life* (New York: Knopf Doubleday Publishing Group, 2011).

237: *The Top Ten Pos-Emotions to Seek Out:* Fredrickson, B. L., Positivity: Top Notch Research Reveals the Upward Spiral That Will Change Your Life (New York: Crown, 2009).

238: *Gratitude in writing . . . higher in mea-surements of well-being:* Emmons, R.A., and M. E. McCullough, "Counting Blessings versus Burdens: An Experimental Investigation of Gratitude and Subjective Well-Being in Daily Life," *Journal of Personality and Social Psychology 84*, no. 2 (2003): 377–389, http://bit.ly/2NnqFs7.

239: *Fake laughter from real laughter:* Bryant, Gregory A., et al., "The Perception of Spontaneous and Volitional Laughter across 21 Societies," *Psychological Science 29*, no. 9 (2018): 1515–1525, https://doi.org/10.1177/0956797618778235.

240: *Upward spiral:* Fredrickson, B. L., and T. Joiner, "Positive Emotions Trigger Upward Spirals toward Emotional Well-Being," *Psychological Science 13*, no. 2 (2002): 172–175, http://doi.org/10.1111/1467-9280.00431.

246: *Lost in Translation List:* Burns, D. D., *Feeling Good: The New Mood Therapy* (New York: Harper Collins, 1999).

248: *Bad moods . . . choosing to believe it:* Burns, *Feeling Good*, 46.

249: *The positive side effects of reappraisal:* Troy, A. S., et al., "Seeing the Silver Lining: Cognitive Reappraisal Ability Moderates the Relationship between Stress and Depressive Symptoms," *Emotion 10*, no. 6 (2010): 783–795, http://doi.org/10.1037/a0020262.

254: *Mindfulness significantly improves:* Brown, K. W., and R. M. Ryan, "The Benefits of Being Present: Mindfulness and Its Role in Psychological Well-Being," *Journal of Personality and Social Psychology 84*, no. 4 (2003): 822–884, http://dx.doi.org/10.1037/0022-3514.84.4.822; Brown, K. W., et al., "Mindfulness Enhances Episodic Memory Performance: Evidence from a Multimethod Investigation," *PLoS ONE 11*, no. 4 (2016): e0153309, http://bit.ly/2MIDd8p; Ding, X., et al., "Improving Creativity Performance by Short-Term Meditation," *Behavioral and Brain Functions 10* (2014): 9, http://doi.org/10.1186/1744-9081-10-9; Loucks, E. B., et al., "Associations of Mindfulness with Glucose Regulation and Diabetes," *American Journal of Health Behavior 40*, no. 2 (2016): 258–267, http://doi.org/10.5993/AJHB.40.2.11; O'Reilly, G. A., et al., "Mindfulness-Based Interventions for Obesity-Related Eating Behaviors: A Literature Review," *Obesity Reviews 15*, no. 6 (2014): 453–461, http://doi.org/10.1111/obr.12156; Zeidan, F., "Mindfulness Meditation Improves Cognition: Evidence of Brief Mental Training," *Consciousness and Cognition 19*, no. 2 (2010): 597–605, http://doi.org/10.1016/j.concog.2010.03.014.

254: *Mindfulness substantially reduces:* Abbott, R. A., et al., "Effectiveness of Mindfulness-Based Stress Reduction and Mindfulness-Based Cognitive Therapy in Vascular Disease: A Systematic Review and Meta-Analysis of Randomised Controlled Trials," *Journal of Psychosomatic Research 76*, no. 5 (2014): 341–351, http://doi.org/10.1016/j.jpsychores.2014.02.012; Deyo, M., et al., "Mindfulness and Rumination: Does Mindfulness Training Lead to Reductions in the Ruminative Thinking Associated with Depression?" *Explore 5*, no. 5 (2009): 265–271, http://doi.org/10.1016/j.explore.2009.06.005; Donald, J. N., et al., "Daily Stress and the Benefits of Mindfulness: Examining the Daily and Longitudinal Relations between Present-Moment Awareness and Stress Responses," *Journal of Research in Personality 65* (2016): 30–37, http://dx.doi.org/10.1016/j.jrp.2016.09.002; Goldin, P., W. Ramel, and J. Gross, "Mindfulness Meditation Training and Self-Referential Processing in Social Anxiety Disorder: Behavioral and Neural Effects," *Journal of Cognitive Psychotherapy 23*, no. 3 (2009): 242–257, http://doi.org/10.1891/0889-8391.23.3.242; Hölzel, B. K., et al., "Mindfulness Practice Leads to Increases in Regional Brain Gray Matter Density," *Psychiatry Research 191*, no. 1 (2011): 36–43, http://doi.org/10.1016/j.pscychresns.2010.08.006; Laneri, D., et al., "Effects of Long-Term Mindfulness Meditation on Brain's White Matter Microstructure and Its Aging," *Frontiers in*

Aging Neuroscience 7 (2016), http://doi.org/10.3389/fnagi.2015.00254; Taren, A. A., et al., "Mindfulness Meditation Training Alters Stress-Related Amygdala Resting State Functional Connectivity: A Randomized Controlled Trial," *Social Cognitive and Affective Neuroscience 10*, no. 12 (2015): 1758–1768, http://doi.org/10.1093/scan/nsv066.

12: Life on Purpose

259: *Lao Tzu got it:* Tzu, Lao, *Tao Te Ching* (Boulder, CO: Shambhala Publications, 2007), 11.

263: *We are incapable of multitasking:* American Psychological Association, "Multitasking: Switching Costs," APA.org, March 20, 2006, https://www.apa.org/research/action/multitask.aspx.

263: *According to neuroscientist and author Dr. Daniel Levitin:* Levitin, D. J., *The Organized Mind: Thinking Straight in the Age of Information Overload* (New York: Plume/Penguin, 2014), 6.

264: *Within an hour of going to sleep:* Deloitte, "Global Mobile Consumer Survey: US edition / The Dawn of the Next Era in Mobile," Deloitte.com, 2017, http://bit.ly/2xwcZjR.

264: *Phones between 86 and 150 times per day:* Deloitte, "Global Mobile Consumer Survey." See also Kleiner Perkins, "Mobile Users Reach to Phone ~150x a Day," "Internet Trends 2013," SlideShare.net, 2013, http://bit.ly/2xvSPXj.

264: *40 percent of our productive time per day switch-tasking:* Iqbal, S. T., and E. Horvitz, "Disruption and Recovery of Computing Tasks: Field Study, Analysis, and Directions," Proceedings of the 2007 Conference on Human Factors in Computing Systems, April 28, 2007, http://erichorvitz.com/CHI_2007_Iqbal_Horvitz.pdf.

265: *Interrupted an average of four times per hour:* Mark, Gloria, "Work Fragmentation as Common Practice: The Paradox of IT Support," Human-Computer Interaction Institute [website], Carnegie Mellon University (n.d.), http://bit.ly/2NnsGob.

265: *"Media multitask" can't pay attention:* Eyal Ophir, E., C. Nass, and A. D. Wagner, "Cognitive Control in Media Multitaskers," Proceedings of the National Academy of Sciences 106, no. 37 (2009): 15583–15587, http://doi.org/10.1073/pnas.0903620106.

13: Pick the Pyros

281: *Rate that person by circling one of the three options:* Levitin, *The Organized Mind*, 144.

284: *More compassionate a person is:* "Brené Brown: 3 Ways to Set Boundaries: The Importance of Knowing When, and How, to Say No," Oprah.com, September 2013, http://bit.ly/2MGknyE.

283: *Someone else's "best" won't meet our expressed needs:* Brown, Brené, *Rising Strong* (New York: Spiegel and Grau, 2015).

285: *As Maya Angelou famously said:* OWN: Oprah Winfrey Network, "One of the Most Important Lessons Dr. Maya Angelou Ever Taught Oprah / The Oprah Winfrey Show | OWN" [online video], May 19, 2014, YouTube, https://www.youtube.com/watch?v=nJgmaHkcFP8.

ACKNOWLEDGMENTS

Bob—this book would not be possible without your unfailing support. Thank you for being a true partner, my person, and for flooding my life with joy. Love you with all my insides.

To my accountabilibuddies, Pookles, Maman, Steph, Angie—this book would not have made its way into the universe without your love, encouragement, and magical ability to call me on my bullshit. Thank you. Love you.

A gigantic thank you to Eva Avery—for seeing this book for what it could be and taking a courageous leap by choosing to be its editor. You taught me that editors could be selfless and transformative, asking thoughtful questions that draw out an author's best writing rather than inserting their own voice. This book would not exist without your patience, keen eye, and humor.

I am eternally grateful to the excellent team at Chronicle who made this book possible: Jennifer Jensen, Christina Loff, Sara Schneider, Ann Spradlin, and Mark Tauber. Thank you also to Jennifer Jordan and Lynda Crawford, for your endless patience with my belligerent misuse of long dashes and quotation marks, and for the insights that helped make this book readable. And Meryl Vedros: your understanding and creativity was the momentum I needed to put this book in the world. Thank you.

And thank YOU—yeah, you reading this page, right now—for making my fuckyeah a reality. Thanks for reading this book and telling everyone you know about how it totally changed your life. That was really cool of you.